# Targeting Senior Voters

# Targeting Senior Voters

*Campaign Outreach to Elders and
Others with Special Needs*

Susan A. MacManus
*with the assistance of
Kariña H. Shields
and support from
The University of South Florida
Institute on Aging*

Foreword by Jim Towey

ROWMAN & LITTLEFIELD PUBLISHERS, INC.
*Lanham • Boulder • New York • Oxford*

ROWMAN & LITTLEFIELD PUBLISHERS, INC.

Published in the United States of America
by Rowman & Littlefield Publishers, Inc.
4720 Boston Way, Lanham, Maryland 20706
http://www.rowmanlittlefield.com

12 Hid's Copse Road, Cumnor Hill, Oxford OX2 9JJ, England

British Cataloging in Publication Information Available

Library of Congress Cataloging-in-Publication Data Available

0-7425-0111-6 (cloth ISBN)
0-7425-0112-4 (paper ISBN)

Printed in the United States of America

♾™ The paper used in this publication meets the minimum requirements of
American National Standard for Information Sciences—Permanence of Paper for
Printed Library Materials, ANSI/NISO Z39.48-1992.

*For my parents*
*Cameron and Elizabeth MacManus,*
*with love.*

# Contents

# Tables

# Figures

# Photographs

# Foreword

There can be little doubt that the defining issue of the twenty-first century for the United States will be how to accommodate the demographic change that is already under way and will accelerate a decade from now when the 78 million members of the baby boom generation begin to retire. How do we deal with this growing elder population without pitting the interests of seniors against those of children? How do we help caregivers who have the needs of their parents and children to balance?

Those who read Susan MacManus's earlier book, *Young v. Old: Generational Combat in the 21st Century*, learned the importance and complexity of these issues and how they might play out in the years ahead. Because she lives in Florida, the epicenter of the age wave where one in five residents is over the age of 65, Susan MacManus has had a front row seat for years and has observed the intricacies of this subject. And as she points out repeatedly in this book, many of these critical policy decisions affecting the social welfare of the young and old will be made at the polls, as one might expect in a democracy. But how?

It is no secret to those seeking elective office that senior voters rule. They show up at the polls. Seniors have clout. They care about issues. They are unaffected by the electoral indifference of younger generations, many of whom don't vote and don't care.

Because senior citizens vote, those seeking higher office or wishing to shape public policy seek to "target" senior voters. They'd be crazy if they didn't. The problem is, they are governed more by sentimental stereotypes of who these voters are, what they are interested in, and how to capture their interest and votes, than by reality. They have failed to stay current on the details of elder life in Florida, where seniors live and under what conditions, what information they need, and how they vote. For that reason, many seeking to influence elections and public policy waste time and money, consistently missing the mark because they misread this pivotal sector of the voting age population.

To the rescue comes Susan MacManus with this new book, *Targeting Senior Voters*. She could have entitled it, "Everything you want to know about senior voters but didn't know what to ask." As you would expect of Susan MacManus's work, *Targeting Senior Voters* is well researched, well documented, and well written. Best of all, it is well timed, because a new round of national elections is at hand and so much is at stake.

But what makes *Targeting Senior Voters* refreshing is that it is downright interesting. I work on senior issues all the time, every day, in my responsibilities as president of Aging with Dignity. I didn't know that targeting voters in assisted living facilities is easier than going to a gated community of relatively healthier seniors. I didn't know that when seniors look at campaign literature, they have a hard time reading red and blue ink, the precise patriotic colors that most candidates use. I would not have guessed that the over-65 group is two times more likely to get news and information on politics from the Web than any other age group of daily on-line users. I have a lot to learn about seniors.

And that is the point of Dr. MacManus's book. We don't know about what makes senior voters tick because no one has taken the time to ask them, to study them, and to listen to them. Until now. That is why *Targeting Senior Voters* will become a must-buy for anyone in the political arena or interested in it. It will be mandatory reading for election officials who must find ways to make the sacred exercise of the right to vote accessible for a growing segment of the senior population that can't just walk to the polls.

I had the privilege to work for Mother Teresa of Calcutta for twelve years. I did her legal work and even worked full time for her for a couple of years. During that time I had occasion to travel with her to a number of American cities because she established over thirty homes in the United States. One time she observed, without the slightest hint of condemnation, that America doesn't treat its elderly very well. That struck me as odd because I had been with her in a home she had for the aged in Mexico, a place where abandoned elderly lived. I knew of her concern about the need to honor our elders, but America? We have Social Security and Medicare, and senior discounts and preferential parking. Surely she would think that we do a better job of caring for seniors than other countries.

But then Mother Teresa's point sunk in. The issue was not the material well-being of the elderly, but their sense of alienation and disconnection from society. Seniors weren't valued like they used to be, and when I searched my own conscience, I knew that what Mother Teresa said was true. Our country acknowledges the political muscle of seniors, but often ignores them because of their perceived weakness. That is the danger of a society that values only the powerful, productive, and efficient.

One of the great features of *Targeting Senior Voters* is the sincere respect and honor that Susan MacManus shows to this generation of citizens who have given America so much. While some in the political process seek to manipulate seniors, and may even try to use them as pawns in the political process, Susan MacManus helps us to understand elders and value them as vibrant and worthy participants in civic life, regardless of their physical capabilities or monetary influence. She describes their importance to society not just in electoral terms—and this book documents that fact with precision—but in cultural and social ones. No one until now has looked at the unique needs of the disabled elderly and identified ways to help them exercise their right to vote. Thank goodness she has.

The stereotype of seniors that we have grown accustomed to, call it the "On Golden Pond" mind-set, is no longer viable. Those in the public policy arena, those in the caregiving business, those who market goods and services to seniors, and those vying for the senior vote, need to hit the "erase" button on what they think they know about seniors, and start over.

*Targeting Senior Voters* is a great place to start.

Jim Towey
President, Aging with Dignity

# Acknowledgments

My parents, Cameron and Elizabeth MacManus, were the real inspiration for this book. Both love politics but have found it increasingly difficult to remain engaged. My mother, 76, recently lost her eyesight, and my father's hearing has worsened with age. He is 78. Watching them struggle to remain informed voters made me aware of how little attention has been paid to the need to make the political system more accessible to older citizens who ultimately experience a sight-, hearing-, and/or mobility-related impairment.

I am grateful to Jim Towey, president of Aging with Dignity, for writing the foreword. His group's research and policy proposals have been incredibly innovative and successful at promoting sensitivity to aging issues in Florida.

The enthusiasm with which people helped me with this project was a real boost. The Institute on Aging at the University of South Florida provided a grant that covered most of the cost of surveys. Survey participants were a great source of ideas on how to improve our electoral system. Dr. Susan Schuler, president of Independent Marketing Research, Inc., conducted the survey and did an outstanding job of capturing lots of open-ended question responses.

A special thanks is due to the 600 Florida seniors who participated in a telephone survey tapping their opinions and recommendations on a wide range of campaign, election, and public policy issues. Thanks are also in order for the Florida supervisors of elections, candidates for state legislative and state cabinet offices, and the activity directors of nursing homes and assisted-living facilities in Hillsborough, Pasco, and Pinellas counties who participated in mail surveys. National survey firms and political consultants offered invaluable recommendations about how to better tap the opinions of seniors. My thanks to Kate Newcomer for surveying the surveyors.

Hillsborough County Elections Supervisor Pam Iorio and Pinellas County Elections Supervisor Dorothy Ruggles helped design the survey distributed to their fellow supervisors across the state. Pasco County Elections Supervisor Kurt Browning provided excellent technical descriptions of the various voting systems and their limitations for the disabled. Ethel Baxter, Chief of Florida's Division of Elections, in the Secretary of State's Office, spent time with me discussing absentee voting procedures and accessibility issues.

Two of my assistants and dear friends spent an inordinate amount of time readying this book for publication. Kariña Shields helped gather, enter, and analyze much of the survey data and prepared all the graphics. Sharon Ostermann kept the vast quantities of source materials in some semblance of order, formatted the text and tables, and constructed the index. Kariña and Sharon both keep me going with their hard work and good humor! Becky Byram helped copy reams of materials when she had some time off her busy high school schedule.

No book could I complete without the helpful editing by my longtime friend-Barbara Langham, an incredibly gifted freelance editor and writer from Austin, Texas. She has made each of my previously published books better, and this one is no exception. I am, as always, eternally grateful for her insights and assistance.

Jennifer Knerr, Rowman & Littlefield editor, has been a real source of inspiration to me in recent years. She edited my previous book, *Young v. Old,* when she was with Westview Press. Working with her on that project made me bound and determined to do so again. She has been a great source of encouragement and assistance. Her assistant, Brenda Hadenfeldt, was also great about giving me guidance on necessary paperwork and formats. Production editor Karen Johnson made sure the book was in excellent shape.

I am particularly indebted to the Pew Research Center for the People & the Press for making data readily accessible to academic researchers. Director Andrew Kohut and research director Kimberly Parker were extremely helpful. I also want to thank the Council on Excellence in Government, especially Sue Ducat, for sharing their survey data with me, and Lee C. Shapiro, of Voter News Service, who provided exit survey data.

Lots of organizations and people played a big role in this book. The AARP (formerly the American Association of Retired Persons) and the National Organization on Disability (NOD) provided lots of background materials. I especially want to thank Adina Topfer, program officer for NOD's VOTE!2000 Campaign for sending materials to me in a rush. William C. Kimberling and Margaret "Peggy" Sims in the Federal Election Commission provided access to their files dealing with disability issues. Diane Lade, senior writer for the Ft. Lauderdale *Sun-Sentinel,* shared her research on senior drivers.

Several academic colleagues were incredibly generous with their data and/or time and expertise: Professors Todd G. Shields, Kay Fletcher Schriner, and Ken Schriner of the University of Arkansas; Professors Douglas L. Kruse and Lisa Schur, Rutgers University; Professor Donna Cohen of the University of South Florida; Ilene Frank of the University of South Florida (USF) Library; Lee Leavengood, Director of USF's Lifelong Learning Institute, and her husband, Victor.

Many of my best students and former students, V. P. Walling, Peter Schorsch, Chris Kohler, Michael Keenan, Kim Grady-Brock, David Engelson, and Dr. Steven Watson of the Florida Department of Health, were involved in some aspect of this research, from tracking down absentee balloting statistics and distributing surveys to coding and analyzing survey data.

Several people spent time looking over this work and made recommendations. For that, I thank John Cutter, freelance writer on elder issues; Jack Hebert, president of the Mallard Group, a political consulting firm; and Rowman & Littlefield reviewers. Thanks to Deb Halpern of WFLA-TV Newschannel 8 for helping me understand television advertising.

I am particularly indebted to Lorene Clay and her son R. T. "Tommy" Clay for helping me secure the wonderful photograph on the cover of this book. It features Lorene, Chance Clay (Tommy's son), and Edna Alderman, 102, Lorene's mother, Tommy's grandmother, and Chance's great-grandmother. The photograph vividly portrays the type of intergenerational ties that will need to be strengthened as our nation ages.

No book can ever be completed without the support of family and friends. A special note of thanks goes to my sister and brother-in-law (Dr. Lou MacManus and Warren Harrison), my brother and sister-in-law (Dr. Cameron MacManus and Julia), my nephew and nieces (Cameron MacManus, Allison MacManus, Susan Harrison, and Genelle Harrison), my aunts and uncles, all my cousins, their spouses and children, my dear friend Kim Strunz, and all the wonderful seniors in the Builders Class at the First United Methodist Church of Lutz.

# 1

+

# Seniors:

## America's Most Consistent Voters

*Photo 1.1   Older voters are the most likely to see voting as a civic responsibility and an act of patriotism.*

The power of older voters is magnified because of a simple fact: They turn out at the polls.

Robin Toner, *New York Times,* June 1, 1999

More than one political pundit has bemoaned the declining turnout in today's elections. Given the low level of public interest, candidates and campaign consultants agree that elections are increasingly being won "at the margins" by targeting specific types of voters.

Among the most heavily targeted are senior voters. Why? Because they register and vote at higher levels than other age groups (see figures 1.1 and 1.2). According to the Federal Election Commission, voters 65 and older turn out

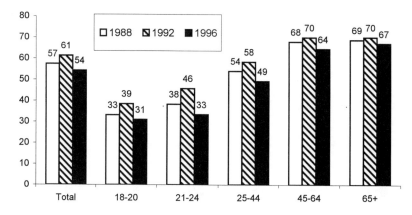

*Figure 1.1    Percent Voted in Presidential Election Years*
*Source: Federal Election Commission.*

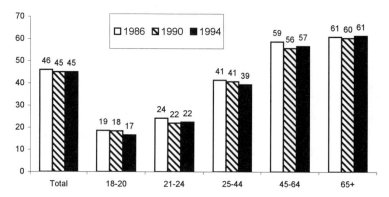

*Figure 1.2    Percent Voted in Midterm Election Years*
*Source: Federal Election Commission.*

in huge proportions for elections, including midterm contests when presidential candidates are not on the ballot. Actually, they register and vote in *all* elections—national, state, and local. A 1999 survey for the Council on Excellence in Government found that among registered voters, 62% of those 65 and older say they vote in all elections, compared to just 14% of the 18-to-34-year-olds. In addition, seniors are more likely than younger voters to cast a *complete* ballot—voting on every item, including all the referenda placed at the bottom of the ballot.

But it's not just voting that makes gray power so potent.

## SENIORS ARE MORE LIKELY TO PARTICIPATE IN ALL ASPECTS OF POLITICS

Older citizens participate in a wide range of political activities. They write letters, lobby, protest, and are not shy about calling on their connections when they want attention paid to their needs.[1] (See table 1.1.) No wonder that today's seniors have been described as the "800-pound gorilla" of generational politics. Consider these facts:

- Older voters are still the most partisan. They more strongly identify with a political party and see sharper differences between the two major parties. They have more explicit likes and dislikes toward each because they have had more years of experience with the political party system.
- Older voters follow national, state, and local politics more closely and rely on a broader range of media (electronic and print) for their information about candidates and issues. Across the nation, older voters are much more likely to pay attention to politics; read and study comparisons and contrasts of candidates on issues of importance to them (newspapers, newsletters, direct mail pieces from candidates); watch a televised debate; and participate in voter opinion surveys.
- Older voters are an important source of campaign contributions and volunteer workers. They are also more willing (and available) than other age groups to participate in focus groups where age-targeted themes, issue stances, and television and radio ads are developed and tested.
- Older voters are more likely to believe it is their civic duty to vote. Survey after survey shows that seniors vote out of a sense of patriotism. In *Gray Dawn*, Peter Peterson observes: "With upbeat names like 'senior citizen,' elders have gained a reputation for civic competence; with cipher names like the 'X' or 'Bof' (as in French for 'who cares?') Generation, youths have gained a reputation for civic withdrawal."[2]

**Table 1.1**

**Personal Interaction With Government**
**Over Past Two Years by Age**
**(Multiple Response Question Set)**

| | All Adults % | 18-29 % | 30-49 % | 50-64 % | 65+ % |
|---|---|---|---|---|---|
| Attended a public hearing or meeting | 46 | 36 | 46 | 58 | 47 |
| Contacted an elected official | 45 | 24 | 46 | 62 | 53 |
| Volunteered time at a local library or school | 42 | 46 | 47 | 38 | 28 |
| Contributed time or money to a political campaign | 34 | 22 | 31 | 47 | 42 |
| Visited a government web site for information | 34 | 40 | 40 | 32 | 13 |
| Participated in a police sponsored community-watch program | 27 | 22 | 29 | 32 | 22 |

*Note: Respondents were asked: "I'm going to mention some different ways that people might have contact with government or be involved with government, and for each, I'd like you to tell me whether you have had the experience within the past two years?"*

*Source: Telephone survey of a random sample of 1,214 U.S. adults conducted May 21–June 1, 1999, for the Council for Excellence in Government by the research firm of Peter D. Hart and Robert Teeter. Used by permission.*

• Older citizens feel more connected to government. A 1999 survey by the Council for Excellence in Government found that seniors feel much more connected to government (56%) than young adults (31%).[3] (See figure 1.3.) Feelings about government affect one's likelihood of voting. For example, the Council's survey found that 50% of "connected" persons vote regularly versus 28% of "disconnected" persons.

## CHANGING THE MESSAGE AND THE MEDIA

The consistent voting and political action patterns of seniors has many implications for professional campaign consultants, candidates for office, political party activists, and others who seek to influence the outcome of elections. In an age when campaigns are hard pressed for time, money, and workers, strategists must target resources toward the senior portion of the electorate. It is unrealistic for candidates and issue advocacy groups to aim at a broad spectrum of registered voters in an effort to reach everyone. Nor is it wise for a candidate or an issue with a more youthful appeal (such as bond issues for public schools) to use tactics that assume disinterest on the part of older voters. Instead, campaigns must address seniors' opinions and concerns and formulate their strategies accordingly. The bottom line is that whether one is running for president, Congress, or the local school board, ignoring the *high-turnout, politically attentive, and informed* senior voter is not a wise—or winning—strategy.

Strategies for reaching senior voters involve method as well as message. Unlike younger voters, those 65 and older are more likely to have sight, hearing, and mobility limitations. Some seniors face challenges with transportation, and

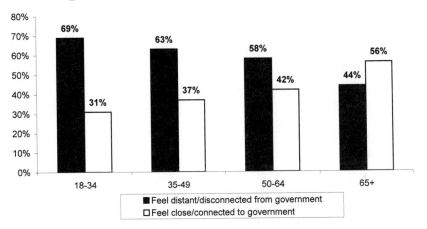

*Figure 1.3    The New Generation Gap: Connection to Government*
*Source: The Council for Excellence in Government, 1999 poll of 1,214 adults conducted May 21–June 1, 1999, by the firms of Peter D. Hart and Robert Teeter, margin of error +/- 3.2 percent. Used with permission.*

some live in concentrated areas such as mobile home communities and nursing homes. As a result, it's fair to ask whether candidates, particularly those with large senior constituencies, have adjusted their campaign tactics. Brochures are a staple of political campaigns. Do candidates print brochures in large type? Do they provide brochure information in audio tapes for the sight-impaired? Advocacy groups often host candidate forums in local schools and town halls. Do they also consider nursing homes as a venue?

The large turnout of seniors in elections has equally important implications for election officials and others charged with implementing registration and voting laws. How are election officials modifying registration procedures and making registration more accessible? What kinds of nontraditional voting methods are used to enable seniors to vote? How do these registration procedures and voting methods respect a voter's limitations while guarding against the potential for fraud?

## ADVOCATING FOR CHANGE

Senior voters have not sat idly by and waited for things to change. The AARP (formerly the American Association of Retired Persons), the largest group that advocates on behalf of seniors, closely follows campaigns and legislative agendas. In the past decade, AARP has established a nonpartisan group, AARP/VOTE, that focuses attention on issues such as Medicare and Social Security. Its volunteers distribute voter guides, host candidate forums, and sponsor voter registration drives.

*Photo 1.2    Eugene Poole, president of the Florida Voters League, Inc., believes "a voteless people is a hopeless people." Get-out-the-vote efforts by groups like the National Organization on Disability will increasingly play an integral role in campaigns.*

In addition, the National Organization on Disability, which works on behalf of all people with disabilities, not just seniors, has embarked on aggressive registration and get-out-the-vote drives. These groups understand that the right to vote is the most basic of all political rights and that efforts to promote voting among all Americans are indispensable to a healthy democracy.

In advocating for change, advocacy groups can benefit from much of the same information needed by candidates, political strategists, and election officials. Data about voting patterns and new laws for expanding access, for example, can empower a group to pursue its objectives. The studies and surveys cited in this book can provide documentation for educational efforts aimed at public officials and private citizens.

## KEY TO WINNING 2000 PRESIDENTIAL AND CONGRESSIONAL CONTESTS

Many election forecasters project a low turnout in the year 2000 presidential and congressional election. This means that senior voters will be courted more than ever because they are likely to be a critical swing vote. Democratic pollster Celinda Lake has said it best: "It's virtually impossible to take back the House or win the presidency without taking back seniors. That makes them the key battleground, and both parties know it."[4]

But reaching seniors in 2000 is a different ball game than in 1996. It will be different for many reasons, including the following:

- The number of seniors has grown. Because there are more of them, they will be an even stronger voting group. (See chapter 2.)
- As the size of the senior electorate has grown, cohesiveness has declined. Although solidly Democratic in the past, seniors are less so now. As one indication, exit surveys have shown that Republicans garnered the 60-and-older vote in U.S. House elections in 1994, 1996, and 1998. Yet Democrats still carried the 65-*and-older* vote in many places. In particular, Florida exit survey data show that 1998 Democratic gubernatorial candidate Buddy MacKay received 52% of the 65-and-older vote, but just 39% of the 60-to-64 vote (and 42% of the 18-to-24 vote).[5] Consequently, both parties will woo senior voters.
- Political campaigns will use more sophisticated targeting in broadcast and direct mail efforts. For example, candidates will run one type of TV commercial during a time slot when seniors are likely to be viewing (mid-morning to early evening) but another type of commercial for younger voters (late night). Cable TV, like radio, has become increasingly segmented, allowing candidates to pitch a different message to different groups by age, religious bent, language, or interest. Direct mail brochures will differ from household to household depending on various demographics such as age, race/ethnicity, and gender.

- Absentee balloting will be heavier as more candidates promote this method as part of their campaign arsenals. Seniors are a prime target for absentee voting—and voting fraud.
- Advocacy groups representing seniors and people with disabilities will engage in more aggressive efforts to get out the vote. Candidates will have to respond to these groups' concerns about accessible registration procedures and voting facilities.
- The smarter candidates will use marketing techniques already being used successfully by the private sector to reach senior consumers with hearing, sight, and mobility impairments. These techniques include audio and video tapes and large-print brochures and sample ballots. Conversely, elements that marketeers have found troublesome for seniors, such as certain colors and sound patterns, will be "corrected" by savvy political consultants.

## BEYOND 2000: A CHANGING SENIOR ELECTORATE

The business of targeting seniors will continue to change as the new millennium unfolds. Indeed, the whole area of senior politics will likely be vastly different from that in the twentieth century.

- The declining cohesiveness that comes with a growing senior electorate will bring some surprises. For example, on high-priority issues such as Medicare and Social Security, seniors will disagree more on how to proceed.
- Stereotypes about senior votes won't apply. Studies suggest that many of tomorrow's senior voters will be more affluent, more educated, and more positively disposed toward the private sector than today's oldest age group. They will also be somewhat more diverse from a racial/ethnic perspective. (See chapter 2.)
- Targeting techniques will become increasingly sophisticated. Political consultants will re-think approaches to direct mail, media advertisements, candidate forums, and even door-to-door campaigning in light of the senior electorate's greater diversity. Some techniques, for example, will cater to the active, affluent, golf-playing set in upscale retirement communities, while other techniques will take into account increases in the number of seniors with seeing, hearing, and mobility limitations.
- Technological innovations will change politics in unforeseen ways. Many seniors are logging on to the Internet to check out candidate Web sites, join chat groups, and obtain information on issues. Apart from the Internet, we can expect changes in many other areas, such as voter identification devices and voting machines, which will have an impact on seniors and targeting.

- Even the definition of an "old" or "senior" voter is changing. The AARP defines it as 50, but others use 55 or 60. Sixty-five continues to be the most widely used marker, but that may change as the retirement age for Social Security rises. Furthermore, the senior category itself will become increasingly stratified. Analysts use a variety of classifications ranging from "near-elderly"[6] and "young-old" to "old-old."[7]

## MAKING THE MOST OF THIS BOOK

Much of the data in this book are the result of surveys that sought to discover the opinions and behaviors of senior voters, candidates, political pollsters, election supervisors, directors of nursing homes and assisted living facilities, and advocacy groups. Other information comes from interviews with political consultants. Data from Florida (the nation's grayest state) are a primary source, but national data are incorporated throughout.

The information in this book can be useful to candidates, political consultants, pollsters who advise candidates, election officials, and government officials. It can be equally useful to advocacy groups that seek to encourage civic participation among the elderly and disabled. It can also be illuminating for journalists, academics, and others who study and observe elections, political phenomena, and social change.

If you are among these readers, you understand—or soon will—that targeting is indispensable to today's elections and, furthermore, that targeting seniors is critical to winning. This book can help broaden your understanding by describing the senior electorate and the characteristics that distinguish this group from other voters. This book can give you insight into identifying and targeting senior voters in campaigns. It can inform you about registration procedures and voting methods that have changed in response to older and disabled voters and, thus, how you might push for more changes. Finally, it can provide information on what seniors think about important issues such as Social Security, Medicare and health insurance options, financial concerns, education, and other issues that can help you craft messages to senior voters.

To begin, let's look at this "800-pound gorilla" and see how it is growing and changing.

# 2

✛

# The Graying Behemoth

*Photo 2.1    Older women still outnumber the men. However, the gender gap among seniors will narrow somewhat in the twenty-first century.*

Of all the demographic trends altering the face of America, the aging of the population will bring about the greatest change.

Frank Wu, *IntellectualCapital.com,* September 9–16, 1999

America has aged rapidly. In 1900, only one in twenty-five Americans was 65 or older, but by 1994, the number had changed to one in eight (33.2 million). If current trends hold, demographers predict that the graying phenomenon will continue. Specifically, by 2040, one in five Americans will be 65 or older (80 million). (See figure 2.1.)

The United States has long considered itself a nation of the young.[1] However, in little more than a generation, that perception will no longer be true. By 2030, persons 65 and older will make up a larger proportion (20%) of the population than those 18 and younger (18%).[2]

Most of the growth in the early twenty-first century will occur between 2010 and 2030 when the baby boom generation turns 65. (Baby boomers are those born between 1946 and 1964.) (See figure 2.2.) Demographers are fond of describing this phenomenon as a "pig moving through a python." Yesterday's baby boom will be tomorrow's senior boom.

A particularly fast-growing group is the centenarians, those 100 and older. During the 1990s, the ranks of centenarians nearly doubled, from about 37,000 in 1990 to more than 70,000 in 1999. U.S. Census Bureau analysts are projecting anywhere from 250,000 to 4.2 million centenarians by 2050.[3]

Peterson in *Gray Dawn* points out that this aging trend characterizes not only America but the rest of the developed world: "For nearly all of history, the elderly never amounted to more than 2 or 3% of the population. With the industrial revolution, the share started to rise. Today, in the developed world, the

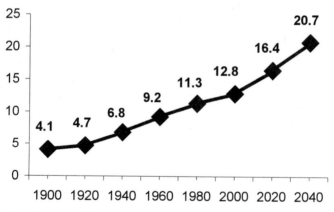

*Figure 2.1    Percent of Total U.S. Population 65-and-over, 1900–2040*
*Source: U.S. Bureau of the Census, 65+ in the United States, 1996.*

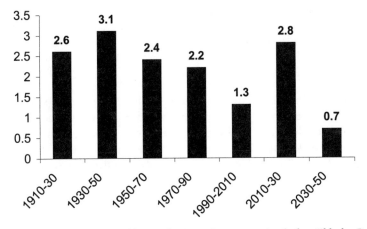

*Figure 2.2 Average Annual Growth Rate (in percent) of the Elderly Population, 1910–1930 to 2030–2050*
Source: *U.S. Bureau of the Census,* 65+ *in the United States. Washington, D.C.: U.S. Department of Commerce, May 1995: 1.*

elderly amount to 14%. By 2030, they will reach 25%—and in some countries, they may be closing in on 30%."[4]

## REASONS FOR THE SENIOR GROWTH SPURT

The fast-paced increase in the size of the senior electorate is occurring for many reasons. Perhaps the three most commonly cited are the following: the aging of the baby boomers, as previously discussed, longer life expectancies, and lower birth rates among younger generations.

### Longer Life Expectancies

Increases in life expectancies are a relatively recent phenomenon. Ken Dychtwald, author of *Age Wave* (1988) and *Age Power* (1999), puts changing life expectancy rates in historical perspective: "Throughout 99 percent of all the years that humans have walked this planet, the average life expectancy at birth was less than 18 years. In the past, most people didn't age—they died. Infectious diseases, accidents, violence, and many other hazards often brought life to an early close."[5]

Even in the United States, life expectancies have not always been as high as they are today. According to Frank Hobbs, author of 65+ *in the United States,* high fertility rates and high mortality rates in the early days of our nation kept the population young:

> Life expectancy at birth was about 35 years when this nation was founded and had increased to perhaps 42 years by the mid-1800s. By 1900, average life expectancy

at birth had increased to 47 years. Life expectancy continued to increase dramatically in the first half of the 20th century, primarily because of decreased mortality among the young, particularly infants. Under the mortality conditions of 1950, life expectancy at birth had jumped to 68 years. . . . [By] 1991, life expectancy at birth had reached a record high of 75.5 years.[6]

Hobbs further reports: "Reductions in mortality have resulted in impressive increases in life expectancy that have contributed to the growth of the older population, especially at the oldest ages." The fastest growing segment of the elderly population is that 85 and older. These elderly totaled 3 million in 1994 (10% of the 65 and older population; 1% of total population). But by 2050, some 19 million Americans will be 85 and older (24% of seniors, 5% of all Americans).

Americans will live even longer in the twenty-first century. According to the Society of Actuaries, Americans born in 1997 can expect to live 76.5 years. By 2050, that life expectancy will rise to 80 and older.[7]

## Lower Birth Rate

In just two decades, the birth rate in the United States has fallen from 16 per 1,000 population (1980) to 14.2 (2000).[8] Americans are having fewer children for lots of reasons. They are marrying later, holding back because of increased costs of child-rearing, and having children at older ages. The increased entry of women into the workforce and improved contraception have also affected the birth rate. In the 1950s and 1960s, the average number of children per family hovered around 3.8, only to dip to 2.1 by the close of the century.

A lower birth rate, longer life expectancies, and the aging of the baby boomers have combined to make seniors a fast-growing group. In addition to growing numbers, gender and race/ethnicity patterns are changing.

## GENDER GAP PERSISTS BUT WILL NARROW

Historically, American women have lived longer than men because of higher death rates among men at every age. The female-male life expectancy gap widened in the twentieth century. From 1900 to 1991, life expectancy at birth increased from 46 to 72 years for men. In contrast, the increase was from 48 to nearly 79 years for women. By 1994, elderly women outnumbered older men by a ratio of 3 to 2. (In numbers, this was 20 million to 14 million.) For the old-old, the gap was even wider: among people 85 and older, women outnumbered men by a ratio of 5 to 2.[9]

However, the gender gap will narrow in the new century. Among the baby boom generation, both genders are expected to live well into their 80s—many into their 90s.[10]

## RACIAL/ETHNIC COMPOSITION OF
## SENIOR POPULATION WILL CHANGE

The senior population is and will remain predominantly white. But the proportions will change by the middle of the century. Census Bureau figures from 1990 show that among the 65-and-older population, 86.7% were white non-Hispanics; this is projected to drop to 66.9% by 2050. Blacks, who made up 2.5% of the senior population in 1990, will grow to 8.4% in 2050. Hispanics, at only 1.1% of the senior population in 1990, will rise to 12.5% in 2050.[11]

Indeed, Hispanics will be the fastest growing segment of the senior population in the first half of the twenty-first century, as shown in figure 2.3.

Whites typically live longer than racial/ethnic minorities.[12] Since 1900, life expectancy at birth has more than doubled for African-Americans, from 33 years to 69 years (1991). However, life expectancy rates at birth are still higher for whites (76 years), although this gap is projected to narrow somewhat.

What do these population trends mean for politics and elections?

## POPULATION PERCENTAGES UNDERSTATE
## POLITICAL CLOUT OF SENIORS

The proportion of seniors in the population understates the group's real political clout. Their vote strength is often magnified, or inflated, because of higher registration and turnout rates.

First, seniors are—and will continue to be—a higher proportion of the voting age population (VAP) than of the population as a whole. In 1996, those 65 and older made up 12.8% of the total U.S. population but 16.5% of the *voting age population*. In 1998, they made up 17.1% of the VAP.

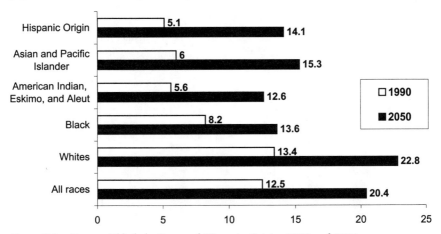

*Figure 2.3   Percent Elderly by Race and Hispanic Origin, 1990 and 2050
Source: U.S. Bureau of the Census.*

*Photo 2.2   Seniors will increasingly become more racially diverse in the twenty-first century.*

Seniors will comprise an even larger percentage of the voting age population in the 2000 presidential election. Their clout at the ballot box will be even greater in the twenty-first century. (See figure 2.4.) From state to state, seniors as a proportion of the voting age population vary because some states have high numbers of elderly residents, as discussed later in this chapter.

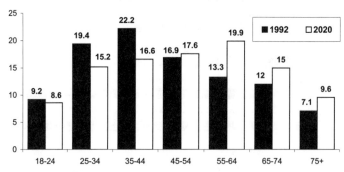

*Figure 2.4   Percent Distribution of Voting Age Population, November 1992 and 2020
Source: U.S. Bureau of the Census.*

Second, seniors are more likely to vote than younger groups. In the 1996 presidential election, seniors (65 and older) made up 16.5% of the VAP but 20% of those who actually voted. Similarly, when the population is narrowed from those of voting age to those who have registered, seniors are also more likely to vote than younger groups. Specifically, in 1996, according to the Census Bureau, more than three-fourths of seniors were registered, and two-thirds voted. In contrast, about half the 18-to-20-year-olds and 21-to-24-year-olds registered; less than a third actually voted.

Older voter clout is even greater in midterm (nonpresidential year) elections. For example, in the 1998 election cycle, figures from the U.S. Census Bureau and Florida Division of Elections showed that persons 65 and older comprised 18% of the state's overall population, 24% of the VAP, but 27% of the state's registered voters.[13]

Furthermore, exit surveys for the 1998 Florida gubernatorial contest reported that people 65 and older accounted for 32% of all who voted. When the group is widened to include people 60 and older, the proportion of those voting rises to 42%.[14]

Senior vote inflation is typically highest at the *local* level, where turnout is often low to begin with. A study of school tax referenda held in several Florida counties in 1995 found that in Hillsborough County, persons 65 and older made up 19% of the registered voters and 29% of those who voted. Comparable figures for Pasco County were 42% and 52% respectively. In Pinellas County, of those who went to the polls on election day, 49% were seniors.[15] And in the 1995 Plant City municipal election, older voters made up 19.5% of the registrants and 43% of those casting ballots. Similar patterns exist across the United States, especially in areas with large concentrations of older residents.

## STATES WITH LARGE SENIOR POPULATIONS ARE POWERFUL IN NATIONAL POLITICS

The states with the largest populations are the most powerful politically. Contrary to what some believe, the most populous states also have the *largest* number of elderly. Actually, the nine states with the highest number of seniors (more than 1 million) have 243 of the 270 Electoral College votes needed to elect the president in 2000.

These states and their Electoral College votes are, in alphabetical order: California (54), Florida (25), Illinois (22), Michigan (18), New Jersey (15), New York (33), Ohio (21), Pennsylvania (23), and Texas (32). The Census Bureau projects that by 2010, more than half (56%) of the nation's 39 million elderly residents will live in these nine states plus North Carolina (14 Electoral College votes).

However, the states with the greatest *proportion* of elderly residents form an entirely different list. (See figure 2.5.) The two exceptions are Florida (19%) and Pennsylvania (16%), which appear on both lists. The other states with higher-than-average percentages of older residents (14% or more) are North Dakota,

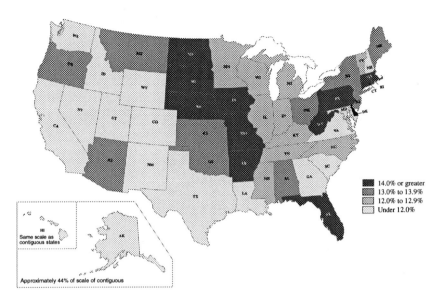

*Figure 2.5   Which States Are the Grayest? Percentage of the Population that Is Aged 65 Years and Over, by State: 1993*
*Source: U.S. Bureau of the Census, 65+ in the United States. Washington, D.C.: U.S. Department of Commerce, May 1995:2.*

South Dakota, Nebraska, Iowa, Missouri, Arkansas, West Virginia, Rhode Island, Massachusetts, and Connecticut. The total votes in the Electoral College for this group is 112.

Wide variations in senior populations exist within a state's boundaries. For example, in Florida, seniors make up a higher percentage of the population in the state's coastal counties and lakefront and golfing communities. Outside the Sunbelt, higher concentrations of seniors, usually poorer, are in rural or inner-city areas.

The newest trend is for seniors to locate near college towns. Moreover, some demographers predict that boomers will be more likely to retire in more remote, less populated, and less age-segregated settings. Thus, the senior population may grow fastest in what now seems the least likely areas (that is—nonretirement communities). As a result, their political clout will expand to all corners of the country.

## REACHING A GROWING MASS WITH SIGHT, HEARING, AND MOBILITY LIMITATIONS

As older Americans live longer, more of them are experiencing chronic, limiting illnesses or conditions.[16] (See figure 2.6.) The number of seniors with sight,

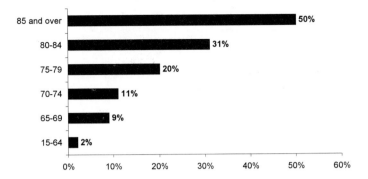

*Figure 2.6.   Percentage of Activities Requiring Assistance by Age Group*
Note: *Activities of daily living include bathing, dressing, eating, walking, toileting, and transferring from a bed/chair*
Source: *U.S. Bureau of the Census,* 65+ in the United States. *Washington, D.C.: U.S. Department of Commerce, May 1995: 3.*

hearing, and mobility limitations is growing and making it difficult for many of them to follow politics as closely and easily as they have before. Research has shown that citizens with disabilities participate at slightly lower rates than those without disabling conditions. (See table 2.1.)

Vulnerability to chronic age-related diseases increases exponentially after middle age. At 50, the risk for many age-related conditions begins to double every five to seven years.[17] In a statewide telephone survey of Florida residents 60 and older, 21% of households had someone with limited vision, 21% had a person with a hearing problem, and 17% had someone with a physical mobility limitation(s).

Because Florida's older population is younger, healthier, and wealthier than that of other states, one can expect these figures to be even higher nationally. Data from the National Institute on Aging, for example, show that about a third of Americans between age 65 and 74 and half of those age 85 and older have hearing problems—either minor (missing certain sounds) or major (total deafness).[18] Similarly, data from the National Center for Health Statistics show that among persons 55 and older, nearly one-third either have difficulty walking (22.3%) or are unable to walk (9.3%). More than one-third say they either have difficulty standing for two hours (27%) or are unable to stand that long (10.3%). With regard to vision impairments, 5% of older Americans say they are unable to read newsprint.[19] Many more have age-related visual impairments such as macular degeneration.

These numbers will swell as the baby boomers age. Smart candidates, interest groups, and consultants must take into account this growing subset of voters and adjust their campaign techniques accordingly.

**Table 2.1**

| Disabled Citizens Participate at Slightly Lower Rates | | |
| --- | --- | --- |
| Form of Political Participation | With disabilities % | Without disabilities % |
| Contributed money to political party or candidate | 13 | 16 |
| Written or spoken to elected representative/official | 30 | 40 |
| Attended political meeting | 13 | 15 |
| Written letter to newspaper | 7 | 9 |
| Contributed money to organization trying to influence government policy or legislation | 16 | 22 |
| Otherwise worked with groups or on one's own to change government laws or politics | 14 | 19 |
| Worked with others on community problem | 24 | 28 |

*Note: Respondents were asked whether they had engaged in each of these seven forms of participation in the past 12 months. The data are from a national random-household survey of 1,240 American citizens of voting age conducted after the November 1998 election. The sample was stratified so that interviews were conducted with 700 people with disabilities and 540 people without disabilities.*

*Source: Douglas L. Kruse, Lisa Schur, Kay Schriner, and Todd Shields.* Empowerment Through Civic Participation: A Study of the Political Behavior of People with Disabilities. *Find Report to the Disability Research Consortium, Bureau of Economic Research, Rutgers University and New Jersey Developmental Disabilities Council.*

## FIGURING OUT THE PERCENTAGE OF SENIOR VOTERS

A first step in planning strategy is to calculate the percentage of senior voters in a given constituency. Therein lies a challenge: How do you define "senior"? The traditional "age 65 and older" may not always apply, as we shall see in the following chapter.

# 3

# ✛

# Identifying and Surveying
# Senior Voters

Photo 3.1  *Among political consultants and pollsters, definitions of a "senior voter" range from 50 to 100. The issue or program being analyzed often dictates the age selected to define a senior.*

Election 2000 "is shaping up as a battle for another pivotal bloc. Call them 'swing seniors.' . . . They're not your father's seniors. They are wealthier and healthier than prior generations of elderly, thanks in part to Social Security and Medicare and more private retirement income. They're more likely to remain active and independent of their children."

Owen Ullmann and Susan Page, *USA Today,* Oct. 25, 1999

Baby boomers puke at the thought of ever becoming seniors.

Ken Dychtwald, *U.S. News & World Report,* April 22, 1996

Identifying and describing people in their golden years has become more difficult than ever. One 62-year-old may be preparing for retirement; another may be starting her first business. One 50-year-old may be buying booties for a new grandchild; another may be buying booties for his own newborn. One 70-year-old may be using a walker to get around; another may be running a 10K.

The difficulty of defining "senior" voters can be especially perplexing for anyone trying to plan strategy for a political campaign. The definition can vary for different reasons and under different circumstances.

## CANDIDATES DON'T JUST DEFINE SENIORS AS 65 PLUS

In political campaigns, candidates trying to reach seniors generally do not limit their efforts to people 65 and older. For example, the plurality (44%) of candidates seeking state legislative or cabinet posts in Florida in 1998 said they thought of people 55 and older as seniors. Only 25% said 65 and older, and 24% said 60 and older.[1]

The size of the senior population in a constituency makes a difference. In areas where persons 65 and older make up *less* than 50% of the population, candidates are more likely to expand the definition of "senior" to include people as young as 55.

More often than not, candidates use multiple definitions, following the advice of professionals assisting in their campaigns.

### Pollsters and Market Researchers Use a Variety of Definitions

In identifying senior voters, 70% of consulting firms use age 65 as the cut point, at least initially. However, when they compile data into categories, the lower cut point varies considerably.[2]

When asked why 65 is the first number they turn to, most firms associate it with what has been the traditional retirement age. Sixty-five, they say, is the age at which one becomes eligible for full Social Security benefits. Others use 65 because it tracks with categories commonly used by the U.S. Census Bureau.

Still others show evidence of 65 as the age at which spending and consumption habits take a markedly different turn.[3]

## Choosing Age Categories

Many public opinion firms with a political bent use four age categories: 18-29, 30-49, 50-64, and 65 and older. The reason is that they can then match political information with socioeconomic data from the Census.

The most common *two-category* age breakdown contrasts 18-to-49-year-olds with persons 50 and older. Proponents of age 50 as the dividing line point to different life experiences that affect the two groups' views of politics. (A more flippant explanation may be that 50 is the age at which people are eligible to join AARP!)

Other firms tailor their categories to the needs of advertisers. Said one representative: "We use 50-65 in our analysis because that age group is the media buying driver."

## Choosing the Lower Cut Point

The choice of the lower cut point varies for many reasons. Some choose 55 as the lower dividing line and group seniors in five-year categories from there—that is, 55-59, 60-64, 65-70 and so forth. Analyzing data in this manner has often revealed generational differences, depending on whether the lower cut point is 55, 60, or 65. For example, survey researchers have discovered partisan differences in support levels for candidates depending upon whether they use "60 and older" (more partisan diverse) or "65 and older" (more solidly Democrat).[4] Likewise, some pollsters report that 55-to-64-year-olds pay even greater attention to candidates' stances on Social Security than those 65 and older. The preretirement group focuses on the issue largely out of fear of the unknown or concern that the system will be changed before they are eligible. In contrast, the 65-and-older crowd knows how Social Security works and impacts their lives. They worry more about health care coverage.

Some pollsters use age 62—the minimum eligibility age for Social Security—as the cut point. Often two-couple senior households have someone 65 or older, usually the male, and a mate a few years younger, typically the female. Either would cause the household to be regarded as occupied by a senior.

Some researchers cite statistics showing that a sizable number of seniors retire prior to age 65 as their rationale for using lower thresholds. One pollster said his firm adds those 55 or older *who are retired* to the pool of persons 65 and older. Another company that focuses on health care and pharmaceutical issues reports always using age 63 because so many people now are retired by that age. Others use 62 for the same reason.

The views of advertising specialists mirror those of the pollsters, primarily because they rely heavily on market research to develop messages. In the words of one: "We have found that at age 55, people are already thinking about retirement issues as they relate to themselves or have parents or elderly relatives who are already there."

### Definition by Clients

A consulting firm's clients affect its definition of "senior." One polling firm whose major clients are nonprofits uses age 55.[5] Its president says this is the age when senior discounts kick in![6] The desire to take advantage of the discounts prods people of this age to acknowledge that they are, indeed, seniors.

Another survey firm with lots of political clients uses three categories: 55-64, 65-74, and 75 and older. The firm's spokesperson described "older seniors" as much different from "younger" and "middle-age" seniors. (There is some evidence that the age at which political participation starts to taper off is 75—although that age is likely to be pushed to the 80s as life spans lengthen in the twenty-first century.)

The chairman of a major political polling firm that specializes in candidate work pointed out that different cut points are used in different venues because states vary in the data base management systems used to classify voters by age. (Keep in mind that these specialist pollsters frequently survey off *registered* voter lists.)

### Definition by Available Resources

Sometimes cost—and, thus, sample size—is a factor. This forces some survey researchers to use age 60 (rather than 50 or 55) as their lower cut point. Age 60 is also used by several national firms that want to compare their findings to those elicited by major exit survey firms such as Voter News Service.

### Definition by Issues

The definition of "senior" varies among the firms that do a great deal of issue polling. Variation by issue was confirmed by the president of a firm that specializes in research for interest groups and the private sector. In conducting surveys and focus groups zeroing in on nursing home issues, for example, his firm never includes anyone younger than 65. Another firm uses age 75 and older when it conducts research related to nursing homes, and age 55 and older when it focuses on issues related to banking.

### Definition by Demographics

Demographics can also play a role in defining a senior. Said one pollster: "Our state has a relatively young population, so we tend to use 60 or 62 to define a senior."

## Marketing Firms More Sophisticated than Political Firms

Marketing/survey firms with a consumer orientation are more attentive to age definitions than politically oriented firms. Consumer marketing firms tend to change the definition of senior depending on the issue or client. For example, one firm's president acknowledged that it uses age 40 as the cut point when conducting surveys for cosmetics firms, but age 60 when the focus is on credit-card-use patterns! When surveying the World War II generation on veterans' issues, another consumer-oriented firm uses age 70 as the lower cut point for seniors. Several firms with both political and private sector clients acknowledge using age 60 for corporate clients but age 65 for political candidates.

Consumer marketing firms have a long history of conducting research on seniors. In a 1991 issue of *Public Relations Journal*, Frank Conaway, the president of a marketing communications firm specializing in corporate programs aimed at the 50-plus market, divided seniors into four segments—55-64 ("older" people), 65-74 ("elderly"), 75-84 ("aged"), and 85 and older ("very old"). He advised marketeers to analyze the time frames in which each segment was reared to determine the values and attitudes its members developed while growing up. For example, the 75-plus segment remembers growing up during the Depression, while the 55-plus segment enjoyed living standards after World War II that far exceeded anything their parents thought possible.[7] Consequently, we might expect one group to be satisfied with a frugal lifestyle while the other would expect all the comforts of modern living.

Researchers typically categorize seniors on the basis of chronological age, but at least one categorizes seniors based on life experiences. This approach, "gerontographics," divides people 55 and older into four segments. "Healthy indulgers" (18%) have experienced the fewest life-changing events such as retirement, widowhood, and chronic health conditions and, as a result, are most likely to behave like younger consumers. "Healthy hermits" (36%) have experienced events affecting their self-concept, such as the death of a spouse, and, thus, feel most comfortable staying put. "Ailing outgoers" (29%) have experienced health problems but maintain a positive self-esteem; still wanting to get the most out of life, they enjoy dining out and wearing attractive clothing. The fourth segment, "Frail recluses" (17%), have experienced physical and social decline and accepted their old-age status, often coping by strengthening their spiritual connections; they are most interested in health care products and services.[8]

These approaches for categorizing seniors—era-determined values and reactions to life-changing experiences—may prove as useful to political campaigns as to consumer marketing efforts. However, both consumer and political strategists may need to continue refining their definitions in light of one emerging trend: the baby boomers' refusal to admit they are growing old.

## Senior Age Definitions Will Change in the 21st Century

As baby boomers age, they will wreak havoc upon definitions of seniors developed up to now. An *American Demographics* magazine article speculates, "Rather than join the mature market, boomers will create a new and vibrant midlife marketplace over the next few decades. . . . Boomers will enter an adventurous life stage called 'midyouth' that will push traditional ideas of a mature market into oblivion. Power players, fun seekers, and matriarchs will typify boomers in their 50s."[9]

The resistance to getting old is not without basis. A 1998 book, summarizing the findings of a $10 million research project funded by the John D. and Catherine T. MacArthur Foundation, reports that older Americans today are in better health than previous generations and can expect to remain so for most of their lives.[10] Many don't feel old and believe they can stave off debilitating conditions with regular exercise, improved nutrition, herbal elixirs, and new drugs.

Some older Americans today can afford life-enhancing measures because they are enjoying greater financial prosperity thanks to Social Security, liberal company pensions, Medicare, a booming economy, and a hefty increase in the value of their homes.[11] As a result, they have become a prime market for luxury cars, upscale homes, exotic cruises, computers, and an assortment of other products and services designed to make their lives more comfortable and enjoyable. Healthy and affluent, they buy eyeglasses (or opt for laser eye surgery) not only to see better but also to look better, and they choose hearing aids that fit invisibly into the ear.

Not surprisingly, aging baby boomers are sensitive to what they are called. Dychtwald advises against calling them "seniors" or referring to them as "mature."[12] Possible new labels include "empty nesters," "primers," or Dychtwald's "middlessence."

## SURVEYING SENIORS

Campaign literature and TV (and radio) ads aimed at seniors are generally based on the findings of surveys and focus groups. A national survey of 103 market researchers and pollsters asked whether the firm conducts surveys of just seniors. Nearly two-thirds said "Yes," although most do so only on occasion.

Gathering the viewpoints of seniors presents some unique difficulties, given the limitations and attitudes discussed earlier. Do polling firms have special training or instructions for persons interviewing the elderly? Nearly half (49%) say "Yes." Among the most common instructions given to the interviewers are the following:

Speak more slowly and loudly; repeat more often.
Tell seniors it is *not* a solicitation call.
Use seniors to talk to seniors.
Advise interviewers of some difficulties (suspicion and fear, gender bias, for example).
Advise interviewers to maintain control of the interview (don't get off track).
If problematic, just hang up.

Let the phone ring seven or more times.
Allow longer for the interview.

While not all pollsters acknowledge giving special instructions, many affirm that surveying older residents (compared to younger ones) can create some special types of problems. (See table 3.1.) Of the pollsters surveyed, a large proportion acknowledge that seniors take longer to interview (89%), need to have questions repeated more often (80%), and may have trouble hearing the interviewer (71%). Nearly three-fourths (71%) of the pollsters say their interviewers have difficulty ending, or exiting, a survey because many seniors like to have someone with whom to chat and share their opinions.

When calling seniors on the telephone, interviewers should keep their voice pitch low. Studies show that older persons often have trouble hearing high-frequency sounds made by the letters "f," "th," "s," and "z." Ironically, shouting can make it harder, not easier, for some seniors to understand words or phrases because it raises voice pitch.[13]

Likewise, repeating a question precisely as asked may not be an effective strategy, particularly if the problem is the pitch. Some specialists advise restating the question using slightly different words.

**Table 3.1**

**Special Problems in Surveying Seniors**

| Problem Encountered | % |
| --- | --- |
| Longer time to interview | 89 |
| Need to repeat questions more often | 80 |
| Hard of hearing | 71 |
| Difficulty exiting survey | 71 |
| More opinionated | 42 |
| More likely to give "DK" or no opinion | 34 |
| More rings to get to the phone | 29 |
| Interviewee is somewhat disoriented | 24 |
| High refusal rates | 17 |
| Interviewee is in nursing home | 12 |

*Note: Respondents were asked: "What types of special problems do you typically encounter when surveying older residents compared to younger ones? Do you sometimes or often experience _____ ? Yes or No?"*

*Source: Telephone survey of 103 public opinion ad market research firms (listed on a national list) conducted September–October, 1999*

If it appears that the respondent is tiring, some firms acknowledge they will call back. Perhaps more than other age groups, seniors expect courtesy and good manners from those tapping their opinions. If not done properly, exiting an interview and/or trying to keep the senior interviewee focused on the specific question at hand can be perceived as rude.

If younger persons are used to solicit information from seniors via telephone, they need to be trained to approach the interview with an open mind. One researcher advised callers to visualize the elderly people they speak to on the phone not as old and frail, but rather as vital and active—like themselves. They need to learn that their own views of seniors may be stereotypical and erroneous: One "may think that all older people are terrific because she has an uncle who's 80 and still climbs mountains." Or another "may think the whole population is gravely ill because his aunt has Alzheimer's disease."[14]

Another touchy issue is how to address older women. One consultant cautions against use of "Ms.": "[I]t's 'Miss' or 'Mrs.' There are no 'Ms.'s' in this crowd."[15] (This will be less of a problem among baby boomers when they reach senior status.)

### Special Techniques for Surveying Seniors with Disabilities?

Just 31% of the pollsters surveyed acknowledged doing anything specific in surveying people with disabilities (sight, hearing, mental). Of those that do telephone surveys, most acknowledge they simply end the interview and drop these people out of the survey, especially the hearing-impaired.

Others are a bit more creative—driven by the topic at hand. One survey firm hired by a utility company to survey disabled persons in order to develop a hurricane evacuation plan sampled from lists of households with teletypewriter technology (TTY). Actually, a number of firms acknowledged using TTY phone lists. Others send out a mail survey to someone who cannot hear well but is interested in participating. Mail surveys can also be an alternative to reach visually impaired individuals; these surveys can be written in either large print or Braille.

Firms relying more on personal interviews and focus groups for gathering data from the disabled report using machines for the hearing-impaired and Braille for the blind. Others use interviewers with disabilities similar to those being interviewed.

When disabled persons are asked to appear for an interview, location becomes an important consideration. First-floor locations (or easy elevator access), close proximity to the parking lot and restrooms, and wheelchair accessibility make it easier for this group to participate. Polling firms are also more likely to provide transportation and food for these participants.

Modifications for surveying people with disabilities is clearly an issue that should be studied more carefully because of an apparent lack of sensitivity on the part of some pollsters. When we asked, "Are there any specific things you do in surveying people with disabilities?" one told us it was "a stupid question." Another who at first acknowledged the firm did nothing, instantly asked, "Are we going to be sued for this?"

## Gender and Safety Issues: Telephone Surveys

More senior-age women than men answer the telephone. Why? First, there are more senior women. Second, even in two-person households, the woman tends to answer the phone because she's in the house and the man often is not.

The oversupply of women respondents means that interviewers are left with some unpleasant options. One is to ask to speak to "the man of the house." To say the least, this can be insulting to a woman because it implies that her opinion is less important than a man's. If, on the other hand, the interviewer hangs up upon hearing a female voice, then dials back and asks for the man of the house, the woman may become frightened.

## Using Focus Groups

Among the pollsters surveyed for this study, 86% acknowledge they use focus groups to gather information from targeted populations. Focus groups generally involve eight to twelve persons brought together to discuss a particular product, issue, or topic under the direction of a moderator. In the world of politics, focus groups are often used to test messages, refine the wording and order of questions used in questionnaires, devise campaign slogans and platforms, and "hone and tone" issue stances.

One researcher, Scott Walker, offers some insight:

> The strengths of a focus group are different from those of a poll. A focus group will not tell you whether a position is mostly favored or mostly opposed by the electorate. A focus group will tell you how voters approach issues, how much thinking they have done about issues, how deeply they care about different issues, what wording resonates best when taking a stand on an issue, and how willing the voters are to accept and believe more information on a topic. By knowing these things, you can select and design messages to persuade and secure voters.[16]

Rea and Parker, in *Designing and Conducting Survey Research*, state that focus groups are best conducted in easily accessible, convenient locations close to the respondents' homes or workplaces.[17] Focus groups should also be conducted at convenient times.[18]

We asked our sample of pollsters who do focus group work if "there are any special things that they do when conducting focus groups composed of seniors?" Here are their responses:

Recruit differently.
Pay more attention to safety issues.
Give better directions to the location.
Make print on handouts and charts bigger.
Use fewer words in written materials.
Choose accessible locations close to where they live.
Hold group sessions during the day—morning or early afternoon.
Take frequent breaks.
Speak louder.
Include instructions to bring their eyeglasses or hearing aids.
Read the material aloud.
Feed them better than other age groups!
Provide transportation. Have drivers pick them up or pay for cabs.
If at night, choose a place with a well-lit and secure parking lot.
Make reminder calls and send letters several times before the session.
Use smaller groups than normal.
Select a moderator with experience interacting with seniors.
Never include young people and 75-year-olds in the same focus group.
Be more patient, kind, and respectful; don't talk down to them.
When first contacting a potential participant, use a trained interviewer to "listen for coherency."
Help participants get to their chairs when they arrive.
Offer extra reassurance about the use of the results; privacy issues come to mind most.
Conduct shorter sessions.
Go slowly, and give good instructions.
When using charts, make them large and mix colors and shapes; don't use highlighters.
Avoid high-tech jargon.
Avoid using electronic or computer-based response mechanisms.

Some focus-group-oriented firms, all of whom do political work, admit that they tend to use rather arbitrary age cut-off points. Several said they do not include persons older than 70 in their focus groups; another uses 80 as the cut point. These firms will likely want to re-think their policies as seniors live longer and in better health.

## SUMMARY AND RECOMMENDATIONS

Aiming for senior voters is sometimes easier said than done. As we have seen in this chapter, there is no universal definition of an "older voter." Definitions vary for various reasons and under different circumstances.

Political pollsters are less attuned to the nuances of age definitions than the more product-driven market researchers. Many political pollsters still rely on the traditional age 65. When the baby boomers reach retirement age, definitions of a senior voter will likely change.

Surveys and focus groups are often the source of data used by the candidate or professional campaign consultant to design campaign literature and TV and radio ads. About half of the professional polling firms surveyed have special training for those charged with interviewing seniors. But most firms acknowledge that seniors take longer to interview, need to have questions repeated more often, and are more difficult to bring to a polite and respectful end.

Telephone surveys require more attention to the pitch of the interviewer's voice as well as certain letters of the alphabet because they are harder for seniors to hear. A long interview may require a call back if the respondent appears to be tiring. Some special attention must be taken when surveying older women—which title to use when addressing them, how to avoid insulting them when asking for the adult male in the household, and how to allay fears about safety if the male is not at home.

Few public opinion firms acknowledge doing anything specific when they survey persons with disabilities. Most telephone survey firms readily admit they simply end the interview when they encounter someone with hearing or mental impairments. Others arbitrarily exclude persons older than a certain age. But some firms employ rather creative techniques—sampling from TTY lists, sending out mail surveys as an alternative, and using similarly disabled persons as interviewers (most often in-person interviews).

Location and access are extremely important considerations when involving seniors in focus groups. First-floor locations, close proximity to the parking lot and restrooms, and wheelchair accessibility are essential. Holding sessions in the morning or early afternoon rather than in the evening, taking frequent breaks, speaking louder, and offering transportation are other important aspects to consider. And facilitators are advised to avoid high-tech jargon and computer-based response mechanisms.

### Candidates Must Do Their Homework before Targeting

Candidates committed to targeting senior voters must realize that a careful analysis of precisely who *are* their senior constituents is essential. At a minimum, checklists must include a calculation of:

Type of community. Identify where age-segregated communities exist within your district.

Type of residential facility. Do seniors reside in mobile home parks, condominiums, townhouses, assisted-living facilities, nursing homes, apartment complexes, single-family dwellings?

Voter registration patterns (Democrat, Republican, third parties, inde-
  pendents).
Voter histories—turnout patterns; candidate support patterns.
Age profile (young-old versus old-old).
Socioeconomic status (income; education; race/ethnicity; retirement status).
Gender ratio (females-to-males).
Health and disability status.
TV and radio stations/programs with larger senior audiences.
Professional organizations with large senior memberships and/or active local
  organizations (for example, AARP, veterans' groups).

Successful candidates and consulting firms build such information household
by household, block by block, and precinct by precinct when available data permits.[19] With limited time and resources, careful identification helps a candidate
decide such things as which neighborhoods to walk, whose door to knock on,
which households to drop targeted mail into, which groups to address, where to
place advertisements, which issues to stress, and whether to offer literature in
different languages. Decisions like these can mean the difference between winning and losing a campaign.

# 4

# ✛

# Campaigning to Seniors:
## *Going after Votes*

*Photo 4.1    Candidates on the campaign trail soon learn to go to functions heavily attended by seniors, such as this dedication of a nursing home for veterans with Alzheimer's.*

34 Chapter 4

Asked why he robbed banks, Willie Sutton said, "Because that's where the money is." The same is true when it comes to targeting voters in an election: You go where the votes are. More precisely, you go after the votes you need to win, the ones that are most readily available to you.

Ron Faucheux, Editor, *Campaigns & Elections,* July 1999

Candidates and campaign professionals know well that targeting is the way to win elections. Targeting is a broad-brushed activity that cuts across all campaign activities:

Simply put, targeting is the method a campaign—large or small—uses to determine where it's going to concentrate direct contact resources (i.e., mailings, telephone calling, door-to-door canvassing, yard sign efforts, neighborhood parties). Most campaigns have a limited amount of time, money and volunteers. So they need to make sure that when the trigger is pulled on a campaign activity—whether it's a candidate canvass, a literature drop, a mailing, a round of persuasion calling or a get-out-the-vote (GOTV) door hanger effort—that they reach the right voters with the right message.[1]

## SENIOR VOTERS ARE THE MOST TARGETED AGE GROUP

No question about it, candidates and campaigns target senior voters more than other age groups. A survey of Florida candidates for state legislative and cabinet posts in the late 1990s asked: "How much did you target your campaign to the following age groups? 18–29? 30–49? 50–64? 65 and older?" The data show that candidates heavily targeted voters in the latter two categories. (See figure 4.1.) While one might say "Yeah, but that's Florida," the pattern held true *regardless* of the percentage of seniors in a given constituency.

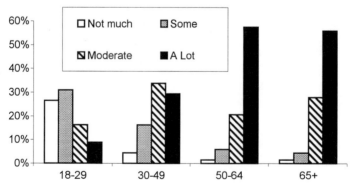

*Figure 4.1   How Much Each Age Group Was Targeted by Candidate*
Source: Mail survey of 68 Florida candidates for statewide cabinet offices and state legislative contests, conducted by the author, December 1998.

Candidates say they know better than anyone else how to reach older voters. When asked: "Who gave you the best advice on how to reach older voters?" (multiple responses possible), nearly three-fourths of the candidates surveyed identified themselves. (See figure 4.2.) The next best sources are professional campaign consultants, campaign coordinators, and elected officials in the area.

Few identify political parties (either at the national or state level) as particularly helpful. This finding is further proof that more candidates are going it alone—running their campaigns independently from the party, although still running with a party label.

Naturally, professional political consultants have a different viewpoint. A study conducted for the Center for Congressional and Presidential Studies at American University found that consultants judge themselves as qualitatively superior to other political actors—candidates, the national political parties, and journalists.[2]

Professional political consultants do, however, concur with the candidates about the declining role of political parties. Researchers asked these pros: "Please tell me whether you strongly agree, somewhat agree, somewhat disagree, or strongly disagree that political consultants have taken the place of political parties in providing [management or strategic advice; media or campaign advertising; polling; direct mail; opposition research; campaign finance or fundraising; get-out-the-vote efforts or field operations]." The majority of the pros either "strongly agree" or "somewhat agree" that consultants outperform parties in *each* of these campaign-related activities. (Of course, the political parties all have their favorite stable of professionals whom they recommend their candidates use.)

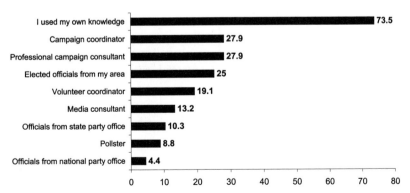

*Figure 4.2   Who Gave Candidate Best Advice on How to Reach Older Voters?*
*Source: Mail survey of 68 candidates for Florida cabinet and state legislative seats, conducted by the author, December 1998.*

## WHERE BEST TO PITCH ONE'S MESSAGE?
## ARE SOME SENIOR SPOTS BETTER THAN OTHERS?

Candidates everywhere "go where the voters are." In Florida, favorite spots are civic clubs with an older membership (50%), senior centers (34%), and retirement communities (25%). Candidates spend little time mingling with younger constituents, although they spend more time with them than with seniors at nursing homes or assisted-living facilities (ALFs). (See table 4.1.) But is it a good idea to bypass these facilities?

### Activity Directors: Ignoring Senior
### Residential Facilities May Not Be Wise

Just 21% of activity directors of nursing homes and ALFs acknowledge that any political candidate came to their facility during the 1998 election cycle.

**Table 4.1**

| Where Candidates Go Most in Search of Votes | | | | |
|---|---|---|---|---|
| **Places visited** | **Never** | **Some** | **A lot** | **No answer** |
| | % | % | % | % |
| Civic clubs with older membership | 3 | 44 | 50 | 3 |
| Senior citizen center | 25 | 38 | 34 | 3 |
| Retirement communities | 21 | 49 | 25 | 6 |
| Civic clubs with younger membership | 16 | 59 | 21 | 4 |
| High schools | 44 | 43 | 10 | 3 |
| Jr./Community colleges | 41 | 49 | 6 | 4 |
| Nursing homes | 34 | 62 | 4 | 0 |
| Assisted living facilities | 34 | 59 | 4 | 3 |
| College/university | 49 | 38 | 4 | 9 |

*Note: Candidates were asked: "How often did you make visits to _____ ? Never, some, or a lot?"*

*Source: Mail survey of 68 candidates for Florida cabinet posts and state legislative seats, conducted by the author December, 1998.*

Most of the visits were initiated by candidates, although some did come at the invitation of the facility's CEO, activity director, or an organized group of residents. (See figure 4.3.)

Some directors take the candidates to task for ignoring senior facilities. One activity director routinely asks candidates to a party for centenarians but says, "They *never* come":

> Seniors take voting very seriously. When a candidate is asked three times to visit a facility and three times has an excuse or doesn't send a representative, seniors will not be interested in them! A flag off the White House does not cut it in my book. Show my residents you care!! They helped make this a free country, participated in campaigns, and saw nearly every invention ever made. So don't they deserve candidates' respect?

Many candidates still stereotype residents of nursing homes and ALFs as "frail and/or demented" and write off their votes. But not all residents of these facilities suffer from dementia or end-stage disease. Actually, these residents often have a wide range of skills and capabilities.

A number of persons living in nursing homes and ALFs are quite capable of following politics and voting, even if they must vote absentee rather than at the polls. But they need candidates to come to them (in some form) because they can no longer go to the candidates—for example, to political forums or debates. And in close elections, every vote counts!

The tendency of candidates to bypass nursing homes and ALFs is likely to change in the near future as more Americans move into them or other types of

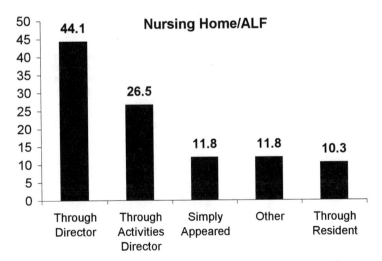

*Figure 4.3    Method by Which Candidate Gained Access to Nursing Home/ALF*
*Source: Mail survey of 68 candidates for Florida cabinet and state legislative seats, conducted by the author, December 1998.*

congregate-care facilities. Nursing home and ALF activity directors[3] and election supervisors[4] believe that candidates should make a greater effort to visit these facilities or provide them with audio- and videotapes and campaign literature.

When asked to identify "Which of the following campaign techniques do you believe would be the most effective in reaching your residents?" nursing home/ALF activity directors identified a wide range of techniques (see figure 4.4) including, among others, large-print ads/brochures (66%), visits by the candidates to meet individually with residents (55%), candidate videos delivered to the facility (33%), candidate forums at the facility (30%), audiocassettes for visually impaired (16%).

Several activity directors offered rather detailed comments about the problems of—and potential solutions for—reaching the elderly in their facilities:

> I feel that candidate videos delivered to the facility would be a great way to reach our residents who are still able to vote. As activities director, I would be in charge of showing the videos, having discussion groups, and letting them decide on their own for whom they would prefer to vote. This past election, some of the residents who voted needed to be more informed about the candidates than they were.

Some suggest that television stations—private and public—make videos of campaign debates available to these facilities. Because most debates are televised at night, many residents are not able to watch them in their entirety. Activity directors say they could replay the debates at a time and in a tempo more in sync with their residents' time clocks and hold discussion groups for interested residents.

Another director observed the spill-over effect of campaigning in nursing home/ALF facilities: "Sitting down on a one-to-one basis is the best way for communication of any type. Even if residents are unable or choose not to vote, the staff, family members, and visitors, as well as volunteers, see that residents in a nursing home are being thought of and their issues discussed" by the candidate.

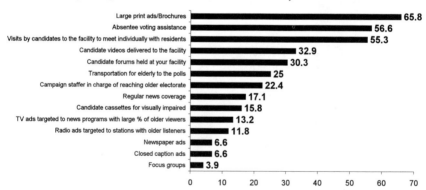

*Figure 4.4   Campaign Techniques Judged to Be Most Effective in Reaching Nursing Home/ ALF Residents*
Note: "From your observations, which of the following campaign techniques do you believe would be most effective in reaching your residents?"
Source: Mail survey of nursing home/ALF activities directors in Hillsborough, Pinellas, and Pasco counties, December 1998.

If candidate forums are held within a senior facility, the candidates should have some knowledge of the mental faculties of the residents. As one director noted, "Forums and debates may get too wordy, complicated, and use too many catch phrases for the cognitive levels of nursing home residents." This does not mean, however, that candidates should talk down to them: "Candidates need to treat older voters as people, not just votes. They should ask [residents] their opinions when and if they visit. Don't cut them [residents] off."

Visits to nursing homes and ALFs, like visits to other venues, can be perceived by the residents as potentially dull and may fail to attract a crowd. Activity directors suggested that one way to inject excitement into candidate visits is giveaways. Regardless of age, everyone—especially someone unable to get out much—likes to get freebies: "Have the candidate or someone from the party visit, hand out stickers, answer questions, shake hands, pass out posters, or maybe even take pictures of the residents (Polaroid) [with the candidate], which they could keep."

Most facilities surveyed (91%) say they do not "have an official policy about political candidates" coming into their facility. Of the few that do, most do *not* allow candidates to campaign in the facility—perhaps a shortsighted policy. Some also require that in the interest of fairness both candidates running in a given race must be present at the same time.

Ironically, senior-dominated mobile home parks in some places raise more prohibitions against campaigning than nursing homes or ALFs. Candidates increasingly complain about encountering resistance from retirement communities. One young woman candidate for the state legislature describes her ordeal:

Photo 4.2   *Gunn Orlander proudly wears an "I Voted" sticker. Seniors turn out to vote in much higher proportions than other age groups, the primary reason for their being targeted by candidates and political parties. Photograph by Scott Iskowitz,* The Tampa Tribune, *used with permission.*

I knew they were a critical constituency. I desperately tried to get access to the mobile home communities—and there are lots in my district. . . . But no matter what I did, it didn't work. They all treated me (the candidate) as a solicitor. And most parks have anti-solicitation policies. But I was not trying to sell anything . . . just to inform them about my issue stances and ask them for their vote.

Much the same is true of gated communities. More seniors are choosing to live in such restricted-access residential areas because they feel safer there than in other neighborhoods and they can afford it.

Residents of such places may be advised to re-think their policies if they want to maximize their political clout. Prohibiting salespersons is a lot different, and more costly, than prohibiting democracy in action.

### Election Officials: Most Recognize the Special Needs of Seniors

Across the country, seminars for election officials have begun focusing on the special needs of seniors, especially those with deteriorating sight, hearing, and mobility. Most of the focus has been on how to make the processes of registration and voting more accessible to these individuals. We surveyed election officials to learn more about some of those issues. But we also asked them in their capacity as *elected* officials, just as we asked candidates and nursing home/ALF activity directors, about outreach techniques.

Many election supervisors acknowledged that some fairly simple tactics would be "somewhat useful" or "very useful" to improve campaign outreach to the elderly with visual, hearing, or mobility limitations. (See figure 4.5.) They heartily endorse the ideas of large-print brochures; more candidate forums in— and visits to—nursing homes, ALFs, and retirement centers; targeted TV and radio ads; and closed-caption TV ads, among others.

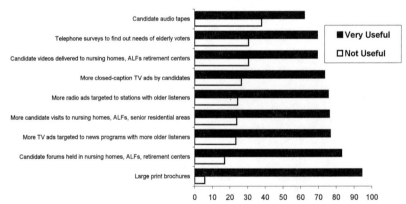

*Figure 4.5   Election Officials' Recommendations: Campaigning to Disabled Voters*
*Note: "How useful are the following for candidates to reach voters who have visual, hearing, or mobility limitations?"*
*Source: Mail survey of Florida Supervisor of Elections, conducted July–September, 1999.*

Among Florida's election officials, consensus is high that each of the above approaches would be helpful in targeting seniors with disabilities. Most lay the responsibility for better outreach squarely in the laps of (1) candidates; (2) advocacy groups; and (3) family, friends, and neighbors.

Other election officials have aired concerns about several of these outreach mechanisms. One supervisor from a county with a fast-growing senior population worries about candidates going to nursing homes whose residents are severely disabled: "I have mixed feelings about having the candidates visit nursing homes. In many cases, nursing home residents might be overwhelmed by the presence of candidates in the home." She prefers that candidates go to senior facilities or ALFs where the voters "are in better shape."

She is not alone. Some 80% of the nursing home and ALF activity directors surveyed say either "some" or "a lot" of their residents suffer from mental problems that affect their ability to follow political campaigns. (See figure 4.6.)

Another election official fears that candidate visits to these types of facilities offer too many opportunities for improprieties with absentee ballots. (We will say more about this problem in the next chapter.)

Several supervisors blame negative TV ads for "confusing" older voters, although they do not detail exactly how this occurs. Florida's seniors concur with this assessment. (More will be said about TV ads later in the chapter.)

In spite of these concerns, most election officials strongly endorse the general idea of improved candidate outreach to older citizens with disabilities. Some see the Internet as one powerful new way to connect confined seniors to campaigns. Several Florida election officials are actively urging advocacy and good government groups to focus on improving the computer—and Internet—literacy of seniors so that they might have access to the range and depth of political information tapped into by other age groups.

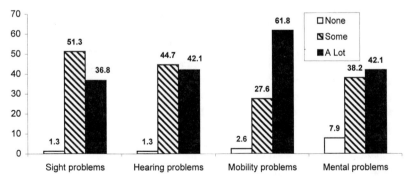

*Figure 4.6   Problems that Affect Nursing Home and Assisted Living Facility Residents' Ability to Follow Political Campaigns*
Note: "Please estimate how many of your residents have the following problems that affect their ability to follow political campaigns?"
Source: Mail survey of nursing home/ALF activities directors in Hillsborough, Pinellas, and Pasco counties, December 1998.

This is a wise recommendation. Once seniors become computer and Internet literate, they are nearly three times more likely to use the Internet to follow politics than younger age groups. (See table 4.2.) This should come as no surprise. Seniors already follow political news via newspapers, magazines, television, and radio. The Internet links all of the above.[5]

## HELPING VOTERS WITH SENSORY DISABILITIES

For some time, the National Council on Disabilities has been studying ways to improve access to multimedia technology (including computers) by people with sensory disabilities.[6] Tech Watch, a community-based, cross-disability task force, routinely advises the National Council on how to accomplish this goal.

Blind and visually impaired persons are the least well served by currently available multimedia technology. These persons also have the most difficulty following politics via the electronic media, especially in state and local races and ballot initiatives. TV and radio news programs typically pick a few "hot" races to cover—and most of those are timed near election day. Detailed coverage of the pros and cons of ballot initiatives is often cursory at best.

While the print media cover a wider range of contests, the visually impaired cannot read these accounts very well, if at all. In the case of newspapers, small or blurred type, the transparency and/or grainy texture of the paper, and the lack of contrast between the paper and the ink are formidable obstacles.

**Table 4.2**

**Everyday On-Line Users Reliance on Web for Political and Evening News**

| Use of Web | Age of Daily On-Line User | | | |
|---|---|---|---|---|
| | 18-29 | 30-49 | 50-64 | 65+ |
| Get news and information on current events, public issues, or politics | 8 | 10 | 8 | 23 |
| Get financial information such as stock quotes or compile information to buy stocks or bonds | 8 | 9 | 16 | 23 |

Note: Respondents were asked: "Please tell me how often, if ever, you engage in each of the following on-line activities. First, how often you go on-line to _____ ? Everyday, 3–5 days per week, 1 or 2 days per week, once every few weeks, less often, or never"?

Source: The Pew Research Center for the People & the Press. Telephone survey of a nationwide sample of adult Internet users who go on-line for news conducted October 26–December 1, 1998. The sampling error is plus or minus 3.5 percentage points.

The National Council on Disabilities has urged those responsible for technological innovations, particularly with regard to computers, to design machines that permit users to do the following:

customize sizes and types of fonts,
customize colors for fonts and backgrounds;
customize interface timings;
focus and enlarge parts of screens;
have a keyboard alternative to a mouse;
interface with speech programs;
choose graphical images with video descriptions;
have more accessible documentation;
have more accessible buttons and keys;
have aural and visual status messages;
detect the presence and direction of hypertext links; and
operate controls without having to see them.[7]

The hearing-impaired can often be reached via TTY (teletypewriter technology) first developed in 1964. With passage of Title IV of the Americans with Disabilities Act (ADA) in 1990, telecommunications relay services were established nationwide, enabling people with TTY phones to communicate with people who have voice telephones.[8]

In 1993, the Television Decoder Circuitry Act became effective, requiring all televisions manufactured in or imported into the United States with 13-inch or larger screens to have built-in decoders capable of displaying closed captions. But despite subsequent legislation requiring closed captioning of television programming, "captioning continues to be viewed as an add-on or postproduction service rather than as a basic right and an integral aspect of the news, information, education, and entertainment milieu. For example, the vast majority of cable television remains uncaptioned."[9] And political candidates are increasingly relying on cable television to reach seniors.

The National Council on Disabilities report, *Access to Multimedia Technology by People with Sensory Disabilities,* also delineates the shortcomings of videos—both for the blind and the hearing-impaired. Most videos are produced with no closed captioning. And the availability of videos for sight-impaired individuals remains bleak.

*Photo 4.3   Sight-impaired individuals have the most difficulty following campaigns, especially "down-ballot" contests which are not featured on television. Few candidates for these offices think to provide audiocassettes to visually impaired constituents.*

Thus, in spite of major technological advancements in multimedia, most have yet to become integral parts of the average political campaign. These shortcomings are evident in our Florida seniors survey.

## WHAT SENIORS SAY ABOUT CAMPAIGNS

According to a growing number of seniors, campaigns today are more negative, a bit more bland and unprovocative, less issue-based, more driven by media and polls, less personal, and far too long. (Other age groups lodge the same criticisms, although not so vociferously.) In spite of these complaints, seniors, more than other age groups, remain interested in the electoral process and committed to participating as much as their health permits.

### National Data: Seniors See More Mud and Less Information

Surveys document the extensiveness of the electorate's disgust and disappointment with current campaign tactics. For example, a post-1998 election survey by the Pew Research Center for the People & the Press found that 68% of those who voted acknowledged that "there was more mudslinging or negative campaigning" compared to the previous election cycle. Seventy-two percent of those 65 and older complained about this trend, but so, too, did the majority of other age groups (66% of the 18-to-29-year-olds, 71% of the 30-to-49-year-olds, and 61% of persons 50 to 64).[10]

The same survey of voters inquired whether "you feel you learned enough about the candidates and the issues to make an informed choice between candidates?" While younger groups are more likely to say they did not learn enough,[11] nearly one-fourth (23%) of those 65 and older have the same complaint.

### Concerns about Media and Pollsters

In general, Americans are divided in their overall impressions of today's campaigns. As shown in table 4.3, nearly half or more of those who *vote* give grades of C, D, or F to every type of participant in the political process. Older voters, compared to other age groups, are slightly more critical of the press and pollsters.

Dissatisfaction with the news media's coverage—not just of politics—is most intense among seniors. For example, one question asked whether "the news organizations get the facts straight or are often inadequate." The "inadequate" response was given by more than half (54%) of the 18-to-29 group, but two-thirds of the seniors.[12]

More than half (56%) of all adults believe that news organizations are "politically biased in their reporting." Older Americans are more likely to have this opinion than younger ones—65% of those 50 and older, compared to 53% of 30-to-49-year-olds and 50% of the 18-to-29-year-olds.[13]

Seniors are still more likely to see a strong watchdog role for the press in keeping politicians honest. For example, 60% of the oldest group, but 55% of the 18-

**Table 4.3**

**Campaign Grades of C, D, F**
**(1998 Election: Voters)**

| Campaign Action | C, D, F Grades | | | |
|---|---|---|---|---|
| | 18-29 % | 30-49 % | 50-64 % | 65+ % |
| Press | 46 | 53 | 52 | 51 |
| Pollsters | 45 | 48 | 47 | 53 |
| Talk show hosts | 60 | 53 | 53 | 45 |
| Campaign consultants | 57 | 54 | 54 | 46 |
| Republican party | 51 | 61 | 68 | 67 |
| Democratic party | 49 | 48 | 42 | 47 |
| Voters | 47 | 51 | 40 | 49 |

Source: *The Pew Research Center for the People & the Press. Post-election survey conducted November 6–10, 1998. The voter subset sample has a sampling error of plus or minus 4.5 percentage points (at the 95% confidence level).*

to-29-year-olds, say that criticism of political leaders by the news media "keeps leaders from doing things that should not be done."

## Media Reliance Patterns during Campaigns

Americans rely heavily on both television and newspapers for their election coverage. More than 80% of seniors say they follow the election through each of these two media. (See table 4.4.) Seniors are less likely than other age groups to rely on radio or on-line sources, although the latter figure will undoubtedly change in the twenty-first century.

Regular news continues to give voters of all ages a better idea of where candidates stand on issues than TV commercials and advertisements. However, TV ads should not be discounted entirely because a sizable proportion—28% (26% of seniors)—say they depend more upon TV ads. Roughly the same proportions say that TV commercials and advertisements give them a better idea of the personal attributes of the candidates. (See table 4.5.) Pew Research Center surveys show that these numbers changed little during the 1990s.

In spite of seniors' criticisms, they still participate at higher rates than other age groups. A survey conducted for the Council on Excellence in Government affirms that older citizens remain the most "connected" to the political process.

**Table 4.4**

**Major Source of Election Campaign News**
**(Those Who Voted)**

| Voters | All | 18-29 | 30-49 | 50-64 | 65+ |
|---|---|---|---|---|---|
| **Television** | 70 | 73 | 62 | 71 | 81 |
| Network | 17 | 21 | 15 | 15 | 18 |
| Local | 41 | 52 | 37 | 39 | 47 |
| Cable | 20 | 17 | 15 | 25 | 27 |
| Other | 1 | - | 1 | 1 | 1 |
| Don't know | 1 | - | 2 | - | 2 |
| **Newspapers** | 74 | 63 | 75 | 69 | 83 |
| **Radio** | 21 | 25 | 26 | 21 | 10 |
| **Magazines** | 7 | 8 | 7 | 8 | 6 |
| **On-line sources** | 6 | 13 | 9 | 3 | 1 |
| **Don't know/refuse** | 2 | 3 | 3 | 2 | 3 |

*Note: Respondents were asked: "How did you get most of your news about the election campaigns in your state and district? From television, from newspapers, from radio, from magazines, or from computer on-line sources. Did you get most of your TV news about the campaign from network TV news, from local TV news, or from cable TV news?*

*Source: The Pew Research Center for the People & the Press. Telephone survey of a nationwide sample of adults 18 years of age and older conducted November 6–10, 1998. The sampling error (at the 95% confidence level) is plus or minus 3.5 percentage points.*

Just one in eight (12%) seniors feels "very disconnected" from government, while nearly one in three (30%) young adults age 18 to 34 feels that way.

## A Closer State-Level Look at Senior Opinions

The Florida senior survey asked: "Compared to past elections, were you more or less interested in this year's election or about the same?" Most said "about the same" (62%) or "more interested" (25%).

However, one in ten said "less interested." The less interested fall into two categories: (1) short-term residents (less than one year); and (2) seniors not living in adult communities. Both patterns are understandable. New residents tend not to vote, particularly in state and local elections, until they get a feel for the lay of the political land. Seniors not living in adult communities may be preoccupied with safety and transportation issues, while seniors in adult communities, even those with health problems, may be more likely to remain engaged and active in the company of like-minded friends and neighbors.

**Table 4.5**

| Usefulness of Candidate Commercials: National Survey 1996 Presidential Contest Voters | | | | |
|---|---|---|---|---|
| **Use** | **18-29** | **30-49** | **50-64** | **65+** |
| **To decide which candidate to vote for** | | | | |
| Very helpful | 8 | 4 | 5 | 3 |
| Somewhat helpful | 21 | 20 | 21 | 23 |
| Not too helpful | 31 | 27 | 26 | 26 |
| Not at all helpful | 40 | 48 | 48 | 43 |
| **To determine what candidates were like personally** | | | | |
| News reports | 60 | 69 | 67 | 67 |
| Candidates' commercials and advertisements | 37 | 26 | 26 | 22 |

*Notes: Don't knows and refused excluded. Respondents were asked: "How helpful were the candidates' commercials to you in deciding which candidates to vote for? Would you say they were very helpful, somewhat helpful, not too helpful, or not at all helpful?" Respondents were also asked: "Which gave you a better idea of what the candidates were like personally—news reports or candidates' TV commercials and advertisements?"*

*Source: The Pew Research Center for the People & the Press. Telephone re-interviews of 1,012 voters conducted November 7–10, 1996. The sampling margin of error (at the 95% confidence level) is plus or minus 3 percentage points.*

## Changes in Their Ability to Follow Political Campaigns

The aging process has made some seniors less able—or willing—to attend candidate forums and debates. It has also created difficulties for them in reading, seeing, or hearing campaign pitches.

*Photo 4.4    Not even slight mobility limitations can keep this woman from attending a political forum. However, a growing number of seniors say they no longer feel comfortable attending such events, primarily for health and safety reasons.*

*Drop in Forum Attendance*

Just 6% of Florida's seniors report attending a political forum or debate during the previous campaign. We asked them to put this in historical perspective: "In recent years, have you gone to candidate forums/debates more, the same, or less than you did five years ago?" While 58% say they have never gone to such events, 22% say they now go less. Only 4% say they go more.

What are the reasons for the drop? As shown in table 4.6, the responses fall into several categories: health, mobility, disinterest or disgust with politics and politicians, and logistics (time, place, distance). Health, mobility, and logistics difficulties are mentioned most by those with limited sight, hearing, and physical abilities.

For example, one retired woman in her early 60s who lives alone said she is less likely to attend forums "Because I'm diabetic now and I've been having trouble with my health." Another woman in her early 70s who lives in an assisted-living facility said, "My husband is very sick and I have to take care of him."

*Difficulties Reading, Seeing, and Hearing*

Florida's seniors were presented with a list of things that might make following campaigns a bit more difficult. They were asked "how big a problem [each] is for you . . . a big problem, somewhat of a problem, or no problem at all?" Reading campaign literature and seeing or hearing TV ads pose problems for some.

Nearly 15% say that *reading campaign literature* is more difficult. One-third of the less-educated, poorer seniors expressed this concern, as did nearly one-third of senior Hispanics, and nearly one-fourth (23%) of those with sight impairments. These patterns, plus additional data, indicate the need to produce literature that is written simply, provided in other languages (when targeting senior immigrants), and written in big print. More will be said about this later in the chapter.

Nearly one in ten Florida seniors reports having trouble *seeing ads on television*. Slightly fewer say they *cannot hear television ads* all that well. Certain colors and speech patterns are problematic for them.

The senior survey corroborated anecdotal evidence that has suggested increased difficulty for seniors in following certain types of races. Ballot initiatives and amendments as well as judicial contests are particularly troublesome. Here are the proportions of seniors reporting some or lots of difficulty following specific types of contests: amendments (30%), judicial contests (25%), school board races (19%), cabinet races (19%), state legislature races (18%), county commission races (18%).

The lower the profile of the office—and the less often television (free and paid) provides close coverage of the race—the more difficulty is reported. This is particularly frustrating for seniors who *want* to be informed. When they have to rely on the printed information, some special problems kick in.

**Table 4.6**

## Why Seniors Go to Candidate Forums and Debates Less

| Reason | % | Reason | % |
|---|---|---|---|
| Health reasons | 15.9 | Already made up my mind before forum | 2.3 |
| Just disinterested, don't want to get involved | 13.6 | New resident | 1.5 |
| Just don't get out much anymore | 12.9 | Candidates come here | .8 |
| Turned off of politics, lost faith in government | 7.6 | Too rehearsed | .8 |
| Aren't as useful as in past or as frequent | 6.8 | Changing partisan balance means it's less interesting | .8 |
| Not enough time, too busy | 6.1 | Inconvenient times and places | .8 |
| Don't like crowds, traffic, distances | 5.3 | Too tired at night | .8 |
| Transportation, can't drive, especially at night | 4.5 | Have never been involved in politics | .8 |
| Candidates are too negative toward each other | 3.0 | Out of town | .8 |
| Easier to watch on TV, read paper | 2.3 | No reason | 12.9 |

*Note: Respondents (22%) wo acknowledged they go to candidate forum/debates less frequently than 5 years ago were asked an open-ended question of "Why?"*

*Source: Telephone survey of a statewide sample of 600 adults 60 years of age or older, conducted December, 1998. The sampling margin of error (at the 95% confidence level) is plus or minus 4 percentage points.*

## RATING CANDIDATE BROCHURES

In *Campaign Strategies and Message Design,* Mary Ann Moffitt acknowledges targeting as an essential campaign tactic: "[In] a campaign situation, each population receives its own, original and specialized message. When conceptualizing and executing the design of messages for a campaign, you want to retain the figure of *each population receiving its own, uniquely designed, messages*" (emphasis added).[14]

Mailed pieces are almost perfect targeting vehicles. As Gold and March acknowledge: "Mail has become a particularly attractive alternative as Census information can now be evenly laid over political subdivisions through new mapping software."[15] Yet another reason is that voter registration and vote history lists are readily available. As a result, one can literally drop different pieces of mail into the same neighborhood, often targeted by age. The authors describe it as follows:

> We are slowly building a household-by-household, voter specific list of people that gives us tremendous knowledge about each household. Things like: their propensity to vote, what issues concern them, what magazines they subscribe to, what kind of refrigerators they own. . . . Some of the characteristics obviously carry more political implications than others, but unexpected correlations can arise if you do . . . extensive survey research with lots of demographic cross-tabs. If you overlay attitudinal responses onto seemingly non-predictive information that is available on the list—things like what kind of car people own, how many weapons are in the household, whether they have a fishing license—you can all of a sudden start seeing some correlations that can enable you to target on an extremely refined basis. That's really important, given the fact that the cost of mail—both postage and production—has gone up substantially in the last six, seven years.[16]

### The Role of Brochures and Direct Mail

Brochures, postcards, and newsletters often arrive in a household via the U.S. mail. Direct mail is one of the most expensive forms of political communication, which makes it even more imperative that the piece be targeted to the right voters. As one direct-mail professional puts it: "Persuasion direct mail is only as good as the names you choose to mail to. Your award winning brochure is worthless if it isn't delivering the right message to the right people."[17]

Direct mail plays a critical role in "targeting voters, developing issues, recruiting volunteers, molding opinions, getting out the vote, and laying the groundwork for future campaigns by establishing a list of donors and supporters."[18] It is particularly important in lower- or down-ballot contests and ballot initiatives, where television ads are either too expensive or reach too broad an audience to be cost-effective.

Robert E. Denton, Jr., and Gary C. Woodward, authors of *Political Communication in America*, say that brochures and direct-mail pieces are most effective under the following circumstances:

- The envelope is attention grabbing.
- A letter, if included, "begins with a startling or dramatic statement by the politician or a celebrity."
- It is conversational in tone.
- It is written in the first person, using a lot of I's and you's.
- It identifies an enemy—an opponent, a group, or an issue position.
- It describes a situation as being "critical, desperate, and urgent."

Others advise coordinating persuasion mail advertisements with television or radio advertisements (where those are used). Usually television or radio advertisements establish the general message with broader appeal, leaving persuasion mail to target a more specific message. But occasionally the reverse is done, especially when the campaign relies on cable television and/or radio stations more heavily than broadcast television to carry a targeted appeal.[19] The explosion of telecommunications has created more segmented electronic media venues, permitting more precise targeting on the basis of age, race or ethnicity, religious preference, and ideology.

The desired chain reaction, once a piece arrives in the mailbox, is to "get attention, arouse interest, stimulate desire, and ask for action."

When analyzing the effectiveness of campaign messages delivered via brochures to seniors, one must examine a wide range of features. Word choice, message length, colors, individuals featured, layout, print font, paper texture and opaqueness, folding techniques, brochure size, as well as the method of delivery (via mail or personal delivery).

## Most Seniors Pay Attention to Brochures

Seniors say they pay attention to the multitude of brochures sent their way. Among Florida seniors, 90% report receiving "a lot of" (45%) or "some" (45%) political ads in the mail. When asked how closely they examine the campaign brochures/ads, nearly three-fourths said either "very closely" (25%) or "somewhat closely" (48%). But more than one-fourth (26%) say they ignored them all. Among the latter group may be seniors suffering from "package fatigue"[20]—too much mail! But some are simply turned off or disinterested in the political process.

We asked Florida's seniors to identify things they like and dislike about campaign brochures through an open-ended question. Most had strong opinions.

### What Seniors Pay Attention to on Candidate Brochures

When asked to "describe the type of candidate brochure that you were the *most* likely to pay attention to" (an open-ended question), the three most common responses were (1) office-specific brochures, especially for down-ballot contests; (2) those that cover issues and platforms, not personalities; and (3) brochures from candidates who share the senior's party identification, ideology, or issue concerns. (See table 4.7.)

## Table 4.7

### Brochures Seniors Are Most Likely to Pay Attention to

| Feature | % | Feature | % |
|---|---|---|---|
| Office-specific (pres.; govr, congress; school bd.) | 16.9 | More colorful ones | 2.0 |
| Cover issues, platforms, not personalities | 15.7 | Those delivered to my door | 2.0 |
| Share my party, ideology, or issue concerns | 11.2 | Large print | 1.6 |
| Candidate biographies | 8.4 | Candidate contrasts | 1.2 |
| Accurate, truthful information & no mudslinging | 8.0 | Someone I don't know | .8 |
| Short, simple, to the point | 7.6 | Include data, surveys | .8 |
| Someone who is familiar | 5.6 | Endorsements by someone other than the candidate | .8 |
| Catchy, eye-appealing, attention grabbing | 4.8 | Contests where I haven't made up my mind yet | .4 |
| Photographs of candidate, family | 4.8 | Ones with summaries at the end | .4 |
| Personal letter & brochures addressed to me | 3.6 | All nonincumbents | .4 |
| Ones that track with newspaper & TV ads | 2.4 | Negative ads | .4 |

*Note: Respondents were asked an open-ended question: "Describe the type of candidate brochure that you were the most likely to pay attention to.*

*Source: Telephone survey of a statewide random sample of 600 adults 60 years of age or older, conducted by the author December, 1998. The sampling margin of error (at 95% confidence level) is plus or minus 4 percentage points.*

For example, one woman in her early 60s who works part time said she likes best those brochures "about the section I live in and what they will do for my town." Similarly, a woman in her late 70s who lives in a mobile home park said: "Well the one that thinks more like I do. I like the ones who are strict with crime and handling things the way they are. Those who are interested in our schools."

For some seniors, what captures their attention is the brochure's design and format. Most preferred are those that are "short, simple, to-the-point," have large print, and are colorful, catchy, and eye-appealing. Also popular are those with photographs of the candidate and his/her family.

Other seniors prefer brochures with a personal touch—either addressed to them personally or given to them by candidates who go from door to door.

One particular type of hand-delivered campaign literature, door hangers, raises the important issue of security. In several public forums at which these data were discussed, some participants expressed concern that campaign literature left hanging on the door or thrown on the porch of a senior lets the world know that he or she wasn't at home. They feared this would increase the chances of being burglarized.

### What Seniors Like Least about Brochures

Florida seniors were asked the flip side of the previous question: "Describe the type of candidate brochure that you were the least likely to pay attention to." At the top of the least helpful list are the brochures that appear to be slinging mud. (See table 4.8.)

However, ads may appear negative only in the eyes of the beholder. As our survey shows, many seniors view as negative any ad that is associated with a party, issue, or personality that they do not personally like. They tend to discard direct mail from these sources before they open it or look at it twice. For example, one woman in her late 70s explained that she was least likely to pay attention to a brochure when she "disagreed with (the candidate's) platform and personality."

Professional campaign consultants tend to defend the often negative tone of direct mail for two reasons. First, they claim it is effective and one of the only ways to catch someone's attention. Second, they argue it often serves a noble purpose. Two defenders of "attack mail" say it well:

> It's a shame when good candidates are attacked for bad reasons. On the other hand, attacking bad candidates for good reason is a public service. Right now, voters are given four choices: vote for the Democrat, or against him or her; vote for the Republican, or against him or her. Take away negative campaigning and you take away half the information voters need to make an informed choice.[21]

While some seniors find office-specific brochures the most helpful, a sizable number also identify them as the least helpful. Moreover, the brochures

**Table 4.8**

**Features of Candidate Brochures Seniors Are Least Likely to Pay Attention to**

| Feature | % | Feature | % |
|---|---|---|---|
| Negative attack ads against other candidate | 26.0 | Photos but little substantive information | 2.6 |
| Candidate who does not share views, party, ideology, no vote | 12.5 | Ones that arrive late in the campaign | 1.6 |
| Office specific | 8.9 | Post cards or half-page flyers | 1.6 |
| Cluttered & confusing | 7.8 | Lack candidate bios, background | 1.6 |
| No substance, too brief, short | 7.3 | Glossy | 1.0 |
| Too many unrealistic promises | 6.3 | Party-sponsored | .5 |
| Fine or small print | 4.2 | Folded brochures | .5 |
| Dull, boring, not catchy or eye-appealing | 3.6 | Those asking for money | .5 |
| Long, verbose | 3.1 | Those from current officeholders | .5 |
| Distortive, biased ads | 3.1 | Stapled | .5 |

Note: Respondents were asked an open-ended question: "Describe the type of candidate brochure that you were least likely to pay attention to."

Source: Telephone survey of a statewide random sample of 600 adults 60 years of age or older, conducted by the author December, 1998. The sampling margin of error (at 95% confidence level) is plus or minus 4 percentage points.

ignored most by Florida seniors are those from judicial candidates. But content is not the only complaint.

## Design and Format Problems

Florida seniors identified special problems related to design and format:

- use of stapled mail-outs; difficult to get open without tearing
- unconventional ways of folding brochures that make them hard to open
- fine or light print
- small print
- curly, round, busy fonts
- too much clutter (Lack of open spaces makes the brochure hard to read.)
- certain colors (Reds and blues are among the most troublesome!)
- postcards; half-page brochures (The type is usually too small.)
- glossy or slick paper (Two problems here—difficult to read because of the glare; difficult to turn pages because of the texture.)
- newsprint (Often this paper is too transparent and there is not enough contrast between the type and the paper, especially when in black and white.)

*Colors*

Six percent of all seniors surveyed acknowledged that they do not see certain types of colors as well as others. The most troublesome are the following, in descending order: blue (24%), black (22%), green (22%), red (20%), brown (4%), yellow (4%), orange (2%), white (2%). Ironically, blues and reds are considered patriotic and, thus, essential by many candidates and consultants!

*Prints or Fonts*

Thirty-five percent of the seniors acknowledged having more trouble seeing certain types of print or fonts. For these older voters, small and very fine print are the most problematic, as indicated here: small print (66%), very fine print (24%), multicolored, flowery (4%), newspaper (3%), very large (1%), old English or script type (1%), glossy (1%).

*Types of Paper*

Seven percent of the seniors surveyed report having more difficulty handling some types of paper than others. Among the most challenging are the following kinds of papers: glossy (44%), newspaper (22%), colored, gift wrap (12%), slick (7%), thick (1%), thin (1%), soft (1%), rough (1%), recycled (1%).

One guidebook designed for health care professionals who interact regularly with seniors affirms what our poll of seniors found. In the book, a health care marketing director advises the following:

> Printed materials intended for seniors—such as direct-mail pieces, newsletters, and even routine forms—should be designed using large, simple type styles and plenty of white space. . . . Avoid glossy paper, text printed on top of background images, and type set in italics or capital letters—all of which reduce readability. Also avoid using type in blue, green, and violet color tones. Seniors may have difficulty distinguishing these colors from one another because the eye lens yellows with aging.[22]

Another marketing consultant quoted in the same guidebook had this advice: "Simple but elegant is a good rule for printed materials. . . . Keep sentences short, and break up text with figures or pictures."

In summary, political consultants and candidates need to be aware that certain colors, prints, fonts, and types of paper affect seniors' ability to read campaign literature. At a minimum, more research needs to be done. It is likely that even higher percentages of seniors would identify some of these factors if they were asked using a close-ended question format.

## NEWSPAPER ENDORSEMENTS

Candidates are advised to seek the editorial endorsements of major newspapers. In *Winning Local and State Elections*, Ann Beaudry and Bob Schaeffer tell potential candidates: "Though most print media do not have nearly the reach or impact of major electronic outlets, they are still followed closely by opinion leaders and *the most likely voters*" (emphasis added).[23]

As previously noted, seniors are avid newspaper readers. Put together the two phenomena and the question arises: How many seniors read these endorsements and what impact do they have on voting decisions?

A little more than half (52%) acknowledge paying attention to which candidates are endorsed by local newspapers. Predictably, higher-educated and upper-income seniors paid more attention to endorsements than others. But do these endorsements influence a senior's vote? When asked "How often did the newspaper endorsements affect who you voted for?" most (46%) said "never." However, a sizable proportion admitted being influenced "sometimes" (39%), and 11% said "often." (See figure 4.7.)

The conditions under which newspaper endorsements affect seniors' vote choices are shown in table 4.9. Often, endorsements are just one more piece of evidence that seniors use to make up their minds. For example, one man in his early 70s said he could be influenced "if I am not familiar with the candidate and if I did not have enough information to make up my own mind." In some cases, the endorsements are the final push needed for wavering voters already leaning in the direction of the paper's favorite candidate.

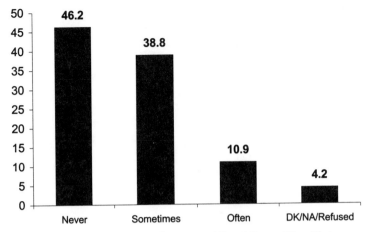

*Figure 4.7  How Often Newspaper Endorsements Affected Seniors' Vote Choice*

*Source: Telephone survey of a random sample of 600 Floridians 60 or older conducted December 1998. Margin of error +/- 4%.*

Typically, newspaper endorsements also play a heavier role in influencing voters when readers know less about a candidate (judicial candidates, for example) or an issue (an amendment or referendum). For example, one man in his early 70s who considered himself independent of party affiliation said he could be influenced "mostly about the candidate I know nothing about."

## RATING TV ADS

In *Air Wars*, Darryl West says what everyone knows: "Elections have become a television game."[24] Television ads are the most expensive part of many campaigns. Optimally, ad producers would like their spots to be so interesting they get covered in regular news broadcasts.

Some advertising professionals point out that "TV ads are tactical and should always be part of a larger strategy. Each ad should evolve from the basic campaign plan. Each ad should reflect the campaign's basic themes. Every time you read an ad script, ask yourself: 'Which of our goals will this ad achieve?'"[25] Sometimes this approach is more difficult than it appears. Television as a medium tends to lead viewers to focus more on a candidate's personal attributes —appearance, voice, demeanor—than on his/her issues.[26]

Ad professional Dean Rindy advises all those who design and film TV ads to ask five questions:[27]

1. Whom do we have to talk to? (That's the audience.)
2. What things do we have to tell them? (That's the message.)
3. What are the most important things? (Discipline that message.)

**Table 4.9**

**Conditions Under Which Seniors Say Newspaper
Endorsements Affected Vote Choices**

| Conditions | % |
| --- | --- |
| In combination with other coverage | 25.0 |
| When voting on low profile races | 19.6 |
| When leaning in direction of paper's choice | 16.3 |
| When they present candidate qualifications | 13.0 |
| When voting on low profile amendments | 7.6 |
| When endorsements cover issues | 6.5 |
| More objectively written ones | 4.3 |
| When too one-sided, I go opposite paper | 3.3 |
| When offer contrasts of candidates & issues (both sides) | 2.2 |
| High profile contests | 2.2 |
| **Total** | **100** |

*Note: Respondents who acknowledged that newspaper endorsements sometimes or often affected how they vote were asked an open-ended question: "In what situations were the newspaper endorsements most likely to affect how you voted?"*

*Source: Telephone survey of a statewide random sample of 600 adults 60 years of age or older, conducted by the author December, 1998. The sampling margin of error (at 95% confidence level) is plus or minus 4 percentage points.*

4. What is the best way to tell them? (Stylize the message.)
5. What is it going to cost? (Ascertain your cost effectiveness.)

In *Manipulation of the American Voter*, authors Karen Johnson-Cartee and Gary Copeland point out that "every word, every visual, every event must be carefully strategized and developed for maximum effect [because] campaigns have become increasingly media affairs rather than party affairs."[28]

When asked how closely they watch political ads on TV, 21% of seniors say "very closely," and 54% say "somewhat closely." Just 24% say "not at all." (See figure 4.8.) Because seniors are often the targeted audience, it is helpful to know which type of TV ads they find most and least helpful. Perhaps most interesting is that some respondents do not differentiate between regular political programming (debates, forums, talk shows—in short, free media) and paid advertisements. This makes it even more desirable to have your candidate appear in as many TV venues as possible.

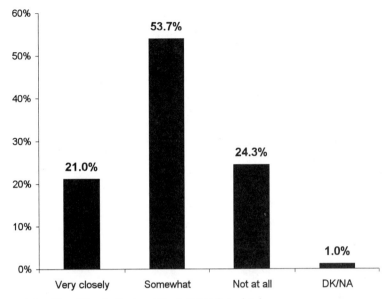

*Figure 4.8    How Closely Seniors Watch TV Political Ads*

*Source: Telephone survey of a random sample of 600 Floridians 60 or older, conducted December 1998. Margin of error +/- 4 percent.*

Consistent with their preferences for print ads, Florida seniors prefer positive ads (no mudslinging, please!) with some meat on them (platforms, promises, issue stances, candidate backgrounds, past voting records). They also like debates and town hall forums. But what seniors find most helpful about TV ads varies considerably. (See table 4.10.)

For example, one woman in her early 60s who worked part time said she liked best those ads "that give the most information without going overboard." Another woman who was in her late 70s liked "ones that told me exactly how they felt and how they would react if they were elected." One man in the 85-and-older category said simply: "The ones that were truthful."

By far the least helpful, from the perspective of seniors, are negative ads. (See table 4.11.) For example, one woman in her early 60s said she disliked most "the ones that run each other down." Another woman who was in her late 70s pointed to "the kind that were trying to undermine the candidate's personal life for no reason." Still another woman in her early 70s complained about "the ones where they talk about each other. They need to tell what they are going to do when (or) if they get in office."

For some voters, highly repetitive ads are annoying. For example, one woman in her late 60s hated "the ones that kept on repeating and repeating, over and over, the same message." For some seniors, this complaint means they cannot hear the ads too well. Short, quick ads, especially 20-second

## Table 4.10

### TV Political Ads Seniors Find Most Helpful

| Ad Feature | % |
| --- | --- |
| Positive ads (not negative ads) | 19.2 |
| Platforms, promises, issue stances given | 14.1 |
| Debates & town meetings | 9.0 |
| Give candidate background, voting records | 7.9 |
| Sincere ads | 7.3 |
| Sufficient information | 6.2 |
| Short, simple, concise | 6.2 |
| Candidates speak for themselves, personal appearances | 4.5 |
| Governor race | 4.5 |
| Share my party, ideology, my preferred candidate | 4.0 |
| Focus on specific clientele groups (children, elderly) | 4.0 |
| Interviews, talk shows, questions to candidates | 3.4 |
| School board & schools | 2.3 |
| Candidate endorsed by someone I respect | 1.7 |
| President | 1.1 |
| Those who told me who is running | 1.7 |
| Ones I could hear | 1.7 |
| Nonrepetitive ads | .6 |
| Those closest to election day | .6 |
| **Total** | **100** |

**Table 4.11**

**Types of Political Ads Least Helpful to Seniors**

| Ad Features | % |
|---|---|
| Negative, attack, mud slingers | 70.3 |
| Slogans constantly repeated | 8.6 |
| Those for candidates of opposite party, ideology | 5.1 |
| Candidates bragging about themselves | 5.1 |
| Platforms & promises | 5.1 |
| Lack of specific information, too general | 4.6 |
| Unknown or unfamiliar candidates | .6 |
| Talk shows & pundits | .6 |
| **Total** | **100** |

*Note: Respondents were asked an open-ended question: "What types of TV ads were the least helpful to you as a citizen?"*

*Source: Telephone survey of a statewide random sample of 600 adults 60 years of age or older, conducted by the author December, 1998. The sampling margin of error (at 95% confidence level) is plus or minus 4 percentage points.*

spots, that constantly repeat the same information are hard for some elderly to hear.

Some 4% of those we surveyed said they had difficulty hearing some types of TV spots more than others. The ones they complained about most were those that are "too loud" and "too fast." Ads with background music, women's or children's voices, and strong accents were also identified by some as troublesome. Interestingly, the same number identified high-pitched voices as hard to hear as low-pitched voices. (Typically, high-pitched voices are the most problematic for older people.)

## WHAT DO CANDIDATES SAY WORKS BEST?

Candidates running for statewide cabinet posts and legislative seats (Senate, House) affirm that they use different techniques to reach different age groups. In general, seniors are much easier to reach than 18-to-29-year-olds using every technique except for the Internet. In most cases, these patterns typically hold true regardless of whether the candidate has won or lost or is an incumbent or challenger. They also hold true regardless of the percentage of senior voters in a candidate's constituency.[29]

Direct mail, door-to-door contact, phone banks, debate forums, assistance in absentee voting, and civic club speeches work best in reaching seniors. (See table 4.12.) (Recall that seniors rank TV and newspapers as the sources they rely upon most.)

Fewer candidates acknowledged that they ran TV advertisements around news programs watched heavily by older voters. In some cases, money was the drawback. But our survey shows that candidates with prior experience running for office were significantly more likely than candidates without such experience to have used that technique (48% versus 30%).

It is not just news programs that make effective venues for political ads. One nursing home activity director advises candidates to focus more on advertising around popular non-news programs, specifically *Wheel of Fortune* and *Jeopardy!*

### Best Combination of Techniques?

There is no one-size-fits-all formula for the best combination of campaign techniques. When asked a final open-ended question: "From your experience, what

**Table 4.12**

**Easier to Reach Senior Voters Using a Variety of Techniques**

| Campaign techniques | 65+ |
| --- | --- |
| Direct mail | 71 |
| Door-to-door contact | 68 |
| Phone banks | 62 |
| Debate forums | 53 |
| Help voting absentee | 53 |
| Civic club speeches | 51 |
| Radio ads | 49 |
| Newspaper ads | 46 |
| TV ads (cable) | 43 |
| TV ads (networks) | 41 |
| Political fairs | 37 |
| Focus groups | 22 |
| Internet | 9 |

*Note: Respondents were asked to "Identify which of the following campaign techniques is effective in reaching different age groups?"*

*Source: Mail survey of 68 candidates for Florida cabinet and state legislative posts, conducted by the author, December, 1998.*

do you find works best in reaching older voters?" many candidates pointed to more than one technique. (See table 4.13.) Certainly, among the most popular are direct mail, door-to-door canvassing, and interaction with seniors at forums, senior centers and residential facilities, and via phone banks.

There were some variations, however. Several candidates, African-Americans, identified churches as a good place to reach older voters—a phenomenon documented by other research. A few others found that helping seniors with the absentee voting process (mainly acquiring ballots and explaining how to complete them) was effective.

Another candidate, a winner, found seeking signatures of registered voters as a way to get on the ballot the best method for reaching older voters. (Florida law allows this technique as an alternative to paying a filing fee.)

Still another candidate who campaigned door-to-door said he often offered to read the campaign brochure or literature to the senior, and that this method was successful. People appreciated him taking time with them, instead of just leaving a brochure and moving on to the next door.

### Reaching Disabled Older Voters

Most candidates encounter persons with disabilities in the course of their campaigns. (See table 4.14.) Candidates are least likely to encounter someone with sight

*Photo 4.5   Attentiveness to facility accessibility affects seniors relying on elaborate walkers, portable oxygen units, as well as wheelchairs.*

**Table 4.13**

**Individual Candidate Assessments of Best Ways to Reach Older Voters**

| What works best in reaching older voters? Winners' answers | % 65+ In Dist. | What works best in reaching older voters? Winners' answers | % 65+ In Dist | What works best in reaching older voters? Winners' answers | % 65+ In Dist |
|---|---|---|---|---|---|
| TV ads- personal/family slant and personal contact | 70 | Ads with a medical theme | 30 | Direct mail | 15 |
| Personal contact | 66 | Depends on the type of residential facility | 30 | Direct mail and door to door | 12 |
| Television | 65 | Door to door canvassing | 30 | Personal touch. Visit residential facility. Radio talk show | NA |
| Mail; door to door | 60 | Direct mail; newspaper, senior citizen groups (visits); door to door | 28 | Absentee assistance / cable TV and targeted direct mail | NA |
| Serving breakfast, phone bank by neighbors, club forums | 55 | Direct contact | 20 | Visiting at their residence, visiting churches, their activities | NA |
| Churches, church groups | 55 | Petitioning to get on ballot | 20 | Door to door, direct mail, phone | NA |
| Visiting facilities, phone banks, brochures | 48 | Door to door | 20 | Door to door, campaigning | NA |
| Direct mail and personal contact | 45 | Personal visit, direct mail, cable TV | 18 | Personal contact | NA |
| Mail | 33 | Direct mail | 15 | | |

Table 4.13 *continued*

## Individual Candidate Assessments of Best Ways to Reach Older Voters

| What do you find works best in reaching older voters? Losers' answers | % 65+ in Dist. | What do you find works best in reaching older voters? Losers' answers | % 65+ in Dist. | What do you find works best in reaching older voters? Losers' answers | % 65+ in Dist. |
|---|---|---|---|---|---|
| Direct mail | 70 | Door to door, church gatherings | 60 | TV most cover, door to door, mailing to targeted age group | 43 |
| Direct mail | 70 | Door to door and radio ads | 55 | Personal visitation or door to door | 42 |
| Direct mail | 60 | Mailing, TV ads, and door to door | 50 | TV ads, direct mail, civic speeches, newspaper ads | 40 |
| Face to face contact - via breakfast groups or other comfortable and convenient settings for them | 60 | Direct mail | 50 | Personal letters | 40 |
| Direct mail; door-to-door | 60 | Door to door | 45 | Forums | 35 |

Table 4.13 *continued.*

# Table 4.13 continued

## Individual Candidate Assessments of Best Ways to Reach Older Voters

| What do you find works best in reaching older voters? Losers' answers | % 65+ in Dist. | What do you find works best in reaching older voters? Losers' answers | % 65+ in Dist. | What do you find works best in reaching older voters? Losers' answers | % 65+ in Dist. |
|---|---|---|---|---|---|
| TV | 35 | Direct mail | 30 | Mail | 10 |
| A friend influencing them | 35 | Phone banks, direct mail, TV | 25 | Word of mouth, condo assoc. | 2 |
| TV appearance as guest of sponsors | 33 | Recruitment of absentee voters - done by my opponent | 25 | Personal contact | NA |
| Civic clubs, personal contact | 33 | Door to door contact | 23 | Direct mail; local cable; local radio | NA |
| Forums/calling | 30 | Directed radio and door to door | 20 | Walking door to door | NA |
| Door to door, direct mailing | 30 | Senior centers | 20 | One-on-one communications/forums | NA |
| Door to door, direct mail | 30 | Door to door contact | 15 | | |

Note: Candidates were asked: "What percentage of your constituency do senior citizens (65+) comprise?" "Did you win or lose?" and an open-ended question: "From your experience, what do you find works best in reaching older voters?"

Source: Mail survey of 68 candidates for Florida cabinet and state legislative posts, conducted by the author, December 1998.

**Table 4.14**

| Frequency With Which Candidates Encountered Constituencies With Disabilities | | | | |
|---|---|---|---|---|
| Disability encountered | No answer | Never | Occasionally | A lot |
| | % | % | % | % |
| With sight problems | 9 | 26 | 54 | 10 |
| With hearing problems | 9 | 13 | 65 | 13 |
| With mobility problems | 7 | 9 | 66 | 18 |

*Note: Candidates were asked: "How often do you encounter constituents with _____ problems?"*

*Source: Mail survey of 68 candidates for Florida cabinet posts and state legislative seats, conducted by the author, December, 1998.*

problems, probably because the sight-impaired are less likely to attend a public forum, fair, or debate, or to answer the door. This and other evidence suggests that sight-impaired voters are the most ignored in the course of regular campaigning.

When asked to identify which techniques their campaigns used to reach older voters *with disabilities*, more than two-thirds identify candidate forums. Slightly more than half identify absentee voting assistance (54%) and telephone surveys (51%). (See table 4.15.) Low on the list, however, are many of the things that seniors say would be helpful—use of large-print ads and brochures (34%), videos to nursing homes (3%), closed-caption ads (0%), and cassettes for visually impaired constituents (0%).

Perhaps the most disturbing finding is that one-fourth or more of the candidates were not able or willing to offer a response to the question.

### Involving Seniors in Campaigns

Seniors have long been recognized as the backbone of a candidate's volunteer corps.[30] We asked candidates how often they used older constituents in their campaigns in various capacities. As shown in figure 4.9, senior volunteers are used most for outreach (working phone banks) and platform or issue development. Fewer relied upon them for the physically intensive work of walking blocks, although more than half still acknowledged seniors walked blocks at least occasionally.

### SUMMARY AND RECOMMENDATIONS

Candidates covet senior voters' attention because of their history of high turnout. Candidates believe they know best—even better than professional cam-

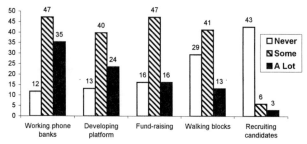

*Figure 4.9    Use of Older Constituents in Campaigns*
Note: "How often did you utilize older constituents in your campaign?"

Source: Mail survey of 68 candidates for Florida cabinet and state legislative seats, conducted by the author, December 1998.

paign consultants—how to reach this age group. But both candidates and professional consultants rate themselves far ahead of political parties. Both groups acknowledge that political parties, particularly at the national level, do little to help candidates reach seniors and even less to guide candidates on how to reach disabled seniors—a growing constituency.

Candidates tend to go to places likely to have large concentrations of seniors—civic clubs, candidate forums and debates, senior centers, and retirement communities. Most ignore seniors in nursing homes and assisted-living facilities. While some residents of these types of facilities suffer from dementia or end-stage diseases, many are quite capable of participating in the political process. It is a mistake for candidates to ignore these residents, especially in close elections when every vote counts. As more Americans take up residence in such places, these votes become even more important. Ignoring them has another side effect—it creates a bad feeling among caretakers, relatives, friends, neighbors, and volunteers who are potential supporters.

Surveys of activity directors at congregate-care facilities and supervisors of elections agree that certain campaign techniques can be effective in reaching these types of voters. These techniques include large-print brochures, candidate visits, audio- and videotapes, and candidate forums held in nursing homes and assisted-living facilities.

Some senior-oriented communities need to re-think their rules on access. Prohibiting candidates from appearing at congregate-care facilities or in age-segregated mobile home parks, condos, and gated neighborhoods may not be wise if seniors want to maximize their political clout.

The Internet is an excellent way to link home-bound seniors with political campaigns. Election officials and elder advocates have begun a pitch to make seniors more computer literate. However, while new multimedia technology is being developed to assist sight- and hearing-impaired persons, it has yet to be widely used. Even closed-captioning is not widely used, especially not on cable TV. Yet candidates are increasingly turning to cable TV because advertising rates are cheaper. Plus, the more segmented audiences enhance a candidate's ability to target seniors.

**Table 4.15**

| Campaign Techniques | No Answer | Didn't use | Considered but did not use | Used |
|---|---|---|---|---|
| | % | % | % | % |
| Candidate forums | 13 | 15 | 3 | 69 |
| Absentee voting assistance | 21 | 19 | 6 | 54 |
| Telephone surveys | 19 | 24 | 6 | 51 |
| Newspaper ads | 24 | 21 | 12 | 44 |
| Transportation of elderly to poll | 18 | 28 | 12 | 43 |
| Radio ads targeted to stations with older listeners | 21 | 28 | 10 | 41 |
| Regular news coverage | 25 | 29 | 7 | 38 |
| TV ads targeted to news programs with large % of older voters | 18 | 32 | 13 | 37 |
| Large print ads/brochures | 21 | 37 | 9 | 34 |
| Campaign staffer in charge of reaching older electorate | 21 | 43 | 10 | 26 |
| Focus groups | 25 | 47 | 7 | 21 |
| Videos to nursing homes | 24 | 66 | 7 | 3 |
| Closed caption ads | 24 | 72 | 4 | 0 |
| Cassettes for visually-impaired | 24 | 72 | 4 | 0 |
| Other | 10 | 4 | 0 | 19 |

What Candidates Used to Reach Older Voters With Disabilities

*Note: Candidates were asked: "Check which of the following techniques your campaign used to reach older voters with disabilities?"*

*Source: Mail survey of 68 candidates for Florida cabinet posts and state legislative seats, conducted by the author December, 1998.*

In general, blind persons have the most difficulty following elections—especially down-ballot, low-profile races, and referenda issues and amendments. The situation has worsened as the electronic media, particularly television, cover only the "hot" races, usually at the top of the ballot.

Candidates, election officials, and political consultants still believe that candidate forums and debates are an excellent venue to interact with seniors. But a relatively small percentage of seniors go to these functions. Health, mobility, and logistics keep many from attending, even though they have in the past. While some of these forums and debates may be televised, they are typically held at night. An excellent form of public service on the part of TV stations carrying these programs would be to distribute videos to nursing homes, ALFs, and senior centers. They could be replayed at times more in sync with senior sleep patterns.

Candidate brochures, either distributed via mail or in person during door-to-door canvassing, need to be more attentive to the interests and needs of seniors. Seniors pay the most attention to brochures that are office-specific (low-profile contests), focused on issues rather than personality, and well-designed. Brochures that are short, simple, to the point, with large print, lots of color (but be careful about blues, reds, and greens), with photographs of the candidate and his/her family are the most attention-grabbing.

Seniors find negative ads the least helpful from a content perspective. From a design point of view, some acknowledge having problems with stapled mail-outs; odd folds; print that is fine, light, or too small; font styles that are too curly or busy; postcard-sized advertisements; glossy or slick paper; and newsprint.

While seniors tend to like the personal touch of meeting a candidate at their front door, some do not like literature to be hung on their doorknobs. They worry about being burglarized because the door hangers either signal to intruders that they are not home, or worse yet, incapacitated.

Candidates for less visible offices are advised to seek the endorsement of their local newspapers. Seniors acknowledge they rely more on newspaper endorsements in such types of contests.

Seniors are more likely to pay attention to political ads on TV than to newspaper editorials or ads. In fact, seniors tend not to differentiate between regular (free) political programming and paid political commercials. As in print, seniors prefer more positive TV ads, with broader coverage of issues and candidate backgrounds.

Some TV ads simply cannot be heard by seniors. The 20-second spot in which the message or candidate's name is rapidly repeated is lost on seniors with hearing impairments. (And louder is not always better either, nor is background music.)

Finally, candidates and professional consultants alike realize how essential seniors are to their success—on the campaign trail as well as at the ballot box. Senior volunteers form the backbone of many campaigns, especially in outreach activities (phone banks) and platform or issue development. When every vote counts, it pays to involve both able and disabled seniors.

# 5

# Helping Seniors
# Register and Vote:

## New Forms of Outreach,
## Accommodation, and Protection

*Photo 5.1   Seniors make up a large portion of poll workers across the U.S. Celeste McConnell and her husband Milton, both 90 years old, have faithfully worked at the polls in Hillsborough County, Florida, for years (Celeste since 1945; Milton for the past 20 years). They stand amidst some 4,000 Votamatic machines stored in the Supervisor of Elections warehouse. Photograph by Phil Sheffield,* The Tampa Tribune, *used with permission.*

> Disabled persons want to have the choice of casting their ballot in the voting
> booth as do non-disabled citizens. . . . [Absentee ballots], while workable
> for some disabled and elderly voters, can remove the spontaneity and sense of
> participation from the voting process. When people are unable to participate
> at the voting site along with others, many would rather not vote.
>
>               National Organization on Disability, *Disabled Citizens at the Polls*

> Picture this: The operators of a nursing home want to curry favor with one
> or more politicians, so they invite the party or campaign to send in an oper-
> ative with a basket full of absentee ballots. He circulates through the
> wards, persuading and cajoling, collecting ballots from the residents, some
> of whom may not be mentally sound, and leaves with a batch of signed bal-
> lots for his candidate.
>
>                                       *The Tampa Tribune,* March 28, 1998

Many seniors thoroughly enjoy going to the polls and prefer voting in person to voting absentee. To them, the polling place is a symbol of democracy at work.

In October 1998, for example, 102-year-old Edna Watkins Alderman voted in person at her precinct polling place in Grandin, Florida. Assisted by a great-grandson who pushed her wheelchair, the white-haired centenarian marked her ballot and placed it in the ballot box. "I think it's quite a privilege," she said. "It's needed to express ourselves."[1]

Voting in person also offers another attraction: It's a great place to socialize with friends and neighbors who are either voting or working at the polls. (Seniors make up the bulk of poll workers and watchers.)

Although seniors are America's most consistent voters, the process of registration and voting can present serious challenges to many of them. Viable options to in-person voting include absentee balloting, early voting, and mail ballot elections—and, in the future, the Internet. But such options must come with safeguards. In the 1990s, unscrupulous party workers, candidates, and interest groups tended to aim their illegal activities at seniors, especially those in nursing homes or those confined for one reason or another to their own home.[2]

## REGISTERING TO VOTE

Seniors register to vote in considerably higher proportions than other age groups in both presidential and congressional (midterm) election years. (See table 5.1.) This pattern has persisted throughout most of the twentieth century. Whether it will continue into the twenty-first century is debatable. Some think that with longer life expectancies, the number of seniors with physical or mental impairments will grow and, thus, the proportion of seniors who register will drop. But others believe that "as more states move to electronic or mail registration systems, the mobility problems of these 'senior-seniors' may be minimized, keeping registration rates fairly stable."[3]

**Table 5.1**

| Percentage Reporting They Registered | | | | | | | |
| --- | --- | --- | --- | --- | --- | --- | --- |

**Presidential Election Years**

| Age | 1972 | 1976 | 1980 | 1984 | 1988 | 1992 | 1996 |
| --- | --- | --- | --- | --- | --- | --- | --- |
| 18-20 | 58 | 47 | 45 | 47 | 45 | 48 | 46 |
| 21-24 | 59 | 55 | 53 | 54 | 51 | 55 | 51 |
| 25-34 | 68 | 62 | 62 | 63 | 58 | 61 | 62 |
| 35-44 | 74 | 70 | 71 | 71 | 69 | 69 | 67 |
| 45-64 | 79 | 76 | 76 | 77 | 76 | 75 | 74 |
| 65+ | 75 | 71 | 75 | 77 | 78 | 78 | 77 |

**Congressional Election Years**

| Age | 1974 | 1978 | 1982 | 1986 | 1990 | 1994 | |
| --- | --- | --- | --- | --- | --- | --- | --- |
| 18-20 | 36 | 35 | 35 | 35 | 35 | 37 | |
| 21-24 | 45 | 45 | 48 | 47 | 43 | 45 | |
| 25-34 | 54 | 56 | 57 | 56 | 52 | 51 | |
| 35-44 | 66 | 67 | 68 | 68 | 66 | 63 | |
| 45-64 | 73 | 74 | 76 | 75 | 71 | 71 | |
| 65+ | 70 | 73 | 75 | 77 | 77 | 76 | |

*Source: U.S. Bureau of the Census, Current Population Reports, Voting and Registration in the Election of November 1976 (Washington, D.C.: U.S. Government Printing Office, 1993), Series P-20, no. 322, 11-12, 14-21, 57, 61; November 1978, no. 344, 8, 11-19, 60, 65; November 1980, no. 370, 10-20, 50, 56; November 1982, no. 383, 1-12, 46, 49; November 1984, no. 405, 13-24, 59; November 1986, no. 414, 11-22, 29, 31; November 1988, no. 440, 13-24, 48, 50; November 1990, no. 453, 1-2, 4, 13-14, 17; November 1992, no. 466, v-vii, 1, 5; November 1994, Table 14, November 1996, PPL-89.*

## Changes in Registration Requirements

Most states in recent years have made it much easier to register.[4] Registration by mail or electronically is quite simple now, thanks to passage of the National Voter Registration Act of 1993 (also known as the Motor Voter Act). It required the Federal Election Commission to develop, and all state and local registrars to accept, a national voter registration postcard.[5] Many states simply adopted the same basic format for their own registration forms.

Actually, many voters apply for registration cards or fill out change-of-address forms at driver's license bureaus. In 1995–1996, according to the Federal Election Commission, 33% of Americans registered at motor vehicle offices, compared to 30% who registered by mail.[6]

Approximately three-fourths of the states permit deputizing ordinary citizens, in addition to election office personnel, to register voters. Deputy registrars, as individuals or in teams, may approach citizens in various locations such as a business or a retirement center. This method holds promise for registering seniors in their homes or senior centers.

In most states, registration cards must be mailed to the election office a certain number of days prior to the election. The postmark on the mailed application is the effective date of receipt.

## Registration Book Closings

"Book closing" dates serve two purposes. First, they give election officials time to prepare official voter registration lists for use by poll workers at each voting precinct. Second, these lists can serve as a fraud-detection device. Signatures on a voter registration card can be compared to sign-in signatures at the polls to make sure the right person is casting a ballot. This is an important safeguard for seniors, who tend to be targeted by vote thieves more than other age groups.[7] (The names of deceased elderly are especially attractive to poachers.)

Typically, states require that citizens register a certain number of days before an election. (See table 5.2.) However, in the case of federal elections, no state can close its registration books more than thirty days prior to the election. Even in states that close their registration books in advance of an election, officials often extend the hours (evenings) and days (weekends) to accommodate last-minute registrants.

## No Advance Registration

A few states have abandoned advance registration entirely. Six states—Idaho, Maine, Minnesota, New Hampshire, Wisconsin, and Wyoming—allow registration on election day. One state—North Dakota—has no registration requirement whatever. In these states, voters merely appear at the polls with proof that they are eligible (18 or older, citizenship, for example).[8]

## Senior Challenges: Keeping Registration Current

Despite the easing of requirements, many seniors still face problems in registering to vote. For example, handwriting may change significantly with age. The original signature on the voter registration card may have been done decades ago. Consequently, election canvassers checking a senior voter's current signature on a ballot (especially an absentee ballot) against the original signature on the registration card may toss out the ballot as invalid. One way to avoid this problem is to have the election office conduct a proactive campaign to update seniors' signatures.[9]

## Table 5.2

## Registration Procedures in the Fifty States and Territories

| State/other jurisdiction | Mail registration | Closing date before election | Absentee eligibility |
|---|---|---|---|
| Alabama | Yes | 10 | M/O |
| Alaska | Yes | 30 | (b) |
| Arizona | Yes | 29 | (b) |
| Arkansas | Yes | 30 | (b) |
| California | Yes | 29 | (b) |
| Colorado | Yes | 29 | (b) |
| Connecticut | Yes | 14 (c) | (b) |
| Delaware | Yes | 20 | (b) |
| Florida | Yes | 29 | (b) |
| Georgia | Yes | (d) | (b) |
| Hawaii | Yes | 30 | (b) |
| Idaho | Yes | (e) | (b) |
| Illinois | Yes | 29 | M/O |
| Indiana | Yes | 29 (f) | C, D, E, M/O, O, P, T |
| Iowa | Yes | 10 | (b) |
| Kansas | Yes | 14 | (b) |
| Kentucky | Yes | 28 | (b) |
| Louisiana | Yes | 24 | D |
| Maine | Yes | Election Day | (b) |
| Maryland | Yes | 29 | (b) |
| Massachusetts | Yes | 20 | (b) |

Table 5.2 *continued.*

Table 5.2 *continued*

## Registration Procedures in the Fifty States and Territories

| State/other jurisdiction | Mail registration | Closing date before election | Absentee eligibility |
|---|---|---|---|
| Michigan | Yes | 30 | (b) |
| Minnesota | Yes | Election Day | (b) |
| Mississippi | Yes | 30 | (b) |
| Missouri | Yes | 28 | (b) |
| Montana | Yes | 30 | (b) |
| Nebraska | Yes | (h) | (b) |
| Nevada | Yes | 30 | M/O |
| New Hampshire | – | 10 (i) | B, D, E, R, S, T |
| New Jersey | Yes | 29 | (b) |
| New Mexico | Yes | 28 | T |
| New York | Yes | 25 | (b) |
| No. Carolina | Yes | 25 | (b) |
| North Dakota | – | (j) | – |
| Ohio | Yes | 30 | (b) |
| Oklahoma | Yes | 24 | M/O |
| Oregon | Yes | 20 | (b) |
| Pennsylvania | Yes | 30 | B, D, M/O, O, P ,R, S, T |
| Rhode Island | Yes | 30 | D |
| So. Carolina | Yes | 30 | (b) |
| South Dakota | Yes | 15 | (b) |
| Tennessee | Yes | 30 | (b) |

Table 5.2 *continued.*

**Table 5.2** *continued*

## Registration Procedures in the Fifty States and Territories

| State/other jurisdiction | Mail registration | Closing date before election | Absentee eligibility |
|---|---|---|---|
| Texas | Yes | 30 | (b) |
| Utah | Yes | 6 (k) | (l) |
| Virginia | Yes | 28 | T |
| Washington | Yes | 30 | M/O |
| West Virginia | Yes | 30 | (b) |
| Wisconsin | Yes | Election Day (k) | (b) |
| Wyoming | – | (g) | (b) |
| Wash. D.C. | Yes | 30 | (b) |
| Am. Samoa | Yes | 30 | M/O |
| Guam | Yes | 10 | (b) |
| Puerto Rico | – | 50 | (b) |
| U.S. Virgin Is. | – | 30 | M/O |

*Note: (a) In this column: B-Absent on business; C-Senior citizen; D-Disabled; E-Not absent, but prevented by employment from registering; M/O-no absentee registration except military and oversees citizens as required by federal law; Out of state; P-Out of precinct; R-Absent for religious reasons; S-Students; T-Temporarily out of jurisdiction. (b) All voters. See column on mail registration. (c) Closing date differs for primary election. In Connecticut, 1 day; Delaware 21 days. (d) Fifth Monday prior to election. (e) With county clerk, within 24 days before an election; eligible voters may also register on election day at polling place. (f) Absent uniformed services voters and overseas voters may be registered until final poll list is prepared up to 10 days before Election Day. (g) Minnesota-21 days or Election Day, or general Election Day. (h) 2<sup>nd</sup> Friday before Election Day. (i) Also, at polls on Election Day. (j) No voter registration. (k) By mail: Utah, 20 days; Wisconsin, 13 days. (l) There are several criteria including religious reasons, disabled, etc., or if the voter otherwise expects to be absent from the precinct on Election Day. (m) Anyone unable to register in person.*

*Source: The Council of State Governments, The Book of the States, 1998–99 Edition, vol. 32, Lexington, KY: The Council of State Governments, 1998: 164–165.*

Another problem is that many seniors move to a different home when they retire or when their health conditions change. Moving, whether from one city or state to another or from a house into an assisted-living facility, often requires changing one's voter registration. The new locale may have different deadlines and procedures than the old one. As a result, a growing number of mobile seniors are failing to make this change in a timely fashion.

Furthermore, those who no longer drive are less likely to be alerted about re-registration at the driver's license bureau. These seniors often need reminders and assistance.

Florida's supervisors of elections affirm the need for such help. As shown in figure 5.1, more than 80% say they sometimes or often get telephone requests from seniors for registration information.[10] More than 90% receive requests from seniors about how to change their address on their voter registration card. Ninety percent of supervisors also believe that both they and candidates should offer more information on how to change one's voter registration.

Among seniors, one-fourth acknowledge that assistance with changing voter registration would be "very" or "somewhat helpful."[11] In many instances, such assistance is available, but the voters are unaware of this service.

The fact that seniors request information by telephone brings up an important point. Government agencies and businesses increasingly rely on automated systems to field and route telephone inquiries. Because seniors are more accustomed to speaking to a person than to a machine, they may hang up at the droning of "Welcome to the Secretary of State's Office." Furthermore, hearing loss and slower cognitive processing make it difficult for them to follow a long series of instructions, such as "Please make your selection from the following menu. For change-of-address forms, please press 2. . . ." Election officers may need to ensure that alternatives to automated answering systems are available to meet senior needs.

One way to better inform persons about a state's or locality's registration rules, procedures, and timetables, as well as the availability of various forms of assistance, would be for election officials to prepare and distribute informational videos.

Ironically, as registration procedures are eased, the potential for improprieties—fraud at the front end of the election process—increases. The options of registering via postcard or changing one's registration (address, party affiliation) by telephone or via the Internet make it easier for sleazy political operatives to prey on seniors, particularly those with failing mental capacities. So, too, does deputizing ordinary citizens.

Along with implementing procedures to help seniors keep their registrations current, election supervisors must institute safeguards to lessen the potential for misdeeds. The design of these safeguards can be a collaborative effort with advocacy groups.

## Registration Site Accessibility

Groups that choose to set up registration for seniors at a physical location, such as a church, school, or office building, need to keep in mind the issue of acces-

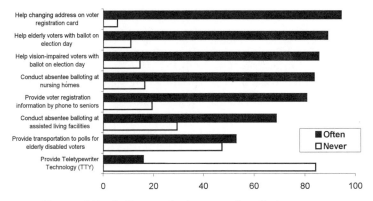

*Figure 5.1    Election Officials: Requests for Assistance from Seniors*
*Note: "How often does your office get contacted to do each of the following?"*

*Source: Mail survey of Florida Supervisor of Elections, conducted July–September 1999.*

sibility for seniors with disabilities. The checklist below can be helpful in making a facility more accessible:[12]

- accessible parking
- accessible paths of travel
- proper signage
- service animal accessible
- Braille available
- interpreters available
- listening and other devices available
- auxiliary aids and services available

*Photo 5.2    Seniors head into the Alice Hall Community Center. Selecting polling places that are accessible and familiar to seniors increases the likelihood that they will vote in person rather than via an absentee ballot. Photograph by Andy Jones,* The Tampa Tribune, *used with permission.*

## Registering Seniors: A Network of Volunteers

The AARP (formerly the American Association of Retired Persons) uses volunteers to run voter registration drives and provide assistance with absentee balloting. This volunteer program, AARP/VOTE, began in 1986 as a pilot project in six states. Each year the program has grown, so that now AARP/VOTE has programs in all fifty states and more than 300 congressional districts.[13]

In addition to conducting voter registration drives, volunteers distribute voter guides, host candidate forums, and engage in other education and advocacy activities. These activities support AARP's legislative goals, but the organization makes it clear that it seeks to inform AARP members and the general public about issues that affect all age groups, not just the elderly. In addition, AARP/VOTE is nonpartisan; it neither contributes money to any political campaign, nor endorses any candidate.

## Registering the Disabled: Targeting Service Providers

Election officials are much more attentive to the special needs of disabled voters than they used to be.[14] The Federal Election Commission offers this advice: "[A]lthough most people, when they hear the word 'disability,' think of wheelchairs, there are actually four broad categories of disability to which election officials will want to be sensitive: impaired vision; impaired mobility; impaired communication, and impaired dexterity."[15]

Attention to the needs of voters with disabilities has been mandated by the following federal laws[16] (see appendix A for an overview):

- Voting Rights Act of 1965 as amended,
- Rehabilitation Act of 1973,
- Federal Voting Accessibility for the Elderly & Handicapped Act of 1984,
- Americans with Disabilities Act of 1990, and
- National Voter Registration Act of 1993.

In the case of registration, these laws cover a wide range of issues, including access to information, registration facilities, and election personnel, among others.[17]

In spite of these gains in accessibility, national studies have found that only 56% of people with disabilities are registered to vote, as compared to 71% of nondisabled individuals.[18] The gap is even greater among seniors.

Significant differences also exist in gender and race. One study has found that "once demographic variables such as income and educational attainment are controlled for, men with disabilities are less likely to register than are women with disabilities and non-disabled persons [and] African-American women with disabilities are more likely to register . . . than white women who are disabled."[19]

Persons with disabilities do not register for a number of reasons. Registering means that one expects to vote, and the prospect of voting can be intimidating. Prior to the 1996 presidential election, for example, election officials in Hillsborough County (Florida) became aware of barriers to registration and voting from the executive director of United Cerebral Palsy of Tampa:

> She says she noticed in talking to some disabled persons that they seemed uninterested in registering to vote. She found that some were daunted by the prospect of finding transportation to the polls. And there were other worries—that the polling place would not be accessible by wheelchair or that lines would be too long. Some feared that registering required a public appearance at the courthouse to request special help. And there are disabled people who have difficulty speaking, so telephoning the supervisor of elections' office for information has been a problem for them.[20]

As a result, the Hillsborough County supervisor of elections implemented a program in which her office places registration applications in the offices of twenty-two agencies that work with the disabled. The idea has spread.

## VOTE!2000 Campaign

One group that has worked aggressively to register persons with disabilities is the National Organization on Disability (NOD). The group attributes the historically poor voter turnout among the disability population at least in part to low registration rates.

NOD's VOTE!2000 Campaign sets out to increase by 700,000 the number of disabled voters. A nationwide registration effort is the first step. A get-out-the-vote drive will follow, along with a careful monitoring of the nation's 120,000 polling places to make sure they are accessible to disabled voters.[21]

The organization has targeted disability service providers, urging them to comply with the National Voter Registration Act (NVRA) that requires them to offer voter registration to their clients. NOD's mail-out to these groups includes the wording of Section 2b of the NVRA: "Each state shall designate as voter registration agencies . . . all offices in the state that provide state-funded programs primarily engaged in providing services to persons with disabilities." NOD interprets this to include shuttle and van service providers, personal assistance providers, home health care providers, sign language interpreters, psychiatric and employment counselors, among others.[22]

NOD has prepared a step-by-step guide for these types of agencies on how to set up a voter registration program. (See table 5.3.) The agencies are also instructed that they are to be nonpartisan. NOD recommends posting a sign that reads: "Our voter registration services are available without regard for the voter's political preference. Information and other assistance regarding registering or voting, including transportation and other services offered, shall not be withheld or refused on the basis of support for or opposition to a particular candidate or particular political party."

*Photo 5.3    Polling place instructions printed in large, bold print, and in different languages where appropriate, are helpful to senior voters. But cluttered signage is often a problem. Photograph by David Kadlubowski, The Tampa Tribune, used with permission.*

Disability advocates point out that the Motor Voter bill requires that disability service providers "must distribute mail voter registration application forms to anyone applying for services, renewing their applications for assistance, or submitting a change of address card."[23]  Certain statements must be included in these forms. (See table 5.4.) People are to be informed that registration is optional and that they will not be denied assistance simply because they choose not to register.

The NOD also has specific recommendations for assisting persons with hearing problems: "Deaf and hearing impaired voters must have access to voting and [detailed] registration information through telecommunications devices for the deaf (TDD's)."[24] Toll-free lines are optimal.

For seniors with mobility and/or sight and hearing problems, informational videos and audiotapes can make some registration-related activities easier. Among Florida's supervisors of elections, more than 60% see the usefulness of videos; 47% of audiotapes.[25] Even those who are less enthusiastic identify cost constraints as the primary reason, not the ineffectiveness of these outreach tools.

## GET-OUT-THE-VOTE (GOTV) EFFORTS: PHONE BANKS, MEDIA ANNOUNCEMENTS

Most Americans appreciate being reminded that an election is just around the corner. For some seniors, these gentle reminders can make the difference in

**Table 5.3**
**Registering Disabled Persons:**
**National Organization on Disability**

---

### INSTRUCTIONS TO NONPROFITS

**Follow these four easy steps**

1.  Appoint one permanent staff person to oversee and coordinate voter registration activities. This person should design the best method for routinely offering voter registration in the intake process, at the reception desk, or during orientation at your agency. This person should ensure that the agency has a regular supply of state mail-in voter registration forms, which can be obtained from the local elections office. Also, this person should register staff to vote.

2.  Agency intake forms and procedures should be amended to include the question, "IF YOU ARE NOT REGISTERED TO VOTE WHERE YOU NOW LIVE, WOULD YOU LIKE TO REGISTER TO VOTE HERE TODAY?" Until it is possible to redesign intake forms, rubber stamps with his question are available for $5 from HUMANSERV, at (212) 854-4053; fax (212) 854-8727.

3.  Clients should always be offered help in completing the voter registration form. Check to be sure the application is properly filled out, and that your agency offers to mail it to the elections office. Obtain answers to commonly asked questions such as, "How will I know if I'm registered?" "Where do I vote?" "How do I get an absentee ballot?" "Do I need an I.D. card to vote?" "Can I register to vote at age 17 if I will be 18 on Election Day?" "If I register now, am I permanently registered?" "Do I have to choose a political party when I register?" "If I vote in a party's primary election, do I have to vote for that party in the general election?"

4.  Record the names and phone numbers of people who register to vote at your agency. This step is for get-out-the-vote efforts. You can also keep track of how many people register to document your success to your staff, board, funders, local coalitions, national affiliates, or the press.

*Source: National Organization on Disability. "NOD Vote! 2000 Campaign: Voter Implementation Guide for Nonprofits." Washington, D.C.: NOD, undated.*

*whether* they vote and *how* they vote (in person, by absentee ballot, in advance [early voting], or by mail—where permitted).

### Phone Banks: When to Call? Well in Advance or at the Last Minute?

Historically, phone banks have been at the heart of get-out-the-vote efforts, according to campaign consultants:

Nothing gets out the vote like a telephone. If you have been meticulous and organized during your campaign phonebanking, you have already identified hundreds or

**Table 5.4**

**Form Statements Required by the Motor Voter Bill**

---

### REQUIRED STATEMENTS

1. "If you are not registered to vote where you live now, would you like to apply to register to vote here today?"
   /_/ Yes      /_/ No

2. (in close proximity to the above boxes, and in prominent type): "IF YOU DO NOT CHECK EITHER BOX, YOU WILL BE CONSIDERED TO HAVE DECIDED NOT TO REGISTER TO VOTE AT THIS TIME."

3. "Applying to register or declining to register to vote will not affect the amount of assistance that you will be provided by this agency."

4. "If you would like help filling out the voter registration application form, we will help you. The decision whether to seek or accept help is yours. You may fill out the application form in private."

5. "If you believe that someone has interfered with your right to register or to decline to register to vote, your right to privacy in deciding whether to register or in applying to register to vote, or your right to choose your political party or other political preference, you may file a complaint with [official's name, address, and telephone number]."

---

Source: Kay Schriner and Todd G. Shields, "Empowerment of the Political Kind: The role of Disability Service Organizations in Encouraging People with Disabilities to Vote, Journal of Rehabilitation (April/May/June 1998): 34.

thousands of voters you are counting on to vote for you. . . . Depending on how many volunteers you have, begin re-calling those voters Saturday in order to reach them all before the polls close on election night.[26]

Candidates generally agree that phone banks are a more effective way to reach older than younger voters. (See figure 5.2.) Twice as many see phone banks as an effective way to reach persons 50 and older than persons 18 to 29 (60%+ versus 30%).

Waiting until the Saturday before an election to reach some seniors may not be wise. For example, those who rely on others to drive them to the polls may need a longer lead time to arrange for transportation. Likewise, those unable to go to the polling place, and preferring to vote absentee, need enough time to secure a ballot, arrange for someone to witness it, and mail it back.

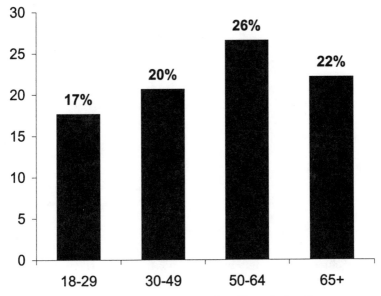

*Figure 5.2   Phone Banks: Effectiveness in Reaching Voters by Age Group*
*Source: Mail survey of 68 candidates for Florida cabinet and state legislative seats, conducted by the author, December 1998.*

But for other seniors always on the go, with full social calendars, a last-minute phone reminder *on election day* may prove worthwhile. The reasoning is that seniors tend to vote in the morning,[27] and poll watchers responsible for checking who has voted can call the no-shows well before the polls close. Seniors who have been too busy or have forgotten about the election can still get there.

Like people of all ages, seniors sometimes forget to vote. In our survey, we asked non-voting Florida seniors 60 and older why they didn't vote in the 1998 election. A small percentage (3%) candidly acknowledged that they forgot. In close elections, that small proportion can be the difference between a candidate winning or losing.

### Postcard and Door Hanger Reminders

Some candidates prefer to send postcards or hang reminders on doorknobs about an upcoming election, along with information about polling places and voting times. The information on where to vote can be critical if the location has changed from the previous election. It is a well-known fact that persons who arrive at an old polling place prepared to vote often go home without voting rather than search for the new location.

Both postcards and door hangers have their shortcomings, as outlined in the previous chapter. Specifically, postcards are too small for some seniors to read, and door hangers can give the appearance that no one is home and, thus, invite burglary. However, for many seniors, these GOTV tactics work just fine.

## TV, Radio, and Internet-Based Informational Efforts

Regular news coverage, public service announcements, and political ads paid for by the party or candidate on TV, radio, or the Internet can raise citizens' awareness of upcoming elections. This is particularly true in low-profile state, local, and referenda (issue) elections.

Compared to young voters, seniors pay closer attention to a wider range of media and to political news in general. Consequently, they can be the most influenced by news stories or advertisements that call attention to impending registration book closings, specific election dates, and changes in precinct lines and voting locations.

News stories and advertisements would also be helpful in publicizing assistance available from the local election office—prior to and on election day. These can include contact numbers (telephone and Internet) for advocacy groups responsible for getting people to the polls. Among Florida's election officials, 92% say it would be quite useful for their offices to have a highly publicized phone number for people to call for voting information. The same percentage favor "more public service announcements informing senior and disabled voters of available assistance."

To date, few media-based GOTV campaigns have informed the public at-large of improvements that have made polling places more accessible for the disabled in the past decade. It shows. One national study of the 1998 election found that

*Photo 5.4    Large directional signs at the polls are very helpful to seniors with sight limitations. Photograph by Kenneth Knight,* The Tampa Tribune, *used with permission.*

disabled persons who have not voted in the past ten years are considerably more likely to anticipate problems at the polling place than those who have voted. (See table 5.5.) The same study found: "Actual or expected problems in voting at a polling place are highest among those who have difficulty going outside alone, and are high among those with severe vision impairments and mental impairments."[28]

## VOTING

Voting is the most direct link between you and your government. Perhaps no one understands this as much as older Americans.

A 1999 survey conducted for the Council for Excellence in Government by the research firms of Peter D. Hart and Robert Teeter shows that nearly two-thirds (62%) of seniors 65 and older vote in *all* elections, compared to just 13% of the 18-to-29-year-olds. (See figure 5.3.) As noted in chapter 1, seniors are also more likely to vote a complete ballot—voting in all contests and on all issues.

Historically, voter turnout rates for seniors have far exceeded those of other age groups. (See table 5.6.) The highest turnout rates are among seniors 65–74 years of age. But even the turnout rates of persons 75 and older are nearly double those of 18-to-20-year-olds in presidential election years and more than three times higher in midterm congressional election years.

**Table 5.5**

### Disabled Non-Voters Expect More Difficulty at the Polling Place

| Difficulty | Disabled Voters Problems encountered if voted in past 10 yrs | Disabled Non-Voters Problems expected if haven't voted in past 10 yrs |
|---|---|---|
| Any difficulty in voting at polling place | 8.2% | 27.5% |
| General mobility (walking, standing) | 1.7% | 10.3% |
| Getting to polling place | 1.6% | 8.8% |
| At polling place (getting inside, using booth/machine, long lines, seeing ballot) | 3.9% | 10.1% |
| Other | 1.4% | 2.9% |

*Note: National random-household survey of 1,240 American citizens of voting age conducted after November, 1998 election. The sample was stratified so that interviews were conducted with 700 people with disabilities and 540 people without disabilities.*

*Source: Douglas L. Kruse, Lisa Schur, Kay Schriner, and Todd Shields,* Empowerment Through Civic Participation: A Study of the Political Behavior of People With Disabilities. *Final report to the Disability Research Consortium, Bureau of Economic Research, Rutgers University and New Jersey Developmental Disabilities Council.*

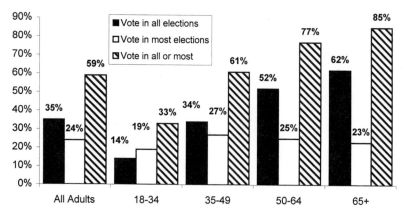

Figure 5.3    Voting Frequency by Age
Source: The Council for Excellence in Government, 1999 Survey of 1,214 adults, conducted
May 21–June 1, by the firms of Peter Hart and Robert Teeter, margin of error +/- 3.2 percent.
Used with permission.

The tapering off of turnout rates among seniors tracks closely with rising disability rates. As shown in figure 5.4, the voting gap between people with and without disabilities widens with age.[29] Data from a national random household telephone survey of 1,240 American citizens of voting age show that 40% of all Americans with some impairment or limitation first experienced it at age 50 or older.[30]

Some observers speculate that the turnout gap between people with and without disabilities may narrow in the next century:

The lower turnout of people with disabilities may be confined to the older generation, who were socialized at a time when disabilities were typically marginalized and

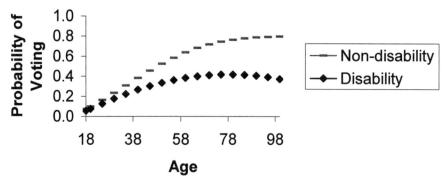

Figure 5.4    Age Patterns in Voter Turnout, November 1998
Source: Douglas L. Kruse, Kay Schriner, Lisa Schur, and Todd Shields, "Empowerment through Civic Participation: A Study of the Political Behavior of People with Disabilities." Final Report to the Disability Research Consortium, Bureau of Economic Research, Rutgers University, and the New Jersey Developmental Disabilities Council, March 1999.

**Table 5.6**

| Percentage Reporting They Voted | | | | | | | |
| --- | --- | --- | --- | --- | --- | --- | --- |
| Presidential Election Years | | | | | | | |
| Age | 1972 | 1976 | 1980 | 1984 | 1988 | 1992 | 1996 |
| 18-20 | 48 | 38 | 36 | 37 | 33 | 38 | 31 |
| 21-24 | 50 | 46 | 43 | 44 | 38 | 46 | 33 |
| 25-34 | 59 | 55 | 55 | 55 | 48 | 53 | 43 |
| 35-44 | 66 | 63 | 64 | 64 | 61 | 64 | 55 |
| 45-64 | 70 | 69 | 69 | 70 | 68 | 70 | 64 |
| 65-74 | 68 | 66 | 69 | 72 | 73 | 74 | 70 |
| 75 + | 56 | 55 | 58 | 61 | 62 | 65 | 63 |
| Congressional Election Years | | | | | | | |
| Age | 1974 | 1978 | 1982 | 1986 | 1990 | 1994 | |
| 18-20 | 20 | 20 | 20 | 19 | 18 | 16 | |
| 21-24 | 26 | 26 | 28 | 24 | 22 | 22 | |
| 25-34 | 37 | 38 | 40 | 35 | 34 | 32 | |
| 35-44 | 49 | 50 | 52 | 49 | 48 | 46 | |
| 45-64 | 56 | 59 | 62 | 59 | 75 | 56 | |
| 65-74 | 56 | 60 | 65 | 65 | 64 | 64 | |
| 75+ | 44 | 48 | 52 | 54 | 54 | 56 | |

*Source: U.S. Bureau of the Census, Current Population Reports, Voting and Registration in the Election of November 1976 (Washington, D.C.: Government Printing Office, 1993), Series P-20, no. 322, 11-12, 14-21, 57, 61; November 1978, no. 344, 8, 11-19, 60, 65; November 1980, no. 370, 10-20, 50, 56; November 1982, no. 383, 1-12, 46, 49; November 1984, no. 405, 13-24, 59; November 1986, no. 414, 11-22, 29, 31; November 1988, no. 440, 13-24, 48, 50; November 1990, no. 453, 1-2, 4, 13-14, 17; November 1992, no. 466, v-vii, 1, 5; November 1994; November, 1996, PPL-89.*

frequently segregated from mainstream society. In contrast, many younger people with disabilities were integrated into the mainstream educational system due to the 1977 Education of all Handicapped Children Act, which helped produce leadership for the disability rights movement.[31]

## Transportation to the Polls

Getting to the polls is one of the biggest obstacles for seniors who either cannot drive or are afraid to drive too far from home and/or in highly congested areas. Some 6% of the Florida seniors we surveyed said that getting to the polls poses a problem for them. Among those who did not vote in the 1998 election, nearly 10% said it was due to transportation difficulties.

Election officials and seniors increasingly see transportation as a key to getting older persons, especially those with disabilities, to the polls. More than half (53%) of Florida's election officials acknowledge that their offices have been contacted either by the senior voter or a friend or neighbor about providing transportation. Nearly one-fifth (17%) of these officials say that when mingling with seniors at political, civic, or social events, they are routinely asked about the availability of transportation.

It is not surprising, then, that 87% of Florida's election officials believe that better transportation to the polls would be a somewhat or very useful way to assist more seniors with visual, hearing, or mobility limitations. Nearly two-thirds (64%) also think that it would be helpful to have a highly publicized election-office telephone number that seniors could call for help in obtaining transportation to the polls. But most election officials candidly admit that they cannot provide transportation because of funding limitations. Instead, they would refer those needing assistance to advocacy groups, churches, and civic organizations.

### Table 5.7

#### How Seniors Get to the Polls

|                              | %    |
|------------------------------|------|
| I got there myself           | 83   |
| Relative drove me            | 12   |
| Neighbor drove me            | 5    |
| Political party pick-up       | 1    |
| Don't know/No answer/Refused | 1    |
| **Total**                    | **100*** |

*Note: Respondents were asked, "Did someone drive you to the polls (if so, who?) or did you get there on your own?"*

*Source: Telephone survey of a random sample of 600 Floridians age 60 or older conducted in December, 1998.*
*\*Statistical discrepancy due to rounding.*

Seniors who rely on someone else to take them to the polls most often depend on relatives and friends. (See table 5.7.) Few report relying on political parties, in spite of the fact that most how-to books on getting out the vote stress the importance of parties and candidates transporting their supporters to the polls. Increasingly, political consultants are advising parties and candidates to be wary of transporting persons because of liability concerns and instead to encourage other groups to carry the load.

The 2000 election has prompted some advocacy groups, such as the National Organization on Disability, to focus more on transportation as a key element of their GOTV efforts. For example, disability provider agencies have been informed that they are permitted to use agency-owned vehicles to take their clients to the polling place. They may also use agency volunteers to provide rides to the polls for those who need them.[32]

## Precinct Location

The closer, and more convenient, the polling place, the easier it is for seniors (and other voters as well) to vote in person. Choosing familiar locations with an easy travel route and a safe place to park is optimal. The Federal Election Commission advises, "Accessible parking with an accessible route to the polling place should be provided. If there is a nearby public transportation stop, there should be an accessible route from the public transportation stop to the polling place site. An accessible passenger loading zone should also be provided."[33]

### Age-Concentrated Neighborhoods

In areas with heavy concentrations of older residents, the ideal is to locate polling places at community senior centers, condo or townhome recreation centers, civic centers, libraries, and churches. The closer to home, the better, and if it's *at* home, that's icing on the cake! More than one-fourth of Florida's seniors say they vote where they live; another 12% vote within walking distance of where they live.

### Mobile Polling Places

Many nursing home and assisted-living facility residents are unable to travel any distance to a polling place. Increasingly, polling places are being brought to them.

Mobile vans staffed by election-office personnel travel to nursing homes and ALFs. In some communities, civic groups, private individuals, foundations, or nonprofits provide the vans as a community service, and the election office provides the drivers. In these arrangements, residents are given a schedule of van arrival and departure times so they can be ready to climb aboard.

Another option is to set up an accessible temporary voting booth inside the facility, with election officials on hand to help the residents vote. This is a some-

*Photo 5.5   Parking accessibility is critical to many seniors, especially those with mobility limitations. Photograph by Gary Rings, The Tampa Tribune, used with permission.*

what different concept than simply sending out election-office personnel to conduct absentee balloting. A temporary voting booth creates the aura of a polling place and gives the residents more psychological satisfaction.

   More than half of Florida's supervisors believe this mobile voting van concept is appealing. More than 30% have already used some type of mobile voting system, although primarily to conduct absentee voting. (Florida law requires that supervisors offer to conduct absentee balloting in nursing homes and assisted-living facilities.) (See appendix B.)

Some elder advocates and election officials believe that making election officials—often a bipartisan team—responsible for voting in these facilities is far superior to leaving absentee balloting in the hands of candidates, political parties, or nursing home personnel. (The fear of absentee ballot fraud will be discussed later in the chapter.)

### Curbside Voting

Another form of taking the voting booth to the person is curbside voting. Curbside voting occurs when "an individual with a mobility impairment . . . cannot enter the polling site because it is inaccessible."[34] When an individual requests curbside voting, a poll worker brings the ballot to the voter's car, then helps the voter complete the ballot if necessary.[35] Such an approach has been ruled allowable under the Americans with Disabilities Act, even when the individual's privacy cannot be guaranteed or a "proximity-to-the-polls" assistance prohibition is violated.

For some disabled seniors, curbside voting is an exciting alternative, the next best thing to actually walking into the polling place. They can witness the frenzy of last-minute campaigning by candidates and their supporters and the excitement of citizens scurrying into the polls.

Some advocacy groups have a different opinion. They see curbside voting as another way to skirt the language and intent of the Americans with Disabilities Act, the effect of which is to discriminate against the disabled: "Voting curbside makes it difficult for the voter with a mobility impairment to enjoy the communitarian benefits of participating in the electoral process. 'Drive by' voting of this sort is a cheapened version of the citizen's ultimate exercise of power and responsibility in a democracy, and does not result in equal benefits for the person with a disability."[36]

Technically, the law requires "that any handicapped voter assigned to an inaccessible polling place will, upon advanced request under established State procedures, either be assigned to an accessible polling place or be provided an alternative means of casting a ballot on election day."[37] It is the "alternative means" that some find undesirable.

### Training of Poll Personnel

In addition to the location of the polls, attention must be given to the people who work there. Their training and behavior can intensify or diminish problems that seniors face in voting.

Actually, poll workers are often seniors themselves. Older adults who have retired have the time to work at the polls, and they enjoy the social contact and participation in the election process. Without them, few elections (other than those conducted by mail) could take place.

The Federal Election Commission, in its publication *Ensuring the Accessibility of the Election Process,* lays out a list of "Common Courtesies and Guidelines" that can easily be distributed to poll workers. (See table 5.8.) A similar list has been developed by the National Organization on Disability and the National Easter Seal Society.[38]

When election officials take time to adequately train poll workers, sensitivity to the special needs of older voters, especially those with disabilities, improves. Election officials can gather useful tips by attending professional association-sponsored workshops addressing these issues.

Elder and disabled advocacy groups can play an important role by volunteering to make presentations at such events. Their input should address both "attitudinal and architectural barriers" that discourage or prevent seniors from voting at the polling place.[39]

Specific problems faced by the mentally impaired, deaf or hard of hearing, blind or visually impaired, and immobile should be discussed because they are *different.* (More will be said about this later in the chapter.)

Video presentations can be especially effective training tools. One state successfully used such an approach following passage of the Voting Accessibility for the Elderly and Handicapped Act of 1984. At that time, the Oklahoma State Election Board prepared a video, *Equal Access for All,* which identified various improvements that could be made at polling places. It was distributed to all county election boards.[40] More such videos, along with pragmatic recommendations, are needed.

These videos would also be an effective way for political parties and professional campaign consultants to advise candidates and volunteers on how to better work the crowd at the polls.

### Layout of the Polling Place

In the 1980s and early 1990s, the Federal Election Commission conducted a number of surveys of polling place accessibility in the American states. Specifically, the surveys examined the accessibility of the following:[41]

parking (designated spaces for disabled; width of parking spaces; level or sloped; paved or not; proximity to polling place; curb cuts; passenger drop-off zones)

walkways or pathways to the building (paved or not; width; curb cuts; ramps; stairs—ramped/sloped; non-slip surfaces; handrails; unobstructed; no overhangs; lighting; signage)

ramps and elevators entering or inside the building (slope; handrails; curbs; wheelchair access; width of elevator cab and doors; height of elevator controls; raised lettering on control panel; proximity to building entrance)

other architectural features (door openings, door handles, stairs, handrails, availability of seating or rest areas, non-slip surfaces)

features within the voting area (visible instructions, wheelchair access—building and voting booth, availability of magnifying devices, lighting, availability of seating)

**Table 5.8**
**Federal Election Commission Guidelines**

**Common Courtesies and Guidelines for**
**Assisting Disabled or Elderly Persons**

- Be considerate of the extra time it might take for a person who is disabled or elderly to get things done, and give unhurried attention to a person who has difficulty speaking.
- Speak directly to the person who has a disability rather than to a companion who may be along.
- Speak calmly, slowly and directly to a person with a hearing problem. Your facial expressions, gestures and body movements help in understanding. Don't shout or speak in the person's ear. If full understanding is doubtful, write a note to the person with a hearing problem.
- Before pushing someone in a wheelchair, ask if you may do so and how you should proceed.
- Greet a person who is visually impaired by letting the person know who and where you are. Provide a guiding device such as a ruler or card for signing forms. When offering walking assistance, allow the person to take your arm and tell him or her if you are approaching steps or inclines.
- Be aware that dogs who assist people with disabilities should be admitted into all buildings. Such dogs are highly trained and need no special care other than provided by the owner.
- Be aware that federal law allows voters with disabilities to be accompanied and to receive assistance by another person in the voting booth.
- Remember that all voters deserve courteous attention in exercising their right as citizens to vote.
- If space allows, provide seating outside the polling place for voters to sit while they wait for rides or for their companions to vote.
- In advance of election day, offer to make available a voting booth to demonstrate to people with disabilities how it works so they can become familiar with its operation and be ready to cast their vote on election day.

*Source: Federal Election Commission,* Ensuring the Accessability of the Election Process: *Innovations in Election Administration, vol. 15, Washington, D.C.: Office of Election Administration, Federal Election Commission, August 1996.*

From the survey results, and in consultation with the National Association of Secretaries of State (NASS) and the Coalition for Voter Accessibility, the Federal Election Commission crafted a set of "sensitivity" recommendations for four types of disabilities: impaired vision, impaired mobility, impaired communication, and impaired dexterity. These are detailed in the Commission's 1996 *Ensuring Disability* report.

The National Organization on Disability has formulated its own "Polling Places Checklist," which incorporates and expands many of the Commission's recommendations. (See table 5.9.)

The National Organization on Disability and others have criticized the Federal Election Commission for not including "learning disabilities, psychiatric impairments, or developmental disabilities such as mental retardation" on its list.[42]

**Table 5.9**

**Polling Places Checklist**

---

## Guidelines

The guidelines contained herein pertain to the removal of architectural barriers so a building may be accessible to the disabled and elderly. The information contained does not address every section of the standards, i.e. restrooms, alarms systems, etc. Therefore accessibility is limited rather than full, and if the following guidelines are adhered to it will constitute an accessible building only for the purpose of voting.

__ **PARKING:** (where provided) Parking spaces should be 8 feet wide with an access aisle of 5 feet. It should be located as close as possible to the entrance.

__ **ACCESS:** The access path from the parking to the entrance should be a pitch of 1 inch to 20 inches and with no sudden change in grade. It should be a minimum of 3 feet wide.

__ **RAMPS:** Ramps may be temporary or permanent. In many cases it is most cost effective to build permanent ramps. Ramps should have a pitch of 1 inch in 12 inches with a minimum width of 3 feet.
There should be a level platform at top and bottom, of 5 feet by 5 feet. They should have a non-slip surface and when a ramp has a vertical rise of greater than 6 inches railings are required. Railings should be 32 inches from the ramp surface to the top of the rail.

__ **ENTRANCE DOORS:** Doors should be a minimum of clear space of 32 inches when the door is open. This would require a 34 inch door or greater.

__ **INTERIOR ACCESS:** There should be an uninterrupted path of at least 3 feet wide from the entrance to the voting area.

---

*Source: National Organization on Disability, 910 Sixteenth Street, NW, Washington, D.C., 20006.*

However, to date, state laws that restrict voting by persons who have legally been declared mentally incompetent and/or are under the care of a guardian have not been declared in violation of the Americans with Disabilities Act.[43]

### Assistance for Persons with Impaired Vision

To better accommodate the needs of the visually impaired at the polling place, the Federal Election Commission recommends good illumination both in the polling place as well as in indoor passageways leading to such facilities. Instructions should be prominently displayed in large, bold type. (Review the previous chapter for a discussion of fonts and colors that pose difficulties to seniors.) Magnifying glasses, magnifying screens, or other viewing devices should be available upon request from a poll worker. Seniors with visual difficulty should be informed that they may request assistance in voting, usually from someone of their own choice (under Section 208 of the Voting Rights Act).[44] Poll workers should be prepared to read or provide an audio recording of any general materials made available to sighted voters by the election office at the polling place.

Election officials and advocates for the blind have additional recommendations. For example, the National Organization on Disability and the National Easter Seal Society suggest using more signage with pictures or symbols. "For example, arrows or a hand point are easier for everyone to understand than signs that say 'voters entrance at the east side.'"[45]

Florida's election supervisors see large-print ballots and a wider distribution of large-type sample ballots before election day as useful services to the visually impaired. More than 86% are "sometimes" or "often" asked to help vision-impaired voters with their ballots on election day.

Britain's "See It Right" campaign has pushed for large print, Braille, and tape versions of the written ballot to be made available to the visually impaired, preferably *before* the election.[46] But to date, taped, recorded, or Braille ballots or other documents cannot be forced on a U.S. locality if an election official certifies that such services would "constitute an undue administrative or financial burden."[47]

Some localities have been more proactive than others in developing ballots for the visually impaired that permit them to vote independently—in private. The experimental system of Marion County, Oregon, "uses tactile markings on a ballot cover (mask) in conjunction with instructions on an audio tape, to allow the visually-impaired voter to vote a ballot without assistance."[48] The system obviously has excited those eligible to use it. While the overall turnout for the first Marion County election (an issue referendum) among all voters was 64%, the turnout among those receiving ballots for the visually impaired was 96%. The second time it was used (a regular election featuring candidates), turnout for the entire county was 39%, compared to 67% among voters with tactile ballots and 41% among voters who returned requested large-print ballots.[49]

Sometimes voting booths cause problems for the visually impaired. The State of Rhode Island re-examined its voting booths, following complaints from voters who relied on someone else to complete their ballots for them. Because there were no curtains, these voters were upset that other voters might hear their choice of candidates as they instructed an assistant to vote.[50] Ironically, the state had just purchased these new voting booths. The lesson here is to allow disability groups to have some input before issuing a purchase order.

The technological revolution, and the swelling ranks of the visually impaired, will undoubtedly spark inventions that aid the blind. As of this writing, a system is already in place that "allows a blind voter to use a touch screen with the assistance of an automated telephone message which directs the voter where to touch the screen to register her choices."[51]A number of electronic voting machine manufacturers are developing talking voting machines that confirm orally the choice a voter has made when he/she presses a button or a screen.[52]

While some may push hard for Braille ballots, it is important to note that they also have one serious drawback. They "would not meet the objective of keeping a vote secret, because [they] would have to be counted separately and would be readily identifiable."[53]

*Assistance for Persons with Impaired Mobility*

Some seniors come to the polls in wheelchairs. Others who are ambulatory rely on walkers, canes, or prosthetic devices to help them get there. Those who suffer from dystrophy, sclerosis, heart ailments, obesity, infirmity of old age, or any number of other conditions also may have mobility impairments. They may be limited in the distance they can walk or the time they can comfortably stand in line.

Wheelchair access is facilitated by curb cuts, ramps, and sufficiently wide walkways, pathways, and doors. The incline of ramps should not be too steep. Voting booths must be of sufficient width and height to allow a person in a wheelchair to fit comfortably into the booth.

The National Organization on Disability and the National Easter Seal Society recommend a 32-inch clearance at nonrevolving doors to enable a person using a wheelchair to enter a building. The best floors are those with smooth and hard surfaces or those covered with a tightly woven carpet with no pad or a thin pad. Tables or voting booths to be used by the wheelchair-bound should have a clear knee space underneath that is at least 29–34 inches high.

The National Organization on Disability also recommends providing parking spaces that are wide enough to open vehicle doors and maneuver a wheelchair or walker between cars.

The Chicago Mayor's Office for People with Disabilities has prepared etiquette tips for poll workers, candidates, and individuals interacting with persons in wheelchairs:[54]

- Do not patronize people in wheelchairs by patting them on the head. Reserve this sign of affection for children, even though the individual's head temptingly rests at about the same height as a child's.
- Leaning or hanging on a person's wheelchair is similar to leaning or hanging on a person and is generally considered annoying. The chair is part of the body space of the person who uses it. Don't hang on it!
- When talking with a person who uses a wheelchair for more than a few minutes, place yourself at their eye level to spare both of you a stiff neck.
- When giving directions to a person who uses a wheelchair, consider distance, weather conditions, and physical obstacles such as stairs, curbs, and steep hills.
- When in doubt about what is or is not an appropriate action, ask the individual who happens to have the disability what is preferred. In other words, extend the same courtesies to a person with a disability as you would to someone without a disability.

For ambulatory persons with limited mobility and stamina, the Federal Election Commission offers the following guidelines in selecting voting locations:

- Avoid long distances to be traversed either within the facility or between the parking lot and the facility. Where distances cannot be avoided, it is useful to have seating along the way to allow seniors to stop and catch their breath. Inside the facility, have plenty of seating in places with waiting lines.
- Do not have doors that are heavy and difficult to open; revolving doors are often a problem as are doors in series.
- Have ramps or an elevator alternative.
- Have non-skid, level walking surfaces, unencumbered with any obstacles over which one might stumble or trip.
- Do not have automatic door closers that shut too quickly.

Other groups have suggested having at least one voting machine with enough knee space to permit voting from a seated position.

What do election officials think would be helpful to better serve the mobility impaired? Among Florida's election supervisors, 87% agree that having more chairs at the polls for the elderly is a good thing, as are more wheelchair-accessible tables and voting booths.

Two other rather novel approaches have some appeal to some Florida election officials: a dedicated time for the disabled to vote (43%) and a dedicated line at the polls for the disabled (46%).

*Assistance for Persons with Impaired Communication*

According to the Federal Election Commission, impaired communication refers to both impaired hearing and to impaired speech. For the hearing-impaired, it is helpful to have interpreters at the polls. Many deaf individuals find sign language easier to understand than written English. For some, their "first language is American Sign Language."[55]

Voters with speech difficulties are often best helped by a poll worker who is trained in how to effectively interact with them or someone with a similar disability.

*Assistance for Persons with Impaired Dexterity*

"Impaired dexterity refers primarily to problems in grasping items in the hand," according to the Commission. In extreme form, it is complete paralysis. Less severe forms include such conditions as muscular disorders and arthritis.

To improve polling place accessibility to the dexterity-impaired, election officials are advised to convert doorknobs into levers, push bar mechanisms, or U-shaped pull handles. It is also important to make sure that any stylus or other ballot-marking instrument has a knob that makes it easy to grasp.

The National Organization on Disability and the National Easter Seal Society also recommend that paper ballots be made available at the polls for persons who cannot operate a voting machine. It is not uncommon for someone at the polls to acknowledge this kind of difficulty. Among Florida's election officials,

*Photo 5.6   Poll workers need to be trained in how to better communicate with hearing-impaired voters. Often, seniors have better hearing in one ear than another. And shouting is often not necessary or very effective.*

89% say they "sometimes" or "often" get contacted to help elderly voters with their ballots on election day. Some types of voting systems pose more problems for seniors and disabled persons than others.

## Ballot Style/Format

According to the Federal Election Commission, ballot systems consist of five major types: paper, mechanical lever machines, punch cards, Marksense (optical scan), and Direct Recording Electronic (DRE) systems. (See table 5.10.)

### Paper Ballots

As of 1998, paper ballots were still used by 4% of the registered voters in the United States. A paper ballot is a printed sheet listing all candidates and issues; a voter uses a pencil to mark choices.

Paper ballots are "the simplest and easiest system for assisting the elderly and wheelchair bound," according to one election supervisor. "The voter can take the ballot to a booth or table and make his/her marks." The major drawback is that counting the ballots takes longer. Naturally, this poses more of a problem in areas with large concentrations of seniors.

Paper ballots also can have many of the same problems of campaign literature. As discussed earlier, large, bold print on nonslick paper is better for many seniors.

### Mechanical Lever Machines

In the 1998 presidential election, mechanical lever machines were used by 18% of the registered voters casting ballots. On these machines, each candidate or issue is assigned a particular lever in a rectangular array of levers on the front of the machine. A set of printed strips visible to the voters identifies the lever assignment for each candidate and issue choice. The voter activates the machine by pulling a lever, which simultaneously closes a privacy curtain.[56]

These types of machines often pose difficulties for seniors with sight, mobility, and/or dexterity limitations. Because the machine's height cannot be adjusted, this type of machine is most difficult for those in wheelchairs. Pulling the lever hard enough to make the curtain close requires a certain amount of strength, which some seniors simply do not have. Small font size can be another problem for seniors with limited vision.

These machines are no longer made, and the trend is to replace them with computer-based Marksense or DRE systems.

### Punch Card Systems

In the 1998 election, punch card systems were used by 36% of all registered voters. These systems use a card (or cards) and a small clipboard-sized device for

**Table 5.10**

**Voting Equipment Usage at the Polls, 1998**

| Voting Type | No. of Counties | % Counties | No. of Precincts | Population | % of Pop | Registered Voters | % Reg. Voters | Change* since 1994 |
|---|---|---|---|---|---|---|---|---|
| Punch card | 635 | 20.23 | 71,027 | 98,259,949 | 36.43 | 53,926,513 | 34.3 | -1.8 |
| Optical Scan | 1,217 | 38.76 | 47,489 | 73,463,341 | 27.24 | 42,129,377 | 27.3 | +5.8 |
| Lever | 480 | 15.29 | 41,907 | 48,973,908 | 18.16 | 28,623,195 | 18.6 | -8.4 |
| DRE | 257 | 8.18 | 14,033 | 23,915,034 | 8.87 | 14,080,560 | 9.1 | +4.8 |
| Paper | 410 | 13.06 | 5,551 | 3,750,397 | 1.39 | 2,427,669 | 1.6 | -1.1 |
| Mixed | 141 | 4.49 | 11,412 | 21,324,009 | 7.91 | 14,033,374 | 9.1 | +0.8 |
| Total | 3,140 | 100.00 | 192,419 | 269,686,638 | 100.00 | 154,220,480 | 100.00 | |

Note: *This figure represents the percentage point change based on usage by the number of registered voters in jurisdictions using this equipment. For example, in 1994, punch cards were used in jurisdictions serving 36.1 percent of the registered voters, in 1998 by 34.3 percent, a decline of 1.8 percentage points.

Source: This table compiled from information provided by Election Data Services, Washington, D.C.

recording votes. The voter punches holes in the card, using a supplied punch device or stylus, opposite the candidate or ballot issue choice. There are two common types of punch cards: the Votomatic and the Datavote.

On the Votomatic, the only information appearing on the card is numbers. Each number represents a candidate or issue choice; the list of candidates and issues are printed in a separate booklet. To vote, a person punches a hole by the number assigned to a particular candidate or issue choice.

On the Datavote, the name of the candidate or description of the issue choice is printed on the card next to the space where the hole is to be punched.[57]

Punch cards are often a problem for seniors with dexterity and sight disabilities. Font sizes are usually small. The stylus is difficult to grip. Hitting the small hole is often difficult for seniors with unsteady hands. Some voters have difficulty aligning the ballot properly and worry that they are "not hitting the right hole" and are thereby "messing up their ballot."

Six percent of Florida's seniors say they have a problem punching ballots. More than half (54%) of the election supervisors acknowledge that punch cards need to be improved because they are too difficult for many seniors and disabled to line up properly. Some officials provide an alternative stylus, a large ball that can be gripped with the whole hand. But many seniors do not know such alternatives are available.

### Marksense

In 1998, Marksense (optical scan) systems were used by 27% of all registered voters. These systems use a ballot card on which candidates and issue choices are preprinted next to an empty rectangle, circle, oval, or an incomplete arrow. Voters record their choices by using a pencil to fill in the rectangle, circle, or oval, or to complete the arrow.[58]

Optical scan systems are similar to a paper ballot in some ways because the voter is physically marking the ballot. The biggest drawback may be the varying degree of scanner sensitivity to the marks. If the mark is too light, or if it does not completely connect the arrows or fill in the circle, it may not be recorded. Seniors with unsteady hands and a weak grip may not record their vote as dark or as completely as someone else.

Another problem is that the arrows, circles, or ovals can be so close together that they create confusion and/or result in a stray mark, thereby creating a situation in which a person over-votes—that is, he or she casts more than one vote in the same contest.

### Direct Recording Electronic (DRE) Systems

In 1998, DRE systems, the newest voting system configuration, were used by 9% of all voters. The percentage is likely to be much higher in the twenty-first century.

DRE systems are an electronic reincarnation of the old mechanical lever machine. There is no ballot. The possible choices are visible to the voter on the front of the machine. The voter directly enters choices into electronic storage with the use of a touch-screen, push buttons, or similar devices.[59]

Some election officials believe this system is the most voter friendly and the most promising for several reasons. First, the type size tends to be larger, as is the rectangular box to be touched when casting a vote. Second, a simple touch records the vote. Third, the system eliminates over-voting; it is impossible to cast two votes in the same contest.

For some seniors these systems are too high tech. They worry that they have not touched the screen properly and fear that their votes have not been recorded. For others, it is old hat—a system they have already encountered at the local library, the ATM machine, or the Internet.

Some election officials recommend taking a DRE machine to senior groups and letting them practice with it before Election Day. As more seniors get "wired," fewer will be intimidated by this type of voting system.

*Mixed Systems*

In the 1998 election, 8% of voters cast their ballots in polling places that provided more than one type of voting machine or system. Depending on the types

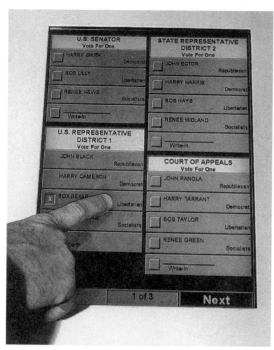

*Photo 5.7    Touch screen voting machines are the newest type of voting system. They are considered to be more "senior friendly" than punch card or mechanical lever voting systems. Photography by Robert Burke, The Tampa Tribune, used with permission.*

of systems provided, this arrangement might make it easier for seniors to cast ballots. At the same time, mixed systems complicate the tabulation process for election officials.

## ALTERNATIVE VOTING ARRANGEMENTS

Going to the polls on election day is out of the question for some seniors, especially the growing number with disabilities. This has prompted election officials and advocacy groups to constantly devise, test, and refine alternative voting arrangements. The three most common approaches currently are absentee voting, mail ballots, and early voting. A fourth on the horizon is Internet voting, which will likely come about because many states and localities already permit on-line voter registration.

### Absentee Ballots

In the past, absentee ballots were reserved for people too ill to go to the polls or those who were out of town on election day. Naturally, older voters relied more on absentee balloting than other age groups.[60] But absentee balloting has expanded tremendously in recent years.

Some states now have what is tantamount to no-fault absentee balloting—anyone can request one and vote accordingly:[61]

> Absentee ballots, once reserved for the small sliver of the electorate who were unavoidably prevented from voting on election day by illness or travel, have become increasingly tools of party strategists and candidates to maximize their votes. In states such as California, huge numbers of absentee votes—most clearly not requested because of travel or other exigency—are cast in every election and have been pivotal in many, including major statewide contests.[62]

Today, voters can apply for an absentee ballot for any reason and without notarization in California, Hawaii, Montana, Oregon, Washington, and Wyoming.[63]

The absentee ballot has changed the whole chemistry of campaigns. Absentee vote contact programs are an effective way to reach voters, especially if you have money. Candidates acknowledge that helping seniors with absentee ballots is a successful campaign technique. (See figure 5.5.)

One political consultant, writing in *Campaigns & Elections* magazine, has advised candidates on how to proceed: "Obtain from election authorities the names of regular absentee voters (e.g., seniors) and voters requesting mail-in ballots. Mail and phone them with a persuasive message. Send target voters pre-stamped applications if absentee voting in your state is open and unrestricted. Phone voters and remind them to mail their application. Still later, visit the house and actually mail the completed ballot."[64]

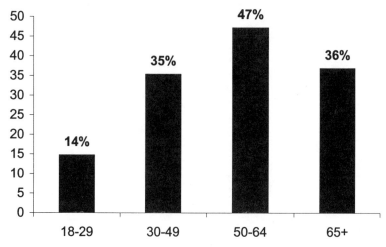

*Figure 5.5    Help Voting Absentee: Effectiveness in Reaching Voters by Age Group*

Source: *Mail survey of 68 candidates for Florida cabinet and state legislative seats, conducted by the author, December, 1998.*

Proponents of no-fault (unrestricted) absentee voting argue that it simply is responsive to today's busy lifestyle. Supporters also point out that the absentee ballot option is favored by persons needing a little more time and preferring a little less congestion.

Opponents believe the absentee ballot further contributes to the disconnectedness between voters and their government: "Standing in line with neighbors to cast a vote on election day is one of the few civic rituals remaining in American democracy. . . . Absentee [voting] is a violation of the sacrament of democracy, which is walking or driving to your polling place and seeing the faces of your fellow citizens."[65]

As with all forms of voting, absentee balloting has its drawbacks for some seniors. These drawbacks range from annoyance and confusion to outright fraud.[66]

## Annoyance and Confusion

Complaints arise when an absentee ballot is mailed in an envelope containing campaign literature. The envelope may bear a greeting such as "Thank you for requesting an absentee ballot." One Florida election supervisor says she receives a number of complaints from seniors who say they requested an absentee ballot from *her* office—not from a political party or candidate. They are either angry or confused.

This scenario emerges because lists of registered voters who have requested absentee ballots are public information under Florida's open records law. Interestingly, among Florida's seniors who voted absentee, 40% say they got their ballot from a political party representative compared to 28% from a supervisor of elections. The remainder either picked up the ballot themselves or obtained one from a relative, friend, or neighbor.

At any rate, questions about absentee ballots are among the most common that senior voters pose to election officials. (See figure 5.6.)

### Fraud

"If vote fraud is going to occur, they say, it's most often attempted via absentee ballots," according to Richard Smolka, editor of *Election Administration Reports*. "Voting absentee isn't supervised as in a voting booth. It's an honor system."[67]

Nursing homes are prime targets for absentee ballot fraud. Vote seekers—in the person of candidates, advocacy group representatives, or even facility personnel—can persuade residents who are a bit disoriented or disabled to accept help in voting. This "help" often takes the form of "completing" the senior's ballot.

In Montgomery, Alabama, "there were the helpful visits to nursing homes before the 1994 elections, when partisans 'assisted' incapacitated and even comatose patients with their ballots."[68] In Hialeah, Florida, campaign workers ordered dozens of absentee ballots by phone and took them to nursing homes looking for willing voters.[69] In Miami, party activists canvassed nursing homes and mental health facilities.[70]

As one safeguard against fraud, many states require that absentee ballots be witnessed. However, techniques for verifying witness signatures are often inadequate. Several recent vote fraud cases have revealed that a bundle of absentee ballots all bore the same witness's name but in different handwriting, suggesting someone else actually witnessed the vote. (We have found some evidence of this in Florida.)

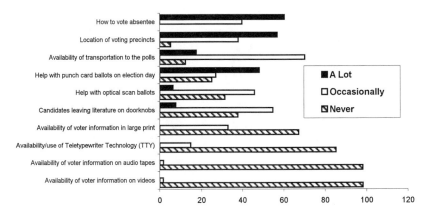

*Figure 5.6   Questions Raised by Senior Voters*
Note: "In the course of interacting with senior voters, how often do you get asked questions about _____ ?"
Source: Mail survey of Florida Supervisor of Elections, conducted July–September 1999.

Because nursing home and ALF residents can be led to vote contrary to their wishes, some election officials prefer to send personnel from their offices to conduct absentee balloting in these facilities. Some facility administrators prefer it as well.

More than 40% of the nursing home/ALF administrators in a three-county area in central Florida acknowledged they have asked their supervisor of elections to conduct absentee balloting at their facilities. (See figure 5.7.) Among those who have not, 42% said they did not know the service was available. (See figure 5.8.) One-third acknowledged that someone in their facility helps residents with the absentee voting process.

Increasingly, states are clamping down on who can request, witness, deliver, or return absentee ballots. The restrictions apply to all persons, not just individuals trying to assist nursing home or ALF residents. (See table 5.11 for absentee ballot procedures in Pinellas County (St. Petersburg), Florida.)

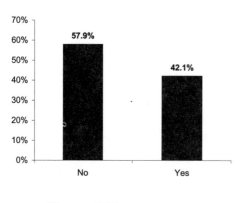

*Figure 5.7    Facility Requested Help Conducting Absentee Balloting from Supervisor of Elections. Note: "Did your facility request that the Supervisor of Elections conduct absentee balloting at your location?" Source: Mail survey of nursing home/assisted-living facility activities directors in Hillsborough, Pinellas, and Pasco counties, conducted December 1998.*

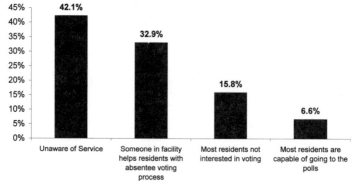

*Figure 5.8    Reasons for Not Requesting Help with Absentee Balloting in Nursing Home/ALF Note: "Did your facility request that the Supervisor of Elections conduct absentee balloting at your location? If No, Why Not?"*
*Source: Mail survey of nursing home/ALF activities directors in Hillsborough, Pinellas, and Pasco counties, conducted December 1998.*

**Table 5.11**

**Absentee Ballot Procedures: Pinellas County, Florida**

---

### REQUESTING AN ABSENTEE BALLOT

**ABSENTEE BALLOT REQUESTS BY TELEPHONE OR IN WRITING [F.S. 101.62(1)]**

From voter: *Voter must provide:*

Name
Address
Date of Birth
Daytime Phone Number
Last 4 digits of Social Security Number
Voter Registration ID Number
Mail Address, if different, and Daytime Phone Number for that address

From other than voter - Must be *immediate family or legal guardian: *Requestor must also provide:*

Relationship to the Voter
Name
Address
Daytime Phone Number
Complete Social Security Number
Driver License Number (optional)

*Immediate family: spouse, parent, child, grandparent, sibling, in-law.

---

Table 5.11 *continued.*

---

**Table 5.11** *continued*

**Absentee Ballot Procedures: Pinellas County, Florida**

---

### REQUESTING AN ABSENTEE BALLOT

Voter may vote in office or carry out their own ballot anytime. [F.S. 101.62(4)(b)(3)]

*Voter must provide:*

Name
Address
Date of Birth
Daytime Phone Number
Last 4 Digits of Social Security Number
Picture and Signature ID
Voter Registration ID Number

**A voter may designate in writing anyone to pick up their ballot no sooner than 4 days prior to Election Day. The designee is limited to 2 ballots for each election other than their own ballot and ballots for their immediate family. [F.S. 101.62(4)(b)(4)]**

CARRYING OUT SOMEONE ELSE'S BALLOT    Voter must sign an authorization designating the person allowed to pick up the ballot. Designee must provide picture ID and complete and office affidavit.

---

Table 5.11 *continued.*

---

**Table 5.11** *continued*

**Absentee Ballot Procedures: Pinellas County, Florida**

---

### RETURNING VOTED BALLOT

Voter may return ballot by mail or in person.

If returned in person, voter *must* provide picture ID.

If returned by someone else, voter *must* sign an authorization designating the person allowed to return the ballot. Designee may only return 2 ballots per election, other than their own ballot and ballots for the *immediate family. Designee *must* provide picture ID.

**Voted absentee ballots can not be accepted at polling places. They must be returned to one of the Supervisor of Elections Offices by 7 p.m. Election Day. [F.S. 101.67(2) and 101.6103(2)]**

Supervisor of Elections Office    Supervisor of Elections Office
Pinellas County Courthouse    County Building
315 Court St. Room 117 150 Fifth St. N. Room 100
Clearwater, FL 33756    St. Petersburg, FL 33710

Supervisor of Elections Office
Election Service Center
14255 49 St. N. Suite 202
Clearwater, FL 33762

**FOR ABSENTEE BALLOT INFORMATION
PHONE: (727) 464-6788**

*Immediate family: spouse, parent, child, grandparent, sibling, in-law.

---

*Source: Supervisor of Elections, Pinellas County, Florida.*

The time to develop more safeguards for absentee balloting in long-term care facilities is now rather later. A 1991 report in the *New England Journal of Medicine* projects that 43% of Americans older than 65 can expect to spend some time in a nursing home. Even more will live in an assisted-living facility or require some form of in-home care. Many of these will choose to vote absentee.

Our analysis of one large Florida county's absentee voting patterns found that roughly 5% of all absentee ballots in the party primaries were cast by residents of nursing homes or assisted-living facilities. In the general election, the percentage was 4%,[71] and these figures are conservative.

### Mail-Ballot Elections

Western states have taken the lead in conducting mail-ballot elections. Colorado, California, Washington, Oregon, Nevada, and North Dakota have used mail balloting in some form or another for several years. In all-mail elections, a ballot is automatically mailed to each registered voter, and voters must return their ballots by election day. The idea has gradually spread to other states. As of 1996, seventeen states, including Florida, permitted such elections at the local level, usually for issue or nonpartisan elections. In January 1996, Oregon became the first state to conduct an all-mail election for a high-profile partisan race featuring a candidate for a federal office (the U.S. Senate).[72]

Mail-ballot elections are appealing for three reasons: "Voters like the ease, election officials save money, and turnout is hiked."[73] The system appears to work well, save states and localities money, and stimulate turnout in lower turnout elections like primaries and referenda. Scholars who have examined voting-by-mail have found that it seems to have the greatest impact among groups who are ordinarily least likely to vote.[74] Others wonder whether this pattern is just a temporary phenomenon.

Not all are totally sold on the idea. It takes longer to report the results of all-mail balloting, especially when a glut of ballots arrives right before or on election day.[75] The reason for the longer reporting time is that in some states, voter signatures must be verified individually to avoid fraud. An alternative has been suggested—processing and opening the ballots before election day. But parties, candidates, and voters fear that these results might be leaked while voting was still taking place, thereby biasing the election.

Others are more philosophically opposed to mail-ballot elections. Robert Sullivan, writing in the *New Republic*, opined: "For me, the big difference between a vote-by-mail election and a regular one is that, once arrived, the ballot in a vote-by-mail election feels more like homework than a civic responsibility, more like a bill to pay."[76]

Groups like the Voting Integrity Project oppose mail-ballot elections because they can easily be manipulated and are not secret ballots:

Just imagine the chicanery possible when a stack of mail arrives at a nursing home, union hall, or church. It wouldn't take long for "ballot parties" to be planned, where members of a group bring their ballots to the hall and "vote the right way" in return for a free meal, entertainment or other rewards. Remember, with voting by mail, there is no more secret ballot, so the voter's current right to vote his or her conscience in the polling booth would be lost.[77]

Candidates have several additional fears—namely, that voting by mail will sharply increase the cost of political campaigning and turn the typical campaign timetable on its head. Among their concerns: "When will people vote and what type of people are they? If your campaign intends to hold back until a final two week blitz, but if half the electorate will have already voted by that point, the tactical problem becomes obvious."[78]

Studies show that older voters and highly partisan voters (these two groups overlap) are the most likely to cast their mail-in ballot earlier in the process.[79]

As is true with all alternative voting arrangements, the potential for mail-ballot fraud is somewhat higher among seniors and disabled citizens. Unscrupulous individuals may offer to help the person complete a mail ballot—but actually do it themselves, counter to the person's instructions, and drop it in the mail.

Some seniors and their advocates believe that some fraud might be eliminated and a higher return rate achieved if a preaddressed, stamped return envelope were provided to the absentee voter. This would, of course, add more costs to the election, but it still might be cheaper than hiring poll workers or buying, maintaining, and storing voting booths and machines. It would erase some opponents' claims that requiring voters to affix a stamp to mail a ballot is equivalent to imposing a poll tax, which is unconstitutional. (As of this writing, the courts have not upheld this argument.)[80]

## Early Voting

Walk-in voting at selected locations within a set time prior to the election began in Texas in 1988. As of 1996, seven other states—Arizona, Colorado, Iowa, Nevada, New Mexico, Oklahoma, and Tennessee—used some variety of early voting.[81] Virginia also permitted it in some locations.[82] Most of these states allow citizens to cast their ballot 20 to 40 days prior to an election.[83]

Early voting has some appeal to seniors, the disabled, and election officials. It lets people vote at a convenient time, when the polling place is less congested, and when election officials have more time to offer assistance. Like mail-ballot elections, those most likely to take advantage of early voting are "primarily engaged party-line, 'most-likely-to-vote' individuals"[84]—older, rather than younger, citizens.

Some Texas-based studies have found that the choice of locations for early voting affects turnout. More people vote early when the opportunity is made available at well-frequented, socially familiar locations.[85]

Early voting—like voting-by-mail—"changes the calculus on polling, targeting, media placement, free media timing, GOTV, and a host of other issues."[86] One Texas political scientist advises candidates to "adopt the strategy of harvesting core supporters early, then proceeding to compete for swing and nonpartisan support with a different but related campaign."[87] Those wanting the senior vote have to go after it early!

Opponents of early voting say it permits candidates to run two different campaigns—one aimed at early voters (that is, seniors) and another at late voters. If inconsistencies appear in the candidate's positions, it then becomes too late for older citizens to switch their votes.

## Cyber or Virtual Voting

The first state to use electronic voting—albeit under unusual circumstances—was Texas. The state permitted an astronaut to e-mail his vote from space in the 1997 City of Houston and constitutional amendment election.[88]

Arizona offered the option of Internet voting during its presidential primary March 11, 2000. Voters could go on-line that day to cast ballots, provided they had registered earlier with polling headquarters via the Internet. In addition, a number of polling sites around the state offered voters the use of a computer (or a traditional paper ballot) so they could send their vote electronically to polling headquarters.[89]

Other states, including California, Florida, Iowa, and Washington, are beginning to consider the prospect of electronic balloting. For example, two counties in Iowa experimented with Internet voting in a pilot project in fall 1999. The project was conducted in eight precincts in Woodbury and Johnson counties among voters who had already cast their ballots. Most of the 1,261 voters who accepted the invitation found the voting easy, even though many, especially elderly voters, had never used the Internet before. In addition, more than 80% of the participants said they would like to be able to vote at *secure* Internet polling sites.[90]

Security remains a key issue. In Florida, when the idea of Internet voting first surfaced in October 1997, a major question was: "How do you guarantee that the recorded vote is the one that was cast and that the person who cast it was the genuine article?"[91] Florida's elections chief responded: "Our technical advisors were telling us about the amount of business that was being conducted over the Internet. If people were trusting their money over the Internet, then voting could be done too, applying existing technology."[92] The idea never got off the ground in the legislature, but some county supervisors are still interested in the concept. Okaloosa County, which has a large number of military residents, is one of these.

The Florida example brings up an important point: Legislatures often must approve all forms of voting. Consequently, advocates for different types of voting systems need to plan a campaign for adoption well in advance of elections.

Heading into the 2000 election, many Americans are hesitant about Internet voting. A July 1999 ABC News poll found that 52% of Americans surveyed oppose it, even if it can be made secure from fraud, and 70% do not believe this will happen for many years. Older citizens are the least likely to endorse cyber voting (19% versus 61% of the 18-to-34-year-olds).[93] Their resistance will likely decline as technology improves. But as noted in an earlier chapter, current technology is not very accessible to sight- and hearing-impaired individuals.

Those who oppose Internet voting, like opponents of other forms of absentee voting, fear that it will further diminish the concept of community and be ridden with fraud.[94]

In an effort to examine issues surrounding the use of Internet voting, two members of Congress in November 1999 introduced the Digital Democracy Study Act (HR3232). The bill calls for study of: (1) the use of on-line technologies within existing voting systems to allow registration and voting, (2) security standards, and (3) effects on voter participation rates.[95] As of this writing, this is the only bill introduced on the subject, but more may follow as virtual voting gains further attention.

## PROTECTING VOTERS AGAINST FRAUD

Until recently, ballot box bandits have not received much attention. But this is changing rapidly, as more incidences of rampant vote fraud are uncovered, and as the public learns that the victims are usually the elderly, poor, and disabled. The rise in vote fraud has led some scholars and political activists to call for reform.

Larry Sabato and Glenn Simpson, authors of *Dirty Little Secrets: The Persistence of Corruption in American Politics*, have offered a number of suggestions for protecting the integrity of the electoral process. They have been joined by a number of good-government groups. Among their recommendations are the following:[96]

Revise the Motor Voter Law. Allow local registration officials to more thoroughly check a person's identification and background to determine eligibility. Allow local election officials to maintain current voter lists and eliminate duplicates.

Create more signature safeguards where mail-ballot elections are conducted.

Use thumbprint scanners to record each voter's thumbprint when he or she first registers. Digitize and store this information for retrieval when a person is casting a ballot, whether at the polls or via an absentee ballot or all-mail ballot.

At the time of registration, require each registrant to provide a number unique to that person (Social Security or driver's license number, for example) that will be printed on the precinct voter lists.

Require that a photo identification card be presented by each voter at the polls.

Require each voter to sign his or her name on the voting roll at the polls, to be compared to the one on the registration form to see if the two signatures match.

Inform all voters of the penalties for fraudulent voting.

Do not separate mail-in ballots or absentee ballots from their cover sheets until the voter's signature has been carefully checked against the registration file signature.

Require every envelope containing an absentee or early-voting mail ballot to be signed by an adult witness whose address should be listed. (Others recommend the signatures be checked as well as a precaution against forgery.)

Do not mail more absentee or mail-in ballots to a single address than the number of voters registered at that address.

Require that an absentee ballot be mailed to the voter's official registration address and no other, unless the voter under oath affirms that he or she will be absent from the locality for the entire duration of the absentee voting period.

Require that states "have a meticulously maintained, centralized list of registered voters that is frequently purged of duplicate registration, the deceased, those who have moved out of the district and out of the state, felons, and non-citizens."

While these reforms would help dramatically, there still is no foolproof system for avoiding fraud, especially mail-ballot-related improprieties. Perhaps the Miami-Dade County supervisor of elections has said it best: "The only way to totally ensure there's no absentee ballot fraud is to have no absentee ballots."[97] He should know!

## SUMMARY AND RECOMMENDATIONS

America's seniors register and vote at considerably higher rates than other age groups. Many prefer voting in person on election day over voting by mail or voting early, where those options are available. But for some, traveling to the polling place is simply out of the question.

Regardless of how or where seniors register and vote, a sizable number will experience some difficulty. They have to rely on—and *trust*—others to request, complete, and return registration materials and ballots for them.

Election officials need to better inform seniors of the improvements that have been made in recent years, especially at the polling place. Many seniors, especially the disabled who have not voted within the past ten years, are simply unaware of the changes. Thus, we recommend considerably more publicity—in the media and at the polls—delineating the various forms of assistance now available at every stage of the electoral process. And more improvements in registration and voting are needed.

State registration laws and procedures vary considerably. Some states permit election day registration, while others cut off registration a set number of days before an election. Seniors who move to a new residence may need more reminding than other age groups about registration deadlines and change-of-address procedures.

Registration rates of disabled persons are lower than those of other citizens. The reasons are many—primarily, transportation difficulties and fears of having to traverse inaccessible facilities to register and vote. Advocacy groups, such as AARP and the National Organization on Disability, have increased efforts to help the elderly and disabled to register and vote.

Get-Out-the-Vote (GOTV) efforts can be a godsend for seniors who appreciate reminders about upcoming elections. But traditional timetables for phone bank GOTV efforts may not be as effective for seniors needing time to request an absentee ballot or arrange transportation to the polls. Other types of voter reminders—postcards and door hangers—have their own shortcomings.

Precinct location, parking, walkways and pathways, ramps and elevators, as well as other architectural features may or may not be "senior friendly." Election officials need to consult accessibility surveys and checklists developed by the Federal Election Commission and disability groups, such as the National Organization on Disability.

In general, more seniors and disabled voters would be positively inclined to vote in person if the polling place prominently displayed large signs (and provided audio recordings) informing them of available assistance. Seniors would, in turn, tell their friends and neighbors.

When seniors arrive at the polling place, well-trained poll workers can help lessen problems. Training sessions should include representatives of elder and disabled advocacy groups, who can play a critical role in sensitizing election officials to the specific problems faced by persons with different types of disabilities. Information and recommendations could be dramatized in videos, which could, in turn, be used by political parties and professional campaign consultants to educate candidates and volunteers.

New voting systems are constantly being developed in response to the growing number of seniors and voters with disabilities. The five types currently in place across the United States are paper ballots, mechanical lever machines, punch cards Marksense (optical scan) systems, and Direct Recording Electronic (DRE) systems. Each has drawbacks, depending upon the individual voter's physical capacities. The two primary concerns of senior and disabled advocates are the flexibility of the ballot format (size, type, presentation) and the degree to which the independence and privacy of the voter are ensured. We recommend that voting machine vendors involve both election officials and voters with disabilities in the design of these machines.

For those who cannot get to the polls on election day, several options are available. The most universal is absentee balloting. A growing number of states and localities are holding all-mail-ballot elections, while some states use early voting. Cyber or virtual voting is likely to emerge as a fourth option in the twenty-first century.

In states that allow early voting, seniors and hard-core partisans vote the earliest. Early voting proponents believe it is a "senior friendly" method because it allows them to vote at a more convenient, less-harried time. However, early voting also forces candidates to run two different campaigns—one aimed at early voters (seniors) and another at late voters.

Whether voting absentee or in a mail-ballot election, seniors, the poor, and the disabled are the most likely to be victims of vote fraud, especially those who reside in nursing homes or other congregate-care facilities. As more vote fraud cases have emerged, states have begun clamping down on all aspects of absentee voting and voting by mail. The biggest challenge in the twenty-first century is to devise better methods to protect the integrity of the electoral system, while accommodating the changing needs of an aging electorate.

# 6

✛

# Crafting the Message:

## *Issues Affecting Seniors*

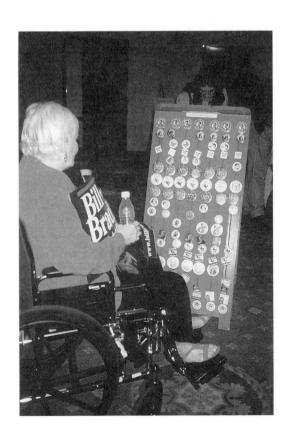

*Photo 6.1    Even political vendors must be attentive to wheelchair access, as this "button man" knows firsthand.*

On January 1, 1996, the first baby boomer turned 50. By the second decade of the 21st century, boomers will evolve into the largest elderly generation in history. Once their oldest members start turning 65 in 2011, the numbers will skyrocket, from approximately 40 million to 70+ million by 2010. As they age, the look, meaning, experience, and purpose of maturity will be transformed.

Ken Dychtwald, *Age Power*

The aging baby boom generation—the Pepsi Generation that would be forever young—is attacking with a vengeance one of the most obvious signs of age: gray hair. . . . The color of choice? Blond, of course. . . . Although only 9 percent of the world's population is born blond, a far, far greater percentage of boomer females in America is going to die that way.

Cindy Starr, Scripps Howard News Service

There's a subtle difference between getting older, a process that people tend to accept more readily, and being old, a status with which some never care to identify.

Robert S. Motika, *American Demographics*

Seniors are the most diverse segment of our society in life-style and activities. . . . Marketers who sell [a product to them] should not talk about their problem, but the solution. Emphasize the fact that it is a product that can improve a life-style or living pattern.

Frank Conaway, President, Primelife

In targeting seniors, candidates and advocacy groups must study older Americans' opinions on issues. Knowing how seniors feel about Social Security, Medicare, and other issues enables candidates to plan campaign tactics and craft the right message.

Certainly, many factors affect message content. These factors may include the health of the economy, the mood of the electorate ("Throw the rascals out!"), the notoriety of the opponent(s), the type of office being sought (governor versus county commissioner, for example), and timing (early versus late in the race).

But often, the message is about issues. Or, at least, that's what most Americans say they want. A 1999 survey by the Pew Research Center for the People & the Press found that all age groups believe a candidate's issue stances are more important than either past accomplishments or what a candidate is like as a person. (See table 6.1.)

Issues such as Social Security, Medicare, and health insurance will continue to dominate the political agenda of many seniors for several years. (See table 6.2.) At the same time, some persistent problems will be redefined and creative solutions sought. New issues will surface as well, driven largely by powerful age-based demographics. It is fair to say that in the new millennium, the focus will be less on the "politics of aging" and more on the "aging of politics and policies."

In examining issues and policies, analysts must be careful not to view seniors as one undifferentiated mass but rather as two age groups—the current generation of seniors and the next one, the baby boomers.

**Table 6.1**

| Election Coverage: Let's Hear About Important Issues! | | | | |
|---|---|---|---|---|
| Preferred Coverage | 18-29 % | 30-49 % | 50-64 % | 65+ % |
| What a candidate believes about important issues | 61 | 65 | 64 | 65 |
| What a candidate has accomplished in the past | 26 | 27 | 27 | 28 |
| What a candidate is like as a person | 12 | 7 | 7 | 2 |
| Don't know/refused | 1 | 1 | 2 | 5 |

Note: Respondents were asked: "In reporting on a presidential candidate, what ONE factor do you think news organizations should pay the most attention to _____ ?"

Source: The Pew Research Center for the People & the Press. Telephone survey of a random sample of 1,032 adults, 18 years of age or older, conducted October 7-11, 1999. The sampling margin of error is plus or minus 3.5 percentage points (at the 95% confidence level).

**Table 6.2**

| Most Important Priority for the Next U.S. President? (First/Second Mentions - Ranked) | | | | |
|---|---|---|---|---|
| Priority | 18-29 % | 30-49 % | 50-64 % | 65+ % |
| Keep Social Security and Medicare financially sound | 17 | 29 | 40 | 51 |
| Improve the educational system | 48 | 31 | 20 | 19 |
| Keep the economy strong | 23 | 31 | 28 | 23 |
| Improve the nation's health care system | 20 | 27 | 31 | 29 |
| Deal with the moral breakdown of the country | 19 | 20 | 20 | 18 |
| Deal with the problems of poor and needy people | 20 | 15 | 13 | 17 |
| Prevent the spread of weapons of mass destruction | 20 | 14 | 12 | 14 |
| Deal with taxes | 8 | 15 | 13 | 7 |
| Work to reduce crime | 17 | 9 | 9 | 8 |
| Other | 5 | 3 | 2 | 1 |
| Don't know/refused | 1 | 1 | 5 | 4 |
| None of the above | 1 | 0 | – | 2 |

Note: Respondents were asked: "Now, as I read from a list, tell me which ONE of the following items is the most important thing for the next President TO DO? Please wait until I read the entire list before you respond. And which should be the President's second highest priority?"

## SOCIAL SECURITY: A HIGH PRIORITY

Social Security has long been regarded as one of America's sacred cows. It is often described as the "third rail of American politics—touch it and chances are good you'll die."[1] Ninety-five percent of American workers are covered by Social Security. It is the single largest item in the federal budget.

Currently, workers become eligible for full retirement benefits at age 65 or for reduced benefits at 62. The program spells economic security for a number of elderly persons—and they are willing to fight for it at the ballot box. Nearly one-third of today's retirees want to protect Social Security at all costs.

Baby boomers and Gen Xers are more skeptical about Social Security being there for them when they retire. A 1999 *Wall Street Journal*/NBC News poll found that only 55% of the baby boomers, and 39% of the Gen Xers are counting on it.[2] Social Security, along with Medicare, pose important moral, social, and political questions to Americans, as observed by the economist Robert J. Samuelson:

> How much should society tax younger (and sometimes poorer) people to subsidize older (and sometimes wealthier) people? Should eligibility ages for Social Security and Medicare be raised? Should benefits for the wealthier elderly be reduced? Will the growing costs of federal retirement programs ultimately crowd out spending for other important national goals (defense, research, education)?[3]

### Is the Solvency of Social Security Severely Threatened? Two Views

The potential economic impacts of an aging population have captured the attention of public policymakers and academicians. To date, there is little agreement on how serious the problem is or how to fix it.

Those with a more alarmist view warn that the program's annual outlays will begin to exceed its annual tax revenues by 2013.[4] When the baby boomers hit retirement age, there will be fewer workers to support them than in the past. For example, in 1945, there were twenty workers to support each Social Security recipient. By 2033, there will be fewer than two (1.8) for each recipient.[5]

Others believe the system will not be stretched that severely. The more optimistic forecasters point to several trends: a slowdown in early retirement, an increase in the tax limits at which people taking Social Security benefits can earn money without being penalized,[6] and higher life expectancy rates that allow people to work longer. These experts are betting that baby boomers will want to remain in the labor force longer, which could "lessen the long-term solvency crisis in Social Security and Medicare and reduce pressure to cut benefits."[7]

### Solutions to the Social Security Problem

Various far-reaching solutions to the Social Security problem have been proposed.[8] Among the most-often discussed are:

- using most of the budget surplus to shore up Social Security;
- raising the retirement age to 70 (It is already being raised slowly from 65 to 67);[9]
- raising taxes on Social Security benefits of those earning $50,000 or more (means testing);
- reducing benefits;
- paying out benefits according to the recipient's financial need (means testing);
- giving individuals other options such as Individual Retirement Accounts (IRAs); and
- letting the government invest some Social Security Trust Funds in the stock market.

Across all age groups, the least popular remedies are raising the retirement age, letting government invest Social Security funds in the stock market, and reducing Social Security benefits.[10] (See table 6.3.)

The market-based alternatives are considerably less popular among seniors than among younger age groups. Two-thirds of seniors strongly oppose allowing the federal government to invest part of the Social Security trust fund surplus in the stock market in hopes of generating a higher return than in government securities. Sixty-one percent are against IRAs.[11]

In the case of IRAs, it is important to note that a majority of every other age group favors letting workers invest some Social Security taxes on their own. This could signal a change in this policy as the baby boomers replace the current senior generation.[12] However, this view could change overnight if the stock market makes a sharp downturn.

In general, the concerns of pre-retirees differ somewhat from retirees. A *Wall Street Journal*/NBC Poll found that among nonretired adults, the two biggest worries about retiring are poor health (33%) and financial problems (30%). But among those who have already retired, a higher percentage cite alienation (23%) or poor health (19%) as their major disappointment, compared to just 10% for financial worries.[13]

For many seniors, financial worries and health care concerns are becoming more intricately connected by the day.

## MEDICARE

Medicare is often described as the difference between life and death for many older Americans. Some 40 million Americans rely on it. Medicare provides health insurance coverage for one in seven persons in the country. Seventy-eight percent are 64–84 years of age, 10% are 85 and older, and 12% are younger than 65 but disabled.

In 1980, Medicare spending consumed around 6% of the federal budget. By 1998, it was 12%.[14] It is projected to constitute between 28 and 38% of the fed-

Table 6.3

## Fixing Social Security's Future Shortfall
(Percentage favoring each proposal)

| Status | Use most of budget surplus to shore up Social Security | Let workers invest some Social Security taxes on their own | Raise taxes on Social Security benefits of those earning $50,000 or more | Gradually raise retirement age to 70 | Have government invest Social Security funds in stock market | Reduce benefits to increase long-term stability of Social Security |
|---|---|---|---|---|---|---|
| All | 73% | 62% | 53% | 34% | 34% | 22% |
| Retired | 80 | 42 | 61 | 38 | 24 | 15 |
| Non-retired | 71 | 68 | 50 | 33 | 38 | 25 |
| Age | | | | | | |
| 18-34 | 67 | 75 | 54 | 26 | 43 | 26 |
| 35-49 | 75 | 65 | 48 | 34 | 36 | 23 |
| 50-64 | 73 | 59 | 53 | 32 | 30 | 19 |
| 65+ | 80 | 39 | 61 | 46 | 24 | 9 |

Source: Wall Street Journal, March 11, 1999. Used with permission of Dow Jones.

eral budget by 2030,[15] if changes are not made to slow its growth and make it more efficient.

Howard Fineman, in *Newsweek*, has put the program in perspective: "After Social Security, it's the costliest and most cherished program in government— and has been ever since LBJ handed the first Medicare cards to Harry and Bess Truman."[16] The two programs together are consuming a larger portion of the federal budget. (See figure 6.1.)

Like Social Security, Medicare is an entitlement program. It has two parts; Part A, financed through the payroll tax, basically covers hospital inpatient care, some skilled nursing facility care, home health after a hospital or nursing home stay, and hospice care. Part B pays for physician services, hospital outpatient services, home health visits not covered under Part A, laboratory tests, and medical equipment. It is funded through a combination of beneficiary premiums and general revenues paid by taxpayers. The breakdown of Medicare expenditures (all parts) is shown in figure 6.2. Importantly, Medicare pays for hospital, physician, and other medical services but does not cover outpatient prescription drugs or long-term care.[17]

The 1997 Balanced Budget Act passed by Congress and signed by the president changed the program somewhat. Under the new Medicare+Choice plan, seniors are offered several options to the original Medicare plan. (See table 6.4.) Regardless of which option he or she chooses, a senior is still a beneficiary of the Medicare program.[18]

### Program Still Has Problems to Solve

The Medicare program faces the same problems as Social Security—fiscal pressures due to the growth in the eligible population (see figure 6.3) and a decline

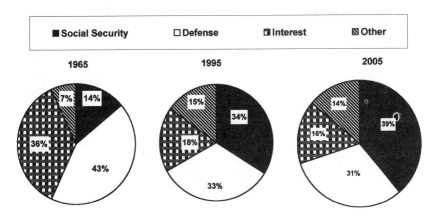

*Figure 6.1   The Shifting American Pie: Budget More to Elderly*
Source: Newsweek, *September 18, 1995, p. 44. Used with permission.*

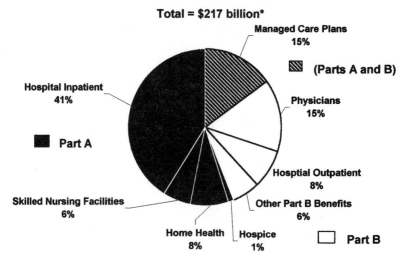

Figure 6.2    Medicare Benefit Payments, 1998
Source: Congressional Budget Office, 1998. *Excludes administrative expenses.

in the number of working-age taxpayers. The Medicare Hospital Insurance Trust Fund that pays for Part A benefits is expected to face a shortfall in the early years of the twenty-first century.

Legislators realized that changes made under the Balanced Budget Act of 1997 were just a quick fix. So Congress created a seventeen-member National Bipartisan Commission on the Future of Medicare. The Commission was charged with studying ways to strengthen and improve Medicare as the baby boom generation (77 million) approaches retirement, beginning in 2010. The panel, composed of lawmakers, policy experts, and citizens, made its initial recommendations to Congress and the president in March 1999.

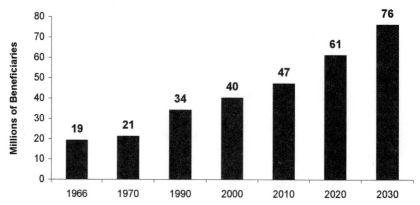

Figure 6.3    The Medicare Population Is Growing Rapidly
Source: Health Care Financing Administration, Office of the Actuary, April 1998.

**Table 6.4**

## Medicare+Choice Health Plan Options

| Option: | What it is: | Things to consider: |
|---|---|---|
| Original Medicare Plan | The traditional pay-per-visit (also called fee-for-service) arrangement available nationwide. | You can go to any provider that accepts Medicare. Some services are not covered and you have to pay some out-of-pocket costs. |
| Original Medicare Plan with Supplemental Policy | The original Medicare Plan, plus one of up to 10 standardized Medicare supplemental insurance policies (also called Medigap insurance) available through private companies. | Depending on the policy you buy, you will have coverage for at least some deductible and coinsurance costs. There may be coverage for extra benefits not otherwise covered by Medicare. You will have to pay a premium for your supplemental policy. |
| Medicare Managed Care Plan | A Medicare approved network of doctors, hospitals, and other health care providers which agrees to give care in return for a set monthly payment from Medicare. They may be managed by a Health Maintenance Organization (HMO), Preferred Provider Organization (PPO) or an HMO with a Point of Service Option (POS). | An HMO or PSO usually asks that you use only doctors and hospitals in their network. If you do, you may have little or no out-of-pocket costs for covered services. A PPO or POS usually lets you use doctors and hospitals outside the plan for an extra out-of-pocket cost. Some managed care plans may offer extra benefits and some may charge a premium. |

Table 6.4 *continued.*

**Table 6.4** *continued*

## Medicare+Choice Health Plan Options

| Option: | What it is: | Things to consider: |
|---|---|---|
| Private Fee for Service Plan (PFFS) | A Medicare-approved private insurance plan. Medicare pays the plan a premium for Medicare covered services, and the PFFS plan provides all Medicare benefits. THIS IS NOT A MEDIGAP PLAN. | The PFFS Plan, not Medicare, decides how much to pay for covered services you receive. They may bill you for more than the plan pays (up to a limit) and you must pay the difference. You will likely have to pay a premium for a PFFS plan. |
| Medicare Medical Savings Account (MSA) | A health insurance policy with a high annual deductible. This is a test program for 390,000 Medicare beneficiaries. Medicare pays the premium for the MSA Plan and deposits money into a separate Medicare MSA you establish. You use the money in the MSA to pay for medical expenses. | You can accumulate money in your Medicare MSA to pay for extra medical costs. Your insurance policy has a high deductible. There are no limits on what providers charge you above what is paid by your Medicare MSA Plan. You can enroll in a Medicare MSA Plan in November. You must stay in it for a full year. |

*Source: Health Care Financing Administration, Medicare & You.*

The rules established by Congress mandated that any recommendation made by the Commission needed eleven votes, but the final list of recommendations submitted was approved by only ten. This is further evidence of the divided nature of public opinion about how to save Medicare. In general, the Commission recommended making the program more market-based by allowing beneficiaries to choose from among competing comprehensive health plans, including one that covers prescription drugs.[19]

Most Americans do not fully understand the changes made in 1997 nor the proposals made by the Commission in 1999. A large-scale study conducted by the League of Women Voters in partnership with the Henry J. Kaiser Family Foundation, found that many Americans are terribly confused about the "basic facts, such as who is enrolled, how Medicare is different from Medicaid, what services are covered and how Medicare is paid for."[20] But they strongly believe that Medicare is an important safety net for the elderly and for people with disabilities.

In the twenty-first century, Medicare faces three basic challenges:

- preserve and improve the program so it will meet the needs of all beneficiaries—especially those with health problems and modest incomes;
- weigh the opportunities and risks of fundamentally restructuring Medicare; and
- balance the need to keep Medicare fiscally strong while assuring access of future generations of elderly and disabled Americans to affordable health care.[21]

## Public Wants More, Not Less, Coverage

Most surveys show that Americans strongly support proposals to expand Medicare but appear "unready . . . to support reforms that would produce major cost savings in public health-care."[22] A 1998 national survey conducted on behalf of the Kaiser Family Foundation and the Harvard School of Public Health produced the following findings:

- 69% favor having Medicare cover long-term nursing home care "even if it means higher premiums or taxes."
- 68% favor having Medicare cover prescription drugs "even if it means higher premiums or taxes."
- 60% favor expanding Medicare so that people aged 62–64 are able to buy into the program before they turn 65.

Conversely, the same study produced these findings:

- 84% oppose requiring seniors to pay a larger share of Medicare costs out-of-pocket.

- 69% opposed a defined-contribution approach that would limit Medicare contributions for an individual to a fixed annual amount.
- 64% oppose increasing worker payroll taxes.
- 63% oppose raising the age of eligibility to 67.
- 56% oppose encouraging seniors in traditional Medicare to move to managed care.[23]

Predictably, the Kaiser Family Foundation/Harvard School of Public Health survey found that support for change is greatest among those not yet eligible for Medicare. Sixty-three percent of those younger than 65 (but only 34% of those 65 and older) agree that we need to make major changes to Medicare soon to keep costs from rising too quickly when the baby boom generation retires. Conversely, 56% of those 65 and older believe that Medicare is basically working well and that only gradual adjustments are needed to preserve the program for future generations.[24]

Americans of all ages agree that Medicare fraud, waste, and abuse need to be eliminated. Seniors are the most adamant about the need to address this problem, as revealed in the Florida seniors survey. When asked how much fraud there is in the Medicare program, 58% say "a lot"; another 25% say "some." (See figure 6.4.) People, doctors, and hospitals are perceived as the biggest perpetrators of fraud and abuse, according to national surveys. Government is seen as the most wasteful because of its poor management of the program.[25]

There is also a fair amount of consensus on using the budget surplus to protect Medicare, according to a survey by the Pew Research Center for the People

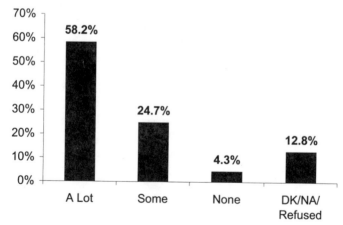

*Figure 6.4    Seniors' Views of Amount of Fraud in Medicare*
Note: "How much fraud do you think there is in our Medicare system in Florida?"
Source: Telephone survey of a random sample of 600 Floridians 60 or older, conducted December 1998, margin of error plus or minus 4%.

& the Press. But this survey, like others, found that persons 65 and older are generally the least enthusiastic about any significant changes in the Medicare system, including those changes proposed by the Clinton administration to "save Medicare." (See table 6.5.)

The changes, whether eventually adopted or not, will not completely resolve senior health care issues. Seniors must still meet deductibles and pay for items not covered under Medicare, notably long-term health care.

## OTHER HEALTH CARE ISSUES: SHORT-TERM, LONG-TERM, AND MANAGED CARE

Medicare covers less than half of all beneficiaries' total health spending,[26] primarily because it does not cover prescription drugs or long-term health care. The costs of each item are escalating rapidly.

### Short-Term Issues: Out-of-Pocket Expenses, Prescription Drugs

Even under Medicare, most beneficiaries have to meet relatively high deductibles and cost-sharing requirements. According to one study, in 1996, beneficiaries spent, on average, more than 20% of their household income to pay for health services directly and for Medicare Part B premiums and private insurance premiums.[27] The breakdown of out-of-pocket spending was as follows: private insurance premiums (31%), Medicare cost-sharing (25%), uncovered services (26%), and Medicare Part B premiums (18%).[28]

**Table 6.5**

**Support for Various Changes to the Medicare System**
(Multiple Response Question - Ranked)

| Change | 18-29 % | 30-49 % | 50-64 % | 65+ % |
|---|---|---|---|---|
| Using part of the projected budget surplus to make Medicare financially secure | 81 | 83 | 85 | 82 |
| Allowing Medicare recipients to buy prescription drug coverage for $24 a month | 82 | 83 | 84 | 59 |
| Eliminating co-payments and deductibles for preventive service, such as pelvic exams and prostate cancer screenings | 69 | 70 | 71 | 51 |
| Allowing those age 62-65 to now purchase Medicare benefits for $300 per month | 68 | 52 | 53 | 30 |
| Increasing the deductible that patients pay for doctor visits by the cost of living | 41 | 44 | 47 | 32 |

*Note: Respondents were asked: "President Clinton has proposed a number of specific changes to the Medicare system. As I read each proposal, please tell me whether you favor or oppose it. How about _____ , do you favor or oppose this proposal?"*

*Source: the Pew Research Center for the People & the Press. Telephone survey of a random sample of 1,200 adults, 18 years of age or older, conducted July 13-18, 1999. The sampling margin of error is plus or minus 3 percentage points.*

Prescription drugs make up a big chunk of the noncovered expenses. People 65 and older comprise 12% of the U.S. population but consume almost 35% of all prescription drugs, according to the AARP. "About 65% of people 65 and older have two or more chronic diseases, as do 80% of people over 85. . . . As a result, one in five elderly people takes at least five prescription drugs a day. About 2.2 million seniors shell out more than $100 a month for medication, and many pay even more."[29] One indication of the gravity of this financial burden is that some seniors don't take their medications as prescribed: They either choose not to buy them at all or to reduce dosages to make their supplies last longer. Undoubtedly, the costs of adding prescription drug coverage to Medicare will be astronomical.

Poorer seniors on Medicare pay an even greater percentage of their income for out-of-pocket health care. (See figure 6.5.) However, about 15% of the lowest-income Medicare beneficiaries get assistance from the Medicaid program.[30] (Medicaid is funded with both federal and state dollars. Unlike Medicare, it is run by the state government and is based on need rather than age.) But Medicaid benefits vary considerably from state to state.[31]

## Long-Term Care: What Is It, Who Pays, and Under What Conditions?

As one sage remarked: "The good news is we're living longer. The bad news is we're dying slower, often in need of assistance and care."[32] When Medicare was established in 1965, men's life expectancy was 67 and women's life expectancy was 73. By 1996, men's life expectancy had increased to 73 and women's life expectancy increased to 79. Plenty of Americans are now living well into their 80s, 90s, and 100s.

Many of these "senior seniors" eventually need help with everyday activities. Activities of Daily Living (ADLs) include bathing, dressing, eating, walking, toileting, and transferring from a bed or chair. (See figure 6.6.) These older seniors

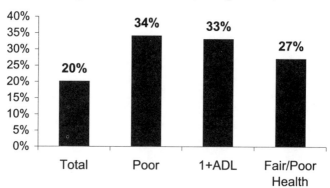

*Figure 6.5   Seniors Pay Nearly a Fifth of Their Income Out-of-Pocket for Health Care— The Most Vulnerable Pay a Larger Share.*
Note: ADL = Activities of Daily Living.
Source: AARP, Public Policy Institute analysis, noninstitutionalized beneficiaries age 65 and over in FFS Medicare using Medicare Benefits Simulation Model (1998 Projections).

may also need assistance with home management chores, or Instrumental Activities of Daily Living (IADLs), such as meal preparation, shopping, money management, using the telephone, and doing housework. Among Americans 85 and older, 35% have trouble with at least one ADL, and 57% experience difficulty with at least one ADL or IADL.

Long-term care needs vary tremendously among the senior population. "For many people, regular or 'long-term' care may mean a little help from family and friends or regular visits by a home health aide. For others who are frail or suffering from dementia, long-term care may involve moving to a place where professional care is available twenty-four hours a day."[33]

Because of the variation in need, a number of different types of long-term care are available, according to the National Institute on Aging. These are home health care, adult day care, adult foster care, meal and transportation programs, assisted living and retirement communities, and traditional nursing homes.

Older Americans who require long-term care often need help paying for it. Medicaid has become the payer of last resort for many for three reasons. First, long-term care is not covered under Medicare or most commercial health insurance plans. Second, most Americans do not have long-term care insurance. Third, many people cannot afford the high cost of nursing home care or other long-term care services over an extended period.[34] In 1995, Americans spent an estimated $91 billion on long-term care; only 60% of that came from public sources.[35] When they exhaust their assets, they turn to Medicaid.

### Medicaid: A Fast-Growing Program Pressuring States' Budgets

Medicaid is one of the fastest growing items in most states' budgets. Nearly two out of three families end up relying on Medicaid to pay nursing home

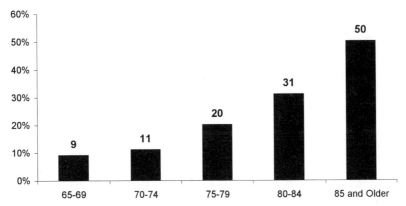

*Figure 6.6    Percentage of Persons Needing Assistance with Activities of Daily Living by Age, 1996*
*Note: Activities of Daily Living (ADLs): The measure of a person's functioning for self-care including: bathing, dressing, eating, walking, toileting, and transferring from a bed or chair. Source: U.S. Census Bureau.*

bills. Consequently, states have been searching for ways to control Medicaid costs. A National Conference of State Legislatures (NCSL) study has identified several cost-containment strategies, most of which are designed to keep elderly persons out of nursing homes as long as possible. NCSL recommends the following:

- providing more home- and community-based services;
- offering more assisted-living arrangements;
- using managed care for Medicaid recipients;
- relying more on adult children of elderly parents; and
- reducing nursing home reimbursement rates.[36]

The options for seniors who either cannot or choose not to live in a single-family home any longer are growing. However, Americans, including seniors, know little about them, except perhaps for nursing homes (technically referred to by Medicare as "skilled-nursing facilities"). But even in the case of nursing homes, knowledge is shallow. Most people know only that a nursing home is the last place they want to end up. Yet, projections are that many of us will find ourselves there in our final years.

A national survey conducted for the Harvard School of Public Health confirms this lack of knowledge. According to the study, nearly 80% of Americans aged 50 and older were familiar with nursing homes/skilled-nursing facilities. Yet 61% had never heard or read about continuing-care retirement communities, 48% were unaware of assisted-living facilities, 49% did not know about congregate living or the existence of specialized facilities for people with Alzheimer's disease.

Among those older than 70, just 18% have visited a continuing-care retirement community; 21%, a congregate senior housing structure; and 23%, an assisted-living residence.[37] (A brief description of these types of senior housing properties appears in table 6.6.) Private-sector-based groups like the American Seniors Housing Association continue to promote these types of housing-health care arrangements as affordable—and better—alternatives to nursing home care for most seniors.

General Accounting Office (GAO) studies show that alternative living arrangements, like nursing homes, will need closer monitoring as their numbers grow. A GAO survey of assisted-living facilities in California, Oregon, Florida, and Ohio found inadequacies in the written information potential residents were given, problems with the quality of care, and problems with the proper administration of medications.[38]

As with nursing homes, not all assisted-living facilities are the same. Monthly fees for ALFs range from $1,000 to $4,000. Only about half will keep residents who develop a need for nursing care. For the other half, the critical question becomes what to do when you reach that point in life.

**Table 6.6**

**Professionally Owned and Managed Seniors Housing Property Types and Estimated U.S. Supply: 1999**
(Alternatives to Nursing Homes)

| Property Type | Description | Est # of Properties | Est # of Units |
|---|---|---|---|
| Senior Apartments | Senior apartments are multifamily residential apartments designed for persons aged 55 years and older. These properties may or may not offer meal service to residents and typically offer a limited array of supportive care services and/or service coordination. | 5,000 | 400,000 |
| Congregate Seniors Housing | Residential developments designed specifically for seniors. Typically, these residences are multifamily structures with 70 to 250 units in high or mid-rise buildings. Individual living units include kitchens and apartments decorated and furnished by the resident. Most residences include extensive common areas, a central kitchen, dining room, and activity spaces. Units are usually rented but may include condominium or cooperative ownership structures with a monthly service fee. Services vary, but often include: building security, activities, meals, scheduled transportation, housekeeping, laundry, 24-hour staff presence, and an on-call nurse or physician. | 5,500 | 660,000 |

Table 6.6 *continued.*

**Table 6.6** *continued*

**Professionally Owned and Managed Seniors Housing Property Types and Estimated U.S. Supply: 1999**
(Alternatives to Nursing Homes)

| Property Type | Description | Est # of Properties | Est # of Units |
|---|---|---|---|
| Assisted Living Residences | Assisted living residences differ from congregate seniors housing in one significant way – they include 24-hour protective oversight and assistance for individuals with functional limitations. Assisted living residences are residential dwellings, typically with less than 100 apartment units and many resemble large single-family homes and house 30 to 60 residents. Most offer private rooms with kitchenettes and common living and dining areas. Services vary, but often include: assistance with activities of daily living; administration of medicine; first-aid and medical care for minor ailments; and round-the-clock protective oversight. | 7,500 | 600,000 |
| Continuing Care Retirement Communities | Continuing Care Retirement Communities (CCRCs) offer a variety of living arrangements and services to accommodate residents of all levels of physical ability and health. The goal of a CCRC is to provide residents with a total range of options to accommodate their changing lifestyle preferences and health care needs as they age. In general, CCRCs make congregate seniors housing, assisted living and skilled nursing available all on one campus. | 2,500 | 600,000 |
| | TOTAL OF PROPERTIES | 19,500 | 2,210,000 |

## Unprepared for Long-Term Care

Most Americans, including seniors, are unprepared for long-term care. A Harvard School of Public Health survey found that 84% of the respondents have not engaged in any type of estate planning for long-term care and that two-thirds have insufficient personal resources to pay for a year of institutional care.

Long-term care insurance is available from the private sector, but it is expensive, and it grows more expensive the longer one waits to buy it. The Health Insurance Association of America estimates the average annual premium covering four years of nursing home and home care (1995) is $1,124 if bought at age 50, $2,560 if bought at age 65, and $8,146 if bought at age 75.[39]

Not surprisingly, many seniors needing long-term care end up in nursing homes, their stays financed through Medicaid.

## Nursing Homes: Residents and Trends

Nursing homes continue to be used by those who need "sophisticated, labor-intensive 24-hour skilled supervision."[40] In the decade between 1985 and 1995, the number of U.S. nursing homes actually declined by 13%, although the number of residents increased by 4% and the number of beds in existing homes increased by 9%. The number of Americans who at some point will need nursing home care is projected to rise, paralleling the aging of the population. However, stays may be shorter as the number of home health care agencies and alternative residential facilities increases.

Most nursing homes (66.1%) are operated for profit, but the number of non-profit-operated nursing homes is increasing (13% and rising). A growing percentage are operated as part of a chain (54%). Seventy percent are certified by both the Medicare and Medicaid programs, which means they will accept eligible elderly.

The 1995 National Nursing Home Survey (NNHS)[41] reported that approximately 1.5 million Americans were receiving care in 16,700 nursing homes. Nearly 90% are 65 years of age and over; more than 35% are 85 and older. The residents are predominantly women (75%), 75 and older (82%), white (89%), and widowed (66%). Elderly women are more likely to be widowed (75%) than elderly men (37%).[42]

The average age of the residents at the time of admission is 82 years, with women typically older (83 years) than men (80 years). Forty-one percent come directly from hospitals; 37 percent live in a private residence before entering the nursing home.

The three most frequent primary admission diagnostic categories are diseases of the circulatory system (27%), mental disorders (17%), and diseases of the nervous system and sense disorders (11%). The vast majority of nursing home residents need help with at least one ADL (97%) and/or one IADL (86%).

Nursing home care is the most costly type of long-term care. Home- and community-based programs are considerably more popular with the public. Public policy makers also like them for their cost-containment potential. But they are often difficult to put in place at sufficient levels. They frequently require action from other levels of government, increased responsibility on the part of states, and/or the reprioritization of state spending. The director of the Health Care Financing Agency (HCFA), the federal agency that runs Medicare, in a speech projecting the future of home- and community-based long-term care, acknowledged this problem: "You have to find a mechanism through which the federal government and the states can renegotiate the terms of the deal in long-term care and the relative balance of responsibilities between Medicare and Medicaid . . . and [w]e're going to have to identify and activate a constituency who can continue to push the political and public policy process."[43]

Despite the importance of solving this problem, the average person is more concerned with the availability of health care and improving its quality.

### Which First: Health Care Insurance or Managed Care Reform?

Public opinion on health care issues fluctuates considerably, with the pendulum swinging from access, to cost, to quality, and back again. As we enter the twenty-first century, the focus is on improving access—making sure more Americans are covered by health insurance. But the pendulum is bound to swing in the other direction, with shifts in the economy and with advocacy groups pushing for new reforms.

Currently, a higher percentage of the public is more concerned with expanding health insurance coverage for those who cannot afford it than in reforming Health Maintenance Organizations and Managed Care Plans. (See table 6.7.) This can be attributed in large part to the growing number of Americans with no health insurance. In 1999, one in six Americans had no health insurance, up from one in seven at the start of the decade.[44]

The explanation for this increase lies in two trends. First, many corporations in the 1990s were downsizing and, consequently, turning to part-time labor precisely to avoid paying for employees' health care and to shore up the bottom line. Second, the decade's booming economy fueled an increase in the number of small businesses. These smaller firms argued they could not pay the current costs of health insurance for their employees and still survive.

At the decade's end, the public no longer agreed with these rationalizations. A *Wall Street Journal*/NBC News poll showed that 67% of Americans think all employers should be required to provide health insurance for their employees. (See figure 6.7.) Interestingly, of all age groups, 50-to-64-year-olds are the most lukewarm toward this notion, although 59% of them agree as well.

The shift to concerns about access does not mean that Americans' frustrations with HMOs and managed care have evaporated. Americans of all ages still get upset "over the refusal of many managed care plans to grant them speedy appointments with doctors, access to specialists, and hospital stays for certain procedures."[45] They also dislike prior approval rules.[46] Predictions are that HMOs will remain "in the political cross-hairs, because Americans want what they have always wanted—better care, higher quality, for less money."[47] But can we afford it all?

**Table 6.7**

### Covering Uninsured More Important Than Reforming HMOs and Managed Care

|  | 18-29 % | 30-49 % | 50-64 % | 65+ % |
|---|---|---|---|---|
| Providing health insurance coverage for those who cannot afford it | 65 | 57 | 54 | 58 |
| Reforming HMOs and managed care plans | 33 | 39 | 43 | 31 |
| Don't know/refused | 2 | 4 | 3 | 11 |
|  | 100 | 100 | 100 | 100 |

*Note: Respondents were asked: "Which of the following health care concerns should be given a higher priority? Is it providing health insurance coverage for those who cannot afford it, or reforming HMOs and managed care plans?"*

*Source: The Pew Research Center for the People & the Press. Telephone survey of a random sample of 1,032 adults, 18 years of age or older, conducted October 7-11, 1999. The sampling margin of error is plus or minus 3.5 percentage points (at the 95% confidence level).*

## Tough Health Care Choices Ahead

Debates over a wide variety of health care issues will surely intensify in the twenty-first century as the burgeoning elderly population forces the cost issue to the front burner. Here are some of the key issues:

- Should advanced, and expensive, medical procedures be limited for persons who are near the end of their lives or older than a certain age?
- Which diseases should be given the highest priority in terms of public research dollars?
- Should children's health care be sacrificed for elder health care?[48]
- Should government-financed health care include remedies outside traditional medicine?
- Should seniors be allowed to choose physician-assisted suicide if they cannot bear the pain of a severe illness? Or should seniors with such illnesses be given whatever drugs are needed to let them live out their lives pain-free?
- Can the public's support for expanded health care and tighter regulation of HMOs and managed care ever overcome its opposition to paying higher taxes for it?
- Will the addition of prescription drugs to Medicare coverage result in fewer new drugs being developed by the pharmaceutical industry?
- How and what are we going to pay with regard to the health care costs incurred by the aging incarcerated population?

## "GRAY" CRIMES

In the twenty-first century, certain types of crimes against the elderly will surely increase. We expect to see higher incidences of physical and mental abuse of the elderly by relatives or caregivers; consumer fraud—including voting; and age and disability discrimination, especially in the workplace. We can also expect more lawsuits brought by seniors and their advocates against various industries—tobacco, alcohol, food, and pharmaceutical. Efforts will be made to show how these industries have allegedly wreaked havoc on an individual's health, shortened life expectancy, ruined quality of life, and looted retirement savings.

### Elder Abuse

Nationally, reports of domestic elder abuse increased a whopping 150% between 1986 and 1996. In Florida alone, more than 29,000 incidents of adult abuse were reported in 1998, an increase of more than 30% from five years earlier. According to the Florida Department of Children and Families, about 70% of those cases involved people 60 and older.[49] And these figures are considered quite conservative because so many abused elders are afraid to report it, for fear they will lose their independence.

More than half of all cases of elder abuse involve neglect. Some 15% involve violence. The rest of the cases involve financial exploitation, emotional abuse, and sexual abuse, according to the National Center on Elder Abuse.[50]

Statistics from Palm Beach County, Florida (an affluent county), show that two-thirds of elderly victims are women. "Women over 80, the most frail among us, are abused, neglected, and exploited more than any other group."[51] The most likely abusers are their children, followed by grandchildren, other family members, and spouses.

Some observers believe elder abuse will increase because of several trends. First, adult children of the elderly are floundering under the weight of greater fiscal pressures. Some feel trapped "in the gap between the cost of long-term care, necessities ranging from private aides to diapers, and the limited amount of government aid to pay for it."[52] Nearly one in four families is already providing some form of assistance to an older relative or friend. If the elder happens to live with relatives—which is happening more every day—economic and care tensions may result in both physical and mental abuse of the senior.

Second, the trend toward smaller families in recent years means there are fewer children and other relatives to serve as potential caregivers. Instead of seven siblings who would take turns caring for Mom and Dad, there will be two. (See figure 6.8.) Having most or all of this responsibility will increase stress for many families. Businesses will suffer, too. A survey by the National Alliance for Caregiving and the AARP found that 14.4 million caregivers work full- or part-time.[53] They cost their employers as much as $29 billion a year in lost produc-

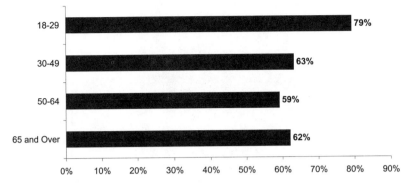

*Figure 6.7   Percentage of People Who Think Employers Should Be Required to Provide Health Insurance*
*Note: Respondents were asked: "Do you think all employers, regardless of size, should be required to provide health insurance for their employees?"*
*Source: The Wall Street Journal, June 25, 1998: A10. Used with permission.*

tivity because they often are late to work, leave early, or take long lunches to carry out their responsibilities. Some businesses have already responded by offering elder care programs. Among major U.S. employers, 30% offered such programs in 1997, up from 13% in 1991.

Nearly 7 million Americans, average age 46, are *long-distance* caregivers for older family members or friends. A survey co-sponsored by the National Council on the Aging and the Pew Charitable Trusts found that more than half of these long-distance caregivers have experienced disruption to their professional, social, or family needs because of their caretaking responsibilities. As the boomers and their parents continue to age, employers will have to address serious employee leave and productivity issues.[54]

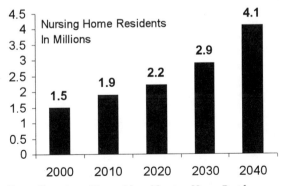

*Figure 6.8a   Fewer Caregivers Means More Nursing Home Residents.*
*Source: AARP Public Policy Institute and the Tampa Tribune. Used with permission.*

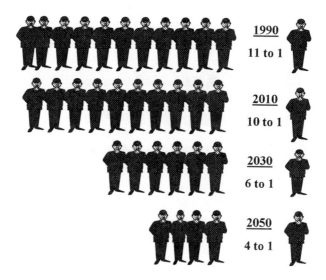

*Figure 6.8b    Potential Caregivers. The ratio of the population 50 to 64 to those 85 and older.*
*Source: AARP Public Policy Institute and the Tampa Tribune. Used with permission.*

Caregivers are not always family members. They can include housekeepers, nurses, friends—"anybody who has the access and the time to get into granny's purse, her closets, her bank account, her stock portfolio."[55] Naturally, not all caregivers have theft or assault on their minds, but it is becoming more of a problem.

Although abuse can occur in almost any kind of care facility, including assisted-living areas and hospitals, most exposés of institutional senior abuse have focused on nursing homes. Here seniors, who usually have more debilitating conditions, are often left unattended and their needs ignored. Government funding cutbacks and the pressure to make a profit have resulted in staff reductions so there are fewer assistants per resident. Newly hired, inexperienced workers are often put on the evening and weekend shifts, with the least supervision. It is the right chemistry for abuse:

> Right now, someone's mother is in a nursing home, hungry and dirty, because no one has time to feed or bathe her. A call bell rings and no one answers. Meanwhile, investors check the stock performance of the company housing her. . . . Nursing home residents aren't just numbers on a balance sheet or nameless bodies in beds, but that's how some are treated when profits come first and protectors fall short.[56]

Another problem is that nursing home administrators often can predict when the state inspection team will appear. They beef up staff until the inspection is over. Some states, like Florida, have begun sending in inspection teams at odd times—late night and weekend shifts.[57] In addition, states are establishing abuse hot lines and publicizing them more widely. Government officials and advocates are bolstering long-term care ombudsman programs.

Many advocates are urging states to become more aggressive in shutting down nursing homes with deficiencies. Others worry that a rush to close nursing homes may not be as effective as the court sending in a temporary manager to solve the problems. Even elder advocates caution that nursing home closures can send residents into "transfer trauma" if they separate them from their families and friends and put them in places that may have even worse problems.[58] But few defend keeping homes open that clearly abuse their residents. Most want them prosecuted and held accountable.

Prosecuting criminals who abuse the elderly can be difficult, however. Alzheimer's victims may not be able to testify. Because seniors bruise more easily than younger adults, physical abuse can be difficult to prove. A senior can have a clear recollection of an incident when it happens and is reported, but may lose it soon thereafter. Nonetheless, we are likely to see more aggressive prosecution of senior abusers in 2000 and beyond.

## Consumer Fraud against the Elderly

Law enforcement officials across the country are actively pursuing individuals and companies that prey on the elderly, taking advantage of their physical and mental infirmities. These scoundrels, typically peddling sweepstakes, financial services, or funeral arrangements, rely on elaborate telemarketing schemes, direct mail (sweepstakes), and home visits to badger seniors into buying phony goods and services with steep price tags.

It is estimated that telemarketers alone bilk Americans out of an estimated $40 billion a year. More than half their victims are older citizens.[59] In the president's words: "The greatest threat that many older Americans face is not a criminal armed with a gun but a telemarketer armed with a deceptive rap. And our most defenseless seniors, those who are sick or disabled and living in nursing homes cannot lock the door against abuse and neglect by people paid to care for them."[60]

A lawyer with the Elder Crimes Task Force in Florida says seniors are often "easy pickings" for sleazy salespersons. "A lot of these seniors are all alone and they trust too much. Remember, this is a generation of people for whom a handshake was a contract."[61]

Court-appointed guardians of elders are also drawing increased scrutiny from state officials across the country. These guardians are appointed to look out for the medical and financial welfare of incapacitated Americans. While most are honest and conscientious, some are not. "Reports of guardians stealing from their wards' bank accounts and otherwise abusing guardianship powers are surfacing with disturbing regularity," according to the AARP.[62]

## Discrimination in the Workplace: Age and Disability

Under federal law, it is illegal to discriminate in any aspect of employment: hiring and firing; compensation, assignment, or classification of employees; transfer, promotion, layoff, or recall; job advertisements; recruitment; testing;

use of company facilities; training and apprenticeship programs; fringe benefits; pay, retirement plans, and disability leave; or other terms and conditions
of employment.

The prohibitions against age discrimination are explicit. The Age Discrimination in Employment Act (ADEA) of 1967 covers workers and job seekers 40 and
older. Expectations are that the number of complaints under this act will escalate in the twenty-first century. Most expect 55-to-64-year-olds to be the most
frequent complainants. As of the year 2000, workers 55 through 64 are the
fastest-growing segment of the labor force, according to AARP research.[63]

Other laws protect the disabled. Title I of the Americans with Disabilities Act
of 1990 prohibits employment discrimination against qualified individuals with
disabilities in the private sector and in state and local governments. Section 501
of the Rehabilitation Act of 1973 prohibits discrimination against qualified individuals with disabilities who work in the federal government.

These laws, along with Title VII of the Civil Rights Act of 1964, the Equal Pay
Act of 1963, and the Civil Rights Act of 1991 also prohibit the following:

- harassment on the basis of race, color, religion, sex, national origin, disability, or age;
- retaliation against an individual for filing a charge of discrimination, participating in an investigation, or opposing discriminatory practices;
- employment decisions based on stereotypes or assumptions about the abilities, traits, or performance of individuals of a certain sex, race, age, religion, or ethnic group, or individuals with disabilities; and
- denying employment opportunities to a person because of marriage to, or
  association with, an individual of a particular race, religion, national origin,
  or an individual with a disability.[64]

The number of age-discrimination claims filed with the Equal Opportunity
Employment Commission (EEOC) reached 19,809 in 1993, but fell to 15,191
in 1998. The number of cases filed under the Americans with Disabilities Act
has fallen slightly from 19,798 in 1995 to 17,806 in 1998. Some attribute the
downward trend in age-discrimination complaints to a 1993 U.S. Supreme
Court ruling that has been interpreted by some to mean "there's no age discrimination if the employer doesn't stereotype older workers as less productive."[65] The downward trends in both disability and age complaints are also due,
in part, to the robust economy of the mid- to late 1990s and the high percentage (more than half) of cases for which the finding was "no reasonable cause."

Many possible victims of discrimination don't file charges because they think
it won't change anything. An AARP survey found that among individuals who
suspected they had been victims of age discrimination, only one in five took any
action. Many said they are afraid of recrimination or losing their jobs. Others
fear they will be stigmatized. Still others lack resources and/or stamina.[66]

Age discrimination cases are extremely hard to prove. As Sara Dix of AARP's Public Policy Institute says, "Employers, if they have any sense, are unlikely to admit that they discriminate against older workers. Subtle and not-so-subtle clues might point to age discrimination, but it is hard to prove, especially in hirings. Age discrimination is easier to detect in terminations, when who was let go and who was retained can be more readily compared."[67]

Senior advocacy groups like AARP are trying to educate employers so they will abandon their negative stereotypes of older workers. Part of the message is that older workers *can* be retrained and *are* accepting restructured jobs. Employers typically praise older workers for such attributes as loyalty, dependability, work attitude, experience, turnover, and absenteeism. But employers give seniors lower marks with regard to flexibility, technological competence, and the ability and willingness to learn new technology.[68] Older workers also tend to be more highly compensated, making them more vulnerable during cost-cutting times.

The number of age-related workplace discrimination charges will increase when any one of the following three conditions occurs:

1. Employers ignore or misinterpret the law.
2. The economy turns down sharply.
3. The number of older workers, able and disabled, rises.

All are likely to occur at some point in the twenty-first century.

## PENSIONS, SAVINGS, AND TAXES

Pocketbook issues will likely take on new dimensions when the boomers begin retiring. We can expect a rewriting of tax laws, probably those dealing with pensions, savings, capital gains, and estates.

### Pensions

Shifts in pension structures are destined to evoke age-discrimination cases, as more workers shift into "cash balance" or "pension equity" plans prompted by employers wanting to save money. Cash balance plans provide all workers with annual credits based on a certain percentage of their pay. That amount is placed into a hypothetical individual "account" that earns interest.

Older workers claim that being switched to these new forms of pensions yields far less money at retirement than they would have accrued under their old plans. They argue they have less time to build up benefits via compounded interest than younger workers. Defenders of such plans say they are not conventional pensions, but savings plans, which are treated differently under federal law.[69]

On another note, the degree to which individual states tax pensions will continue to be an important consideration when workers choose where they want to spend their retirement years.[70]

**Taxes**

The sources of retirement income will be different for tomorrow's retirees. Future retirees say they expect to rely more on income from private savings, IRAs, and 401(k) or 403(b) plans, and less on Social Security.[71] (See figure 6.9.) Any attempts to raise taxes on these private-sector-based revenues will evoke tremendous political battles. The baby boomers have come to trust Wall Street more than the federal government and to despise the Internal Revenue Service.[72]

Even attitudes toward taxing business (which historically have been quite positive) may change as more Americans invest in the stock market. A little more than three decades ago, only one in ten American adults owned stock. Today, more than half of all adults own at least $5,000 in stock. Those who have been in the workforce longer—that is, adults older than 35—are more likely to own stock (61%). Interestingly, stock ownership—either directly or through mutual funds or retirement accounts—is higher among registered voters than adults in general.[73] Consequently, candidates may find it in their best interests to tread lightly on the issue of taxing businesses.

The fact that many of the newest investors are lower- and middle-income families has prompted some analysts to predict that this new "investor class" will be "interested in nest-egg protection, not social engineering by an activist government."[74] Thus, tomorrow's seniors may be more resistant to higher taxes on businesses and on their own personal capital gains.

A sizable portion of the baby boomers will also find the estate tax, as currently structured, unpalatable when they retire, precisely because they have saved and invested wisely. As one scholar has noted:

[A] slew of politically active middle-class voters, proud that they have built up assets by saving and investing, will be faced with the prospect that all they have sacrificed to

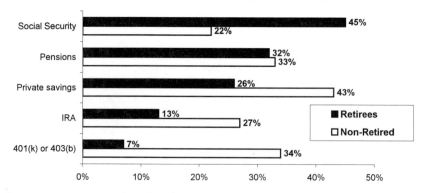

*Figure 6.9    Percentage of People Who Say the Following Are or Will Be a Major Source of Retirement Income*
Source: The Wall Street Journal/NBC News Poll. Telephone survey of 2,012 adults conducted March 4–7, 1999, by the polling organizations of Peter Hart and Robert Teeter. Margin of error+ or -2.2 percentage points. Used with permission.

accumulate may be virtually confiscated [by the federal government's estate tax]. They heeded the rules and norms—saving, not spending. Their reward is to have it snatched away before their kids can touch it. These are not people who consider themselves rich. They will not be happy that politicians have labeled them as such.[75]

Today's retirees, who rely more heavily on Social Security, are more likely to oppose new or higher *state and local* taxes than federal taxes. This is primarily because they benefit more directly from programs funded by federal taxes (e.g., Social Security and Medicare).[76] Even during periods of budget surpluses, these seniors favor putting more money into Social Security and Medicare over funding other programs or cutting taxes. (See table 6.8.)

## EDUCATION: OLD VIEWS, NEW FORMS

Seniors often are stereotyped as being against education. Specifically, when seniors vote against local taxes to pay for schools, media commentators and school advocates tend to pull out labels like "greedy" and "self-centered." But actually

**Table 6.8**

**What to Do with the Federal Budget Surplus?**

| Preferred Action | 18-29 % | 30-49 % | 50-64 % | 65+ % |
|---|---|---|---|---|
| Cut taxes | 16 | 16 | 9 | 12 |
| Pay off the national debt more quickly | 11 | 14 | 10 | 8 |
| Increase spending on health/education/environment | 34 | 24 | 11 | 9 |
| Help make Social Security/Medicare programs financially sound | 37 | 42 | 67 | 67 |
| Don't know/refused | 2 | 4 | 3 | 4 |
| | 100 | 100 | 100 | 100 |

Note: *Respondents were asked: "If it turns out that the federal government has a budget SURPLUS this year, in your opinion, which ONE of the following should be done with the available money? Should it be used: For a tax cut, to pay off the national debt more quickly, for increased spending on domestic programs such as health, education, and the environment, or to help make the Social Security and Medicare programs financially sound?"*

Source: *The Pew Research Center for the People & the Press. Telephone survey of a random sample of 1,500 adults, 18 years of age or older, conducted January 19-25, 1999. The sampling margin of error is plus or minus 3 percentage points (at the 95% confidence level).*

seniors are no more self-centered than the younger age groups who dispropor-
tionately favor more spending on schools to benefit their children.

The truth is that polls consistently show a significant portion of the senior population, like other age groups, in favor of improving America's educational system.
For example, a survey by the Pew Research Center for the People & the Press found
that 69% of those age 65 and older say that improving the educational system
should be a top priority national issue.[77] A similarly high percentage (66%) of the
young-old (those 50 to 64 years old) feel the same way. As one might expect, these
figures are not as high as those of younger age groups (85% of 18-to-29-year-olds
and 73% of 30-to-49-year-olds), but are high nonetheless.

## School Taxes and Bond Elections

In general, most Americans agree that our educational system is broken and
needs fixing. The age groups differ, however, with regard to *what* each thinks has
caused the problem and *how* it should be fixed. Their views are tempered by
their *own experiences* with the educational system.

Past studies of why the elderly tend to vote against school tax and bond referenda have shown that most have not had any personal interaction with the
school system for years.[78] Many no longer have children in school. And even
though many have grandchildren, they have observed that these youngsters
seem to have a poor grasp of the basics—reading, writing, and arithmetic.

Seniors, being more attentive to news coverage than other groups, are quite
aware of two contrary facts. First, the performance of American students, relative to other industrialized nations, has generally declined. Second, the
amount of money expended on education during the past several decades has
increased sharply.

Exit polls asking why some seniors vote against higher school taxes show that
they do so for a variety of reasons. But the overriding reason is that they do not
want to spend more money on something that appears to be broken. They see
today's schools as being poorly run by top-heavy administrations. Seniors also
blame today's parents for not becoming more involved in their children's education. (See table 6.9.)

Other polls show that seniors, more than other age groups, favor more discipline in the classroom; prayer in schools; character, values, and morality instruc-
tion; and higher performance standards—for students and teachers. However,
seniors still believe in public schools and public education and, thus, are less
supportive of vouchers and other private-sector-based approaches to educational
reform. This is less true of the baby boomers.

## Schools: How to Involve Seniors?

Teachers and school administrators know that as the baby boomers retire, an
even higher percentage of seniors will have no children in school. (In Florida

## Table 6.9

### Major Reasons Given for Voting "Against" Sales Tax for Schools by Age Group

| Reason | 18-29 % | 30-49 % | 50-64 % | 65+ % |
|---|---|---|---|---|
| Taxes are already too high in Hillsborough County.* | 98 | 73 | 75 | 87 |
| I don't believe the tax will be temporary.* | 98 | 63 | 72 | 90 |
| A tax increase will negatively affect Hillsborough County businesses because surrounding counties have lower sales taxes | 38 | 41 | 41 | 55 |
| Schools waste too much money; they could manage on current revenues if they'd operate more efficiently.* | 35 | 77 | 77 | 88 |
| The lottery has not paid for schools as promised. | 68 | 74 | 84 | 88 |
| Schools are not teaching the basics.* | 11 | 32 | 49 | 68 |
| More money is not the answer, better run schools are.* | 16 | 77 | 87 | 89 |
| Schools are turning out kids who can't read, write or add or subtract.* | 57 | 51 | 75 | 81 |

Table 6.9 *continued*.

Table 6.9 continued

## Major Reasons Given for Voting "Against" Sales Tax for Schools by Age Group

| Reason | 18-29 % | 30-49 % | 50-64 % | 65+ % |
|---|---|---|---|---|
| Schools spend too much on administration.* | 43 | 58 | 76 | 88 |
| Parents should be more responsible for their kids education; schools can't do everything.* | 15 | 47 | 56 | 81 |
| I resent school officials campaigning for the tax increase at taxpayers' expense* | 19 | 41 | 72 | 70 |
| Schools should be more aggressive in getting business/PTA to raise money/donate money to pay for computer and technological improvements.* | 10 | 24 | 36 | 52 |
| I don't have much confidence that the money will be spent for what the school board says it will fund.* | 49 | 44 | 92 | 87 |
| The money will go for construction but buildings don't guarantee kids will learn more.* | 39 | 48 | 64 | 76 |
| Holding a special election is a waste of taxpayers's money, especially when officials know turnout is usually low.* | 10 | 24 | 65 | 70 |

**Table 6.9** *continued*

**Major Reasons Given for Voting "Against" Sales Tax for Schools by Age Group**

| Reason | 18-29 % | 30-49 % | 50-64 % | 65+ % |
|---|---|---|---|---|
| More money is not the answer, more parental interest and involvement is* | 43 | 36 | 59 | 73 |
| The teachers union is too strong and has too much influence on elected officials.* | 9 | 12 | 44 | 46 |
| Too much is spent building lavish schools; plain and simple buildings would do just fine.* | 4 | 18 | 48 | 63 |
| Not enough teachers have been trained on how to use computers to teach.* | 16 | 8 | 46 | 40 |
| Kids will just use computers to play games, not to learn.* | 34 | 4 | 40 | 47 |
| Too much money was spent by supporters of the tax increase who will directly benefit from it.* | 34 | 27 | 64 | 64 |
| Other | 9 | 16 | 9 | 10 |

*Note: Percentages add to greater than 100% due to multiple response question format. Respondents who indicated they voted "Against" the one-half cent sales tax increase for schools were asked, "Which of the following were major reasons you voted 'Against'? Check all that apply."*
*\* Indicates the relationship between age and the reason given for voting is statistically significant at the .05 level or lower.*

*Source: Exit survey, Hillsborough County, September 12, 1995, by Susan A. MacManus, University of South Florida, 962 respondents, margin of error of plus/minus 3.5 percent.*

today, two-thirds of all voters have no children in school.) Educators from kindergarten through the twelfth grade are aggressively seeking ways to involve seniors. Programs are being developed to involve retirees in tutoring, mentoring, volunteering, and teaching youngsters—anything to bring the seniors onto school grounds. Schools are also opening their facilities for community use on evenings and weekends.

Surveys show that younger retirees, boomers included, are keenly interested in continuing their education after leaving the workforce. As a result, colleges and universities are establishing and expanding senior-oriented lifelong learning institutes. Some are supporting retirement communities. In the words of one such retiree, university-affiliated retirement homes "testify to an appetite among educated, affluent retirees for more than golf and sunshine, more than 'fishing, drinking, and going to Wal-Mart'."[79] In turn, universities "get a living laboratory for students in the exploding field of gerontology . . . , patients for their medical centers, and a loyal body of alumni more likely to bequeath their substantial wealth if they live just steps from the university's fund-raising office."[80]

Two demographic trends indicate an unprecedented demand for teachers (more than 2 million in the next decade). The first trend is a "baby boom echo"—the wave of baby boom offspring entering the schools. The second is the graying of the education workforce. Thousands of people—including many teachers and principals—will retire in the near future.[81] Because of this teacher shortage, the education community is rethinking teacher certification requirements so that it will be less difficult for someone without an education degree or certificate to teach in the public schools. Among those who might be enticed to teach are well-educated retirees.

But much has changed in the average classroom since these elders sat there. Technology, cultural diversity, widening income disparities, mainstreaming of disabled children, more lawsuits against teachers, less latitude on imposing discipline, less parental involvement, and changing social mores make today's classrooms considerably more complex. Most experts acknowledge the need to provide training on these changes before seniors venture onto today's campuses.

## MORAL AND SOCIAL ISSUES: A WIDE GENERATIONAL DIVIDE?

On political issues in general, seniors are a little more conservative than younger persons and label themselves as such. However, most people in each age group tend to describe themselves as moderates. (See table 6.10.) This pattern has persisted across time.

Of all age groups, older Americans are the most concerned with a perceived moral breakdown in the country. Sixty-three percent believe this issue is a top priority for the nation. In contrast, just 42% of 18-to-29-year-olds rank this issue that highly.[82]

Actually, in the decade of the 1990s, all age groups tended to link rising social problems with declining morals. Many lay the blame for increases in juvenile crime, teenage pregnancies, and substance abuse on television, the entertainment industry, and, now, the Internet. However, older Americans are a bit more critical of these media and industries. Seniors are also more prone to attribute moral decay to the decline of the traditional family structure, while the young blame it on economics.[83]

New forms of individual expression and lifestyles have always generated intense debates. Lifestyle issues are often cast as a choice between protecting individual rights or protecting society at-large. The young are more interested in individual rights; the old, in protecting society at-large.

At the close of the twentieth century, gay rights, parental consent for an abortion, gun control, and unrestricted "speech" on the Internet were among the most

**Table 6.10**

**Seniors Are Slightly More Conservative**

|  | 18-29 % | 30-49 % | 50-64 % | 65+ % |
|---|---|---|---|---|
| **Conservative** | 24 | 35 | 38 | 35 |
| Very Conservative | 5 | 9 | 9 | 7 |
| Conservative | 20 | 27 | 29 | 28 |
| **Moderate** | 45 | 40 | 40 | 41 |
| **Liberal** | 28 | 22 | 17 | 15 |
| Liberal | 20 | 18 | 11 | 10 |
| Very Liberal | 8 | 5 | 6 | 5 |
| **Don't know/refused** | 3 | 3 | 5 | 9 |
|  | 100 | 100 | 100 | 100 |

*Note: Respondents were asked: "In general, would you describe your political views as _____ ?"*

*Source: The Pew Research Center for the People & the Press. Telephone survey of a random sample of 1,032 adults, 18 years of age or older, conducted October 7-11, 1999. The sampling error is plus or minus 3.5 percentage points (at the 95% confidence level).*

"divisive" issues. But age-group preferences differed more in *degree* rather than direction. Seniors were somewhat stronger in their support for parental consent for abortion[84] and protecting the right to bear arms (versus gun control).[85] Younger groups were more supportive of gay rights[86] and an unregulated Internet.

By the beginning of the twenty-first century, opinions had narrowed considerably on previously contentious issues such as gender roles, racial equality, and environmental protection. The narrowing of the opinion gap demonstrates another phenomenon: What is considered liberal by one generation may be accepted as moderate or mainstream by succeeding generations.

A number of intense morality-oriented battles of the future will center on seniors. These battles may involve issues such as the following:

- Health rationing: Which age group or disease gets highest priority for medical treatment? Who gets organ donations first?
- Euthanasia: Does a person have a right to physician-assisted suicide?
- Pain: Does someone suffering from a terminal illness have the right to spend the last days of life in a pain-free manner? Should illegal substances be approved for medicinal use in such circumstances?
- Grandparents' rights: Should parents, often divorced and remarried, have the right to restrict grandparents' visitation?
- Privacy: Are individuals' medical and financial records private property? Can access via the Internet be restricted?

The privacy issue is one that may connect, rather than divide, generations as Internet use expands. However, it too will be a classic struggle between individual and societal rights, especially when the outcome may affect the nation's health and security.

## FOREIGN AFFAIRS AND DEFENSE

Older Americans continue to be more interested in, and more knowledgeable about, international affairs than younger groups. Nearly two-thirds closely follow international news most of the time. Younger persons are more likely to pay attention "only when something important or interesting is happening." (See table 6.11.)

When asked to identify top-priority foreign policy problems, seniors tend to mention security-related issues. Seniors see as the five most important problems international drug trafficking (87%), reducing the threat of international terrorism (75%), getting Saddam Hussein out of Iraq (69%), keeping a close watch on the development of China as a world power (65%), and stopping the spread of AIDs around the world (62%). (See table 6.12.)

The next generation of seniors (50-64) is more committed than the other age groups to protecting America's economy and its trading partners. The youngest

**Table 6.11**

### Seniors Closely Follow International Affairs

| How Often Follow | 18-29 % | 30-49 % | 50-64 % | 65+ % |
|---|---|---|---|---|
| Only when something important or interesting is happening | 59 | 49 | 35 | 26 |
| Closely most of the time | 40 | 49 | 63 | 66 |
| Don't know/refused | 1 | 2 | 3 | 8 |
| | 100 | 100 | 100 | 100 |

*Note: Respondents were asked: "Which of the following two statements best describes you: 'I follow INTERNATIONAL news closely ONLY when something important or interesting is happening,' OR 'I follow INTERNATIONAL news closely most of the time, whether or not something important or interesting is happening?'"*

*Source: The Pew Research Center for the People & the Press. Telephone survey of a random sample of 1,008 adults 18 years of age or older, conducted March 30, 1999. The sampling margin of error is plus or minus 3.5 percentage points (at the 95% confidence level).*

voting age adults (18-to-29-year-olds) rank health, environmental, and human rights concerns ahead of security or economic concerns.

Most Americans (77%) believe that government should continue to play a *major* role in maintaining a strong defense in the twenty-first century. (See table 6.13.) Surveys also consistently show that support for increasing defense spending is higher among those 50 and older. Older Americans are also the most likely to question peacekeeping and drug interdiction roles for the military—roles they perceive as having a negative impact on the military's defense readiness.

The fear that Third World countries are developing weapons of mass destruction—biological and chemical warfare—is rising across all generations. So, too, is the fear of nuclear testing by India, Pakistan, and North Korea. But most Americans don't think they personally can do anything about such developments.

Military veterans' health care is another matter. Veterans groups, dominated by seniors, have been quite successful in fighting for medical benefits and services. Interest in veterans' health care issues will intensify and take on new dimensions as the World War II generation faces long-term care choices, and as new research links the problems of Vietnam and Desert Storm generations to exposure to "external agents." We can expect mounting pressure to do the following:

**Table 6.12**

**Top Priority Foreign Policy Problems**
(Multiple Response Question)

| Problem | 18-29 % | 30-49 % | 50-64 % | 65+ % |
|---|---|---|---|---|
| Reducing the threat of international terrorism | 62 | 80 | 82 | 75 |
| Stopping international drug trafficking | 60 | 68 | 79 | 87 |
| Stopping the spread of AIDS around the world | 73 | 63 | 64 | 62 |
| Protecting the global environment | 65 | 61 | 64 | 56 |
| Making the world financial system more stable | 58 | 60 | 63 | 60 |
| Getting Saddam Hussein out of Iraq | 53 | 57 | 64 | 69 |
| Keeping a close watch on the development of China as a world power | 40 | 50 | 62 | 65 |
| Monitoring the emergence of China as a world power | 26 | 39 | 57 | 52 |
| Better managing our trade and economic disputes with Europe | 27 | 39 | 51 | 49 |
| Better managing our trade and economic disputes with Japan | 26 | 40 | 42 | 44 |

Table 6.12 *continued.*

- build more long-term care facilities for veterans;
- fund more research on diseases—physical and mental—contracted by veterans in the Vietnam and Gulf Wars;
- better compensate veterans exposed to chemicals or biological agents, inflicted either by foreign nations or our own government's immunization programs, during tours of duty.

Establishing such programs may be harder to achieve than in earlier times because the number of veterans in Congress has diminished in recent years. Veterans groups might have more success at the state level, especially in places where they make up a large portion of the voting population. For example, Florida has responded (albeit with some federal assistance) to pressure from veterans groups by opening several nursing home facilities to veterans with Alzheimer's disease.

**Table 6.12** *continued*

## Top Priority Foreign Policy Problems for U.S.
### (Multiple Response Question)

| Problem | 18-29 % | 30-49 % | 50-64 % | 65+ % |
|---|---|---|---|---|
| Preventing human rights abuses in other countries | 39 | 40 | 34 | 35 |
| Bringing about a permanent settlement between Israel and the Arabs | 26 | 31 | 46 | 46 |
| Ending the warfare in the Balkans | 28 | 29 | 41 | 44 |
| Insuring democracy succeeds in Russia and the other former Soviet states | 22 | 32 | 36 | 32 |
| Countering the threat of North Korean militarism | 25 | 30 | 27 | 35 |

*Note: Respondents were asked: "As I read a list of SPECIFIC foreign policy problems, tell me whether each should have top priority in the U.S. government, a priority but not top priority, or no priority."*

*Source: The Pew Research Center for the People & the Press. Telephone survey of a random sample of 1,786 adults, 18 years of age or older, conducted March 24-30, 1999. The sampling margin of error for the split samples of 893 is plus or minus 4 percentage points.*

## STATES ON THE HOT SEAT: WHAT TO DO ABOUT OLDER DRIVERS?

Americans of all ages love their cars. When to stop driving is one of the most agonizing decisions any American must make. "Simply put, transportation is key to our personal independence and freedom."[87] For seniors, their "automobility" is a major concern.

### Accident Rates

Statistics show that driving becomes more hazardous with age. (See figures 6.10 and 6.11.) The aging process impacts vision, reflex time, physical strength, memory, and other capabilities, causing accident rates to increase after age 65. The type of accident varies by age group. For example, younger drivers are more likely to hit trees and utility or light poles, while seniors are more likely to hit pedestrians, bicyclists, and parked cars.[88]

**Table 6.13**

**Major Roles for Government in the 21ˢᵗ Century**

| Government's Role | All Adults | 18-34 | 35-49 | 50-64 | 65+ |
|---|---|---|---|---|---|
| | % | % | % | % | % |
| Maintaining a strong defense | 77 | 70 | 79 | 84 | 80 |
| Improving education | 70 | 81 | 70 | 67 | 53 |
| Making college affordable | 68 | 80 | 68 | 55 | 58 |
| Helping senior citizens | 67 | 69 | 68 | 69 | 58 |
| Finding a cure for diseases | 67 | 74 | 58 | 68 | 67 |
| Reducing violence | 66 | 75 | 65 | 63 | 56 |
| Cleaning up the environment | 63 | 71 | 61 | 58 | 53 |
| Expand health ins. coverage | 58 | 61 | 58 | 55 | 58 |
| Fighting discrimination | 57 | 65 | 58 | 48 | 49 |
| Reducing poverty | 57 | 63 | 61 | 48 | 47 |
| Supporting scientific research | 53 | 56 | 49 | 45 | 59 |
| Improving moral values | 46 | 49 | 41 | 41 | 50 |
| Helping people buy homes | 38 | 41 | 42 | 30 | 36 |
| Exploring outer space | 30 | 34 | 30 | 37 | 25 |
| Assisting poor nations | 21 | 25 | 20 | 19 | 18 |

Note: "Still looking ahead to the next century, I would like to know how big a role you think that government should play on different issues, as opposed to business, community organizations, or other institutions that might also deal with these issues. In the future, do you think that government should play a minor role, a medium role, or a major role in the following areas?"

Source: The Council for Excellence in Government, 1999 Survey.

As might be expected, driving becomes particularly hazardous for older seniors. Drivers 80 and older, studies show, are the most likely to get ticketed for causing an accident. Furthermore, a driver 85 or older is about four times more likely than a youth to die in an accident. Even so, seniors resist the idea of giving up their cars.

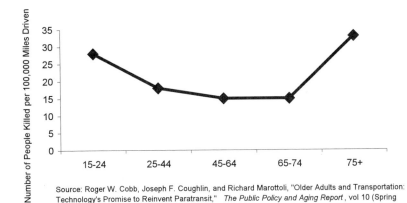

*Figure 6.10 Fatality Rates per 100,000 Miles Driven by Age Group, 1996*
*Source: Roger W. Cobb, Joseph F. Coughlin, and Richard Marottoli, "Older Adults and Transportation: Technology's Promise to Reinvent Paratransit,"* The Public Policy and Aging Report, *vol. 10 (Spring 1999): 10. Used with permission.*

## More Frequent Testing, Shorter Renewal Periods

Bills have been introduced in a number of states to address the older-driver issue but have encountered formidable opposition. Groups like the AARP have opposed differential licensing periods and testing based on age. As of this writing, three states—Arizona, Florida, and West Virginia—had considered legislation requiring more frequent testing of older drivers. All three efforts failed. In fact, when the bill was introduced in the Florida Legislature, lawmakers quickly labeled it "the suicide bill."[89] (Florida has one of the nation's most lenient driver's licensing systems. Any licensed driver can obtain a renewal for another six years by phone or mail two consecutive times, provided he or she has not been cited for a moving violation. That means that for eighteen years, there is no way to check for any impairment that might hinder one's ability to drive.)

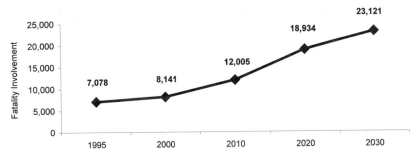

*Figure 6.11 Projected Senior Driver Fatality Involvement Rate, 1995–2030*
*Source: Roger W. Cobb, Joseph F. Coughlin, and Richard Marottoli, "Older Adults and Transportation: Technology's Promise to Reinvent Paratransit,"* The Public Policy and Aging Report, *vol. 10 (Spring 1999): 10. Used with permission.*

If Florida's senior drivers are any example, change will not come easily. They are evenly divided on the issue of shorter licensing periods for older persons, with about half for and half against. (See figure 6.12.) Women are more likely than men (49% versus 41%) to favor shorter licensing periods for elders. (When asked why, many women cite their experiences as passengers in cars driven by older males!) Among seniors who favor shorter licensing periods, the vast majority prefers 65 as the baseline age. Others say it should be 70.[90]

Apart from shortening licensing periods, a few states are looking at restricting older drivers if they have serious impairments. Four states—Arizona, California, Illinois, and Pennsylvania—have been somewhat successful in imposing vision test requirements for seniors.[91] Little, however, has been done about hearing problems among senior drivers.

Other states, perhaps recognizing the inevitability of seniors behind the wheel, are beginning to study how to make traffic signs and roads safer and more accessible for older drivers.

### A Discrimination or Safety Issue?

Until recently, many seniors saw driver-related legislation as a form of discrimination. This is slowly changing as more seniors view requirements such as vision testing as *safety* issues. The Florida legislator (age 73) who unsuccessfully sponsored a bill to require hearing and vision tests every three years for drivers 75 and older sums up the safety arguments best: "I really don't understand how any person or group claiming to advocate for the elderly can oppose this. If you want to keep seniors alive, by God don't put them behind the wheel of a car if they don't belong there."[92]

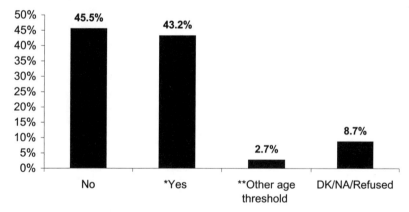

*Figure 6.12    Shorter Licensing Period for Seniors?*
Note: "Do you favor shorter licensing periods for persons 65 or older seeking drivers license renewals?" *Indicates at age 65  **Indicates at ages 70, 80, and 90.
Source: Telephone survey of a random sample of 600 Floridians 60 or older, conducted December 1998.

## Driver-Improvement Courses: Mandatory versus Voluntary

The key to reducing accident rates among the elderly, some experts say, is re-education. But many seniors oppose *mandatory* programs that might prompt their driver's license to be revoked, even when they are offered carrots, like insurance discounts. In 1997, for example, six states—Alabama, Iowa, Maryland, Vermont, Wisconsin, and Minnesota—considered bills to offer insurance discounts to seniors who successfully completed driver-improvement courses. All six failed to get either through the legislature or past the governor's veto pen. Those fighting such legislation, besides the insurance industry, were seniors who perceived that driver-improvement programs would become mandatory and that, in the course of taking one, they would be singled out for needing their licenses revoked.

Voluntary retraining programs evoke far less controversy than mandatory programs. The AARP now offers an alternative course for persons 50 and older. This 55 Alive/Mature Driving refresher course covers age-related physical changes, rules of the road, and safety precautions (defensive driving). In 1997, 640,000 persons completed the course, most out of concern for their own safety, but some drawn by an insurance discount incentive. Other groups like the National Safety Council and most chapters of the American Automobile Association also have popular "mature driver programs."

None of these programs, however, conducts any vision, mental function, or road testing.[93] Thus, the effectiveness of these classes in actually reducing accident rates among seniors is open to question.

## What Are the Alternatives?

Eventually for most adults, there comes a time to hand over the car keys. At that point, say transportation policy experts, seniors are left with three principal choices. One is riding with friends and family. A second is public transportation—buses, light rail, and subways. The third is paratransit,[94] which typically consists of door-to-door services with a van or automobile. With this type, scheduling is demand-response—that is, the rider calls ahead to schedule a ride, and the provider responds as quickly as possible, given constraints such as vehicle availability and rider itinerary.

Senior advocates argue: "It's pointless and heartless for states to impose stricter licensing guidelines for seniors unless they have auto [or other] alternatives far beyond getting a ride from a son or daughter." Many seniors live in suburbs or rural areas where mass transit availability is limited and likely to remain so. That leaves paratransit as the more viable option.[95] (See table 6.14.)

Up to now, the biggest barriers to senior use of paratransit options have been cost and vehicle design. But transportation experts are predicting the development of affordable, low-floor, size-appropriate vehicles that will be universally recognized as a mobility option.[96] One thing is certain: the growing number of

**Table 6.14**

## What to Do When You Can't Drive

| Alternative Transportation | 18-29 % | 30-49 % | 50-64 % | 65-74 % | 75+ % |
|---|---|---|---|---|---|
| A friend | 27.4 | 19.8 | 18.1 | 21.4 | 23.6 |
| Relative in same household | 42.7 | 38.8 | 40.6 | 37.9 | 12.7 |
| Relative living elsewhere | 6.8 | 7.2 | 8.0 | 14.6 | 14.5 |
| Taxi or paid driver | 3.4 | 6.8 | 9.4 | 7.8 | 20.0 |
| Bus | 12.8 | 15.5 | 8.0 | 6.8 | 3.6 |
| Metrorail or Tri-Rail | 2.6 | 2.2 | .7 | .0 | 1.8 |
| Train | .0 | .4 | .0 | .0 | .0 |
| Wouldn't go many places | 1.7 | 6.5 | 8.7 | 8.7 | 10.9 |
| No response/refused to comment | 2.6 | 2.9 | 6.5 | 2.9 | 12.7 |

Note: Respondents were asked: "Suppose you suddenly had a serious accident or illness or lost your eyesight or couldn't drive anymore. How do you think you would get to work or wherever you needed to go? Would you primarily rely on _____?"

Source: Public Transportation in Florida, a Survey of Resident Use Patterns, Assessments and Preferences, prepared for the Florida Department of Transportation, by the author, 1997.

seniors needing transportation assistance is bound to give the automobile industry sufficient incentive.

In the years ahead, public policy makers will face tough decisions: Should they support paratransit options, or should they expand traditional public transportation? Who will pay for these options? Will senior transportation become another large, government-financed entitlement program?

### GOVERNMENT AND POLITICIANS: DESPAIR BUT NOT DISINTEREST

Americans in general are frustrated with government and politicians. Nearly three-fourths of the public long for elected officials who have honesty and integrity and who put the public interest ahead of their own. (See table 6.15.) The call for honesty and integrity is particularly strong among those 65 and older.

**Table 6.15**

## Qualities Most Needed in Our Elected Officials Today

| Preferred Quality | All Adults % | 18-29 % | 30-49 % | 50-64 % | 65+ % |
|---|---|---|---|---|---|
| Having honesty and integrity | 48 | 43 | 47 | 48 | 56 |
| Putting the public interest ahead of personal interest | 23 | 28 | 19 | 30 | 19 |
| Putting a priority on performance and results | 8 | 11 | 10 | 5 | 3 |
| Having the ability to inspire people | 6 | 12 | 5 | 1 | 3 |
| All/None | 13 | 3 | 17 | 14 | 15 |
| Not sure | 2 | 3 | 1 | 2 | 4 |

*Note: Respondents were asked: "Which of these qualities do you think is most needed in our elected officials today?"*

*Source: Telephone survey of a random sample of 1,214 U.S. adults conducted May 21-June 1, 1999 for the Council for Excellence in Government by the research firm of Peter D. Hart and Robert Teeter. Used by permission.*

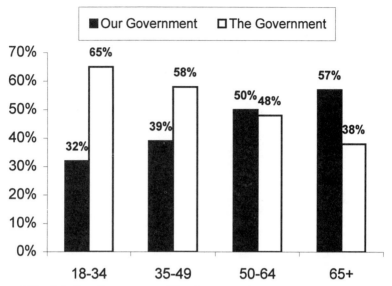

*Figure 6.13    Is It Our Government or The Government?*
Note: "When you think and talk about government, do you tend to think of it more as 'THE government' or more as 'OUR government'?"
Source: The Council for Excellence in Government, 1999 poll of 1,214 adults conducted May 21–June 1, margin of error +/- 3.2 percent.

A majority of adults (55%) no longer think of government as their own—"of, by, and for" the people. (See figure 6.13.) They blame special interest groups, the media, elected officials, and political parties for what's wrong with government today. (See table 6.16.) Americans perceive that each of these groups has undue influence over public policy making.

There is even a widespread belief among citizens that they have lost control over the presidential nomination process. In their opinion, large political donors, news organizations, and party leaders now exert more influence on which candidate wins their party's nomination than the average voter. (See table 6.17.)

Does this mean that voters no longer care which party's candidate wins the race for president? Absolutely not! (See table 6.18.) Does this mean they perceive little difference between the Republican and Democratic parties? No! By and large, Americans care a great deal about the outcome of the presidential race and view the two parties as different. But those who care the most and see the greatest differences are seniors, a further indication of their commitment to voting.

## What Voters Want to Know about Candidates

What do voters want to know about presidential candidates? A majority of each age group wants to know three things: reputation for honesty, ability to connect with average people, and voting record/policy positions. (See table 6.19.) More

## Table 6.16

### "Who Is Most Responsible for What's Wrong With Government Today?"

| Responsible | All Adults % | 18-29 % | 30-49 % | 50-64 % | 65+ % |
|---|---|---|---|---|---|
| Special Interest Groups | 36 | 24 | 43 | 40 | 40 |
| The Media | 29 | 34 | 25 | 33 | 28 |
| Elected Officials | 24 | 24 | 24 | 22 | 26 |
| Political Parties | 24 | 16 | 28 | 21 | 26 |
| The Public | 14 | 17 | 13 | 13 | 11 |
| Government Employees | 6 | 8 | 6 | 5 | 4 |
| None/Other/All | 8 | 8 | 9 | 9 | 6 |
| Not Sure | 2 | 3 | 2 | 2 | 3 |

Note: Respondents were asked: "Among the following, which one of two would you say are most responsible for what is wrong with government today?"

Source: Form A (n = 585): Telephone survey of a random sample of 1,214 U.S. adults conducted May 21-June 1, 1999 for the Council for Excellence in Government by the research firm of Peter D. Hart and Robert Teeter. Used by permission.

## Table 6.17

### Who Has *Too Much* Influence on Which Candidates Become Presidential Nominees?

| Influence | 18-29 % | 30-49 % | 50-64 % | 65+ % |
|---|---|---|---|---|
| Large political donors | 65 | 73 | 82 | 76 |
| News organizations | 56 | 68 | 65 | 63 |
| Party leader | 34 | 44 | 53 | 57 |
| Average voters | 12 | 8 | 5 | 8 |

Note: Respondents were asked: "How much influence do you think news organizations have on which candidates become presidential nominees: too much, too little, or about the right amount?" Same question asked about political donors, the average voter, and party leaders.

Source: The Pew Research Center for the People & the Press. Telephone survey of a random sample of 1,205 adults, 18 years of age or older, conducted September 1-12, 1999. The sampling error is plus or minus 3 percentage points (at the 95% confidence level).

**Table 6.18**

### Presidential Election 2000 Outlook: Political Parties

#### Care Which Political Party Wins?

| Preferences | 18-29 % | 30-49 % | 50-64 % | 65+ % |
|---|---|---|---|---|
| Care a good deal | 56 | 62 | 61 | 69 |
| Don't care very much | 44 | 35 | 37 | 25 |
| Don't know/refused | 1 | 3 | 2 | 6 |
| | 100 | 100 | 100 | 100 |

#### Are Political Parties Different?

| Viewpoint | 18-29 % | 30-49 % | 50-64 % | 65+ % |
|---|---|---|---|---|
| Differ greatly | 26 | 34 | 36 | 38 |
| Differ a fair amount | 55 | 44 | 44 | 40 |
| Hardly any difference | 16 | 19 | 19 | 19 |
| Don't know/refused | 3 | 3 | 1 | 3 |
| | 100 | 100 | 100 | 100 |

Note: Respondents were asked: "Generally speaking, would you say that you personally care a good deal WHO wins the presidential election in the year 2000 or that
you don't care very much who wins?" and "Thinking about the Democratic and
Republican parties, would you say there is a great deal of difference in what they
stand for, a fair amount of difference, or hardly any difference at all?"

Source: The Pew Research Center for the People & the Press. Telephone survey of a
random sample of 1,203 adults, 18 years of age or older, conducted February 18-21,
1999. The sampling margin of error of the split sample of 603 is plus or minus 4.5
percentage points (at the 95% confidence level).

older than younger voters also want to know about a candidate's church membership, military service, professional background, experiences growing up,
spouse, and children. These details have long been standard information that
candidates give about themselves.

But what about details of a more personal nature that have to do with private
behavior? What does the public think about the obligation of the press to report
candidates' spousal abuse, tax evasion, falsification of records, extramarital
affairs, homosexual lifestyles, substance abuse, mental problems, depression, or
abortions, regardless of how long ago these had taken place?

**Table 6.19**

| What Do You Want to Know About Presidential Candidates? | 18-29 % | 30-49 % | 50-64 % | 65+ % |
|---|---|---|---|---|
| Candidate's reputation and honesty | 77 | 78 | 84 | 80 |
| How well a candidate connects with average people | 76 | 67 | 67 | 79 |
| Candidate's voting record or policy positions in public offices he or she previously held | 55 | 63 | 62 | 63 |
| Candidate's major campaign contributors | 40 | 38 | 36 | 39 |
| Whether a candidate is an active church member | 16 | 24 | 26 | 30 |
| Clubs and organizations a candidate belongs to | 33 | 21 | 18 | 21 |
| Personal qualities of the candidate's spouse | 18 | 17 | 11 | 28 |
| Candidate's military background | 11 | 10 | 23 | 32 |
| Candidate's experiences growing up | 13 | 16 | 18 | 24 |
| Professional background of a candidate's spouse | 8 | 12 | 12 | 21 |
| Candidate's personal finances | 8 | 13 | 16 | 13 |
| Candidate's children | 6 | 7 | 5 | 17 |

*Note: Respondents were asked: "Thinking about the presidential candidates and what you will learn about them over the next year, please rate the importance of each of the following things. How important is it for YOU to learn about _____? Very important, somewhat important, not too important, or not at all important?*

*Source: The Pew Research Center for the People & the Press. Telephone survey of a random sample of 1,032 adults, 18 years of age or older, conducted October 7-11, 1999. The sampling margin of error is plus or minus 4 percentage points for the registered voter subset of 739 (at the 95% confidence level). .*

As shown in table 6.20, a majority of all age groups believe that certain things should "almost always" be reported. These things are spousal abuse, tax evasion, and falsification of records (academic and military).

Older voters are considerably more interested in a candidate's current extramarital affairs, homosexuality, substance abuse, and mental problems than younger voters. Only small percentages of any age group believe abor-

**Table 6.20**

### Presidential Candidate Behavior:
### What Should Almost Always Be Reported?

| Specific Behavior | 18-29 % | 30-49 % | 50-64 % | 65+ % |
|---|---|---|---|---|
| A candidate is known to have physically abused a spouse | 66 | 71 | 75 | 71 |
| A candidate is found to have not paid federal income tax once in the past | 57 | 67 | 66 | 68 |
| A candidate is found to have exaggerated his or her record of military service | 55 | 64 | 67 | 57 |
| A candidate is found to have exaggerated his or her academic record | 58 | 60 | 65 | 59 |
| A candidate is having an extramarital affair | 39 | 38 | 46 | 53 |
| A candidate is a homosexual | 31 | 34 | 46 | 48 |
| A candidate is found to have had a drinking problem in the past | 32 | 32 | 42 | 42 |

Table 6.20 *continued.*

tions, depression, past extramarital affairs, or youthful substance abuse are very newsworthy.

### Are News Reports Fair?

Does the public perceive that news organizations are fair in covering different types of presidential candidates? Or are news organizations too tough on certain candidate types? Perception varies by age group. As shown in table 6.21, older voters are less likely than other age groups to perceive too-tough coverage of candidates, indicating a greater trust in media reporting. About a third of older voters, however, do perceive that coverage is too tough on certain types of candidates—those who are trailing, those affiliated with a religious group, female candidates, or conservative candidates, in that order.

Younger voters, by contrast, are more likely to perceive coverage as too tough, and they rank candidates receiving this treatment in different order—namely, female candidates first, then African-Americans, trailing candidates, and those affiliated with a religious group.

### Timing: When Voters Make Up Their Minds

Candidates who want to win the senior vote must start early. Older voters make up their minds much more quickly in the presidential election cycle. In 1996,

**Table 6.20** *continued*

**Presidential Candidate Behavior:
What Should Almost Always Be Reported?**

| Specific Behavior | 18-29 % | 30-49 % | 50-64 % | 65+ % |
|---|---|---|---|---|
| A candidate is found to have used cocaine as a young adult | 35 | 34 | 38 | 35 |
| A candidate is found to have been treated by a psychiatrist in the past | 26 | 24 | 31 | 41 |
| A candidate is found to have had an extramarital affair in the past | 20 | 24 | 22 | 28 |
| A candidate is found to have used marijuana as a young adult | 20 | 23 | 22 | 30 |
| A candidate is found to have taken anti-depressants | 18 | 24 | 16 | 22 |
| A female candidate is found to have had an abortion | 16 | 16 | 15 | 21 |

Note: *Respondents were asked: "For each of the following stories about presidential candidates, please tell me whether you feel it should almost always be reported, whether it should sometimes be reported depending on the particular circumstances, or whether it should almost never be reported?*

Source: *The Pew Research Center for the People & the Press. Telephone survey of a random sample of 1,205 adults, 18 years of age or older, conducted September 1-12, 1999. The sampling error for the split samples of 592 or 613 is plus or minus 4.5 percentage points (at the 95% confidence level).*

nearly half had decided on their choice in the year preceding the election. (See table 6.22.) Seniors are more likely to vote in line with their long-held party affiliation; they are stronger partisans.

Candidates cannot count on impressive performances in the presidential debates to sway the voting decisions of many seniors. Part of the reason presidential debates are more helpful to younger voters (see table 6.23) is that most older voters have already made their vote choice by the time the debates take place.

The pattern of earlier vote decisions among seniors will probably persist in Election 2000, especially with the front-loading of the party primaries. However, the emergence of a strong third-party candidate could alter the pattern somewhat.

Will these patterns change in the near future? Here are key questions to ponder:

- Once the baby boomers reach retirement age, will their voting habits resemble those of today's senior voters? Will they be more or less partisan?

**Table 6.21**

**Presidential Candidates:**
**Who Gets News Coverage That Is Too Tough?**

| Type of Candidate | 18-29 % | 30-49 % | 50-64 % | 65+ % |
|---|---|---|---|---|
| The frontrunner | 21 | 22 | 26 | 19 |
| Far behind in the race | 47 | 41 | 34 | 33 |
| Female | 54 | 48 | 40 | 32 |
| African-American | 48 | 45 | 31 | 24 |
| Liberal views | 31 | 32 | 23 | 22 |
| Conservative views | 29 | 32 | 30 | 30 |
| Associated with a religious group | 42 | 40 | 40 | 33 |

Note: Respondents were asked: "All in all, do you think that news organizations are too easy, too tough, or are they generally fair in their coverage of the following types of presidential candidates?"

Source: The Pew Research Center for the People & the Press. Telephone survey of a random of 1,205 adults, 18 years of age or older, conducted September 1-12, 1999. The sampling error is plus or minus 3 percentage points (at the 95% confidence level).

- Will coverage of certain aspects of a candidate's personal life ever be of so little interest that the press does not cover them? If so, what . . . and when?
- What impact will "electronic democracy" have on voter turnout and their opinions of government? Will Internet voting improve both, or will it make matters worse?[97]
- How much will the senior issues discussed in this chapter dominate the political agenda of the twenty-first century—at national, state, and local levels?

## SUMMARY AND PROJECTIONS FOR THE NEW MILLENNIUM

Powerful age-driven demographics will affect virtually every public policy in 2000 and beyond. Issue stances favored by current seniors, in many cases, will shift somewhat when the baby boomers begin retiring.

Three issues will remain top priorities for seniors: Social Security, Medicare, and health care (short- and long-term). Disagreements over the severity of fiscal shortfalls abound. Demographers and policy analysts have different perspectives on just about everything, including the basics: How many workers will be avail-

**Table 6.22**

**Time Voter Made Presidential Decision**

| 1996 Voters | 18-29 | 30-49 | 50-64 | 65+ |
|---|---|---|---|---|
| | % | % | % | % |
| Before 1996 | 34 | 37 | 48 | 48 |
| Before summer, during the primaries | 15 | 16 | 13 | 11 |
| During or after the Republican Conv. | 6 | 9 | 10 | 5 |
| During or after the Democratic Conv. | 1 | 1 | 1 | 1 |
| September, after the conventions | 22 | 12 | 11 | 11 |
| During or just after the Pres. debates | 4 | 4 | 1 | 3 |
| In the last week before the election | 7 | 7 | 5 | 6 |
| Over last week-end prior to Elec Day | 1 | 2 | 1 | 4 |
| On Monday (day before Elec Day) | 1 | 4 | 2 | 3 |
| On Election Day | 5 | 7 | 6 | 6 |
| Don't know/can't remember | 4 | 2 | 2 | 2 |

Note: *Respondents were asked: "When did you make up your mind definitely to vote for* _____ *?" The responses were aggregated.*

Source: *The Pew Research Center for the People & the Press, "Campaign '96 Gets Lower Grades from Voters." Washington, D.C.: author, November 15, 1996. From a telephone survey of sample of 1,102 registered voters 18 years of age or older conducted November 7-10, 1996. The sampling error is plus or minus 3 percentage points (at the 95% confidence level).*

able to support each Social Security and Medicare recipient? Will the bulk of the baby boomers retire early, or will they stay in the workforce longer than today's retirees? How much have the boomers really saved for their retirements? Will the boomers' enthusiasm for market-based solutions wane if the market tumbles? Will working-age Americans ever be willing to pay substantially more in taxes and insurance premiums to support entitlement programs?

For today's seniors, Social Security is a sacred cow. Even in the face of Social Security bankruptcy projections, few seniors are willing to substantially alter the program's structure by raising the eligibility age, permitting government to invest Social Security funds in the stock market, or reducing benefits. They adamantly oppose plans that would let individuals invest their own retirement funds in the

**Table 6.23**

**Helpfulness of the Presidential Debates: Declining
1992 v. 1996**

| Among Voters | 1992 | | | 1996 | | |
|---|---|---|---|---|---|---|
| | Helpful | Not helpful | Didn't Watch | Helpful | Not Helpful | Didn't Watch |
| **Age** | % | % | % | % | % | % |
| Under 30 | 81 | 16 | 3 | 50 | 47 | 4 |
| 30-49 | 73 | 21 | 6 | 39 | 48 | 12 |
| 50-64 | 64 | 32 | 5 | 34 | 48 | 16 |
| 65+ | 59 | 31 | 5 | 46 | 46 | 5 |

*Note: Respondents were asked: "How helpful were the presidential debates to you in deciding which candidates to vote for? Would you say they were very helpful, somewhat helpful, not too helpful, or not at all helpful?"*

*Source: The Pew Research Center for the People & the Press, "Campaign '96 Gets Lower Grades from Voters," Washington, D.C.: author, November 15, 1996. From a telephone survey of sample 1,102 registered voters 18 years of age or older conducted November 7-10, 1996. The sampling error is plus or minus 3 percentage points (at the 95% confidence level).*

market. But when the boomers begin retiring, opposition may soften because boomers more readily embrace market-based options.

Medicare, considered a life-or-death program by many elderly, is widely criticized for what it does *not* cover—particularly prescription drugs and long-term health care. It is too soon to say definitively whether the new Medicare+Choice plan will effectively reduce costs. Most Americans, including seniors, do not understand their options. Nor do they fully comprehend the basics of the Medicare program—who is eligible, which services are covered, and how services are paid for.

Some analysts are convinced the Medicare program must be restructured considerably to save it for the next generation of retirees. But when major reforms are put before the public, they receive only a lukewarm reception once citizens are informed of the costs. The vast majority of Americans, especially working-age adults, favor expanding the program to include long-term care and prescription drugs. The bad news is that they oppose higher co-payments. The good news is that younger Americans, including the baby boomers, are more open to drastic changes in the program to reduce costs, such as raising the eligibility age.

A far greater consensus exists on the degree of fraud, waste, and abuse in the Medicare program. Seniors are the most adamant that the current program is heavily abused by doctors, hospitals, and beneficiaries themselves and is poorly run by the government.

Many seniors are frustrated with ever-rising out-of-pocket health care expenses. High deductibles and cost-sharing requirements of the Medicare program and out-of-pocket expenses for prescriptions squeeze the finances of many seniors, especially the poorer ones. However, the lowest-income Medicare beneficiaries do receive help from the Medicaid program, although benefits vary considerably from state to state.

Because most seniors have not planned for long-term care and are unaware that other types of housing for seniors are available, most migrate to nursing homes when they can no longer live at home. Residing in a nursing home can quickly exhaust one's savings or assets, which means many seniors move onto the Medicaid rolls. Nearly two out of three families end up relying on Medicaid to pay nursing homes, putting a tremendous strain on state budgets. Attempts at cost control, such as home- and community-based care, often get lost in the deep divide of intergovernmental relations. But the concepts remain quite popular with the public at-large.

Public opinions on health care issues fluctuate considerably, depending upon the state of the economy, changes in corporate and government benefits packages, and pressures from various actors in the health care system (e.g., physicians, hospitals, insurance companies, average citizens). The opinion pendulum swings from concern about access, to cost, to quality, and back again. By the end of the 1990s, the biggest concern was access. But concerns about cost could quickly surface if Medicare and Medicaid are expanded. Quality issues, too, will get more attention as more seniors face the realities of managed care and/or affordable long-term care.

Health maintenance organizations (HMOs) and managed care plans are constantly under attack by some seniors. They are upset that they must wait longer to see a doctor, often cannot choose the doctor they wish to see, are limited in their access to specialists, and subject to limits on their length of stay in a hospital. Long-term care, especially skilled-nursing, facilities are also criticized for their neglect and abuse of residents.

"Gray" crimes will surely increase in the new millennium. The types of elder crimes most likely to escalate are physical and mental abuse of the elderly by relatives and other caregivers, consumer fraud, and age and disability discrimination (especially at the workplace). Seniors will also be at the center of class-action suits against various industries—tobacco, alcohol, food, and pharmaceutical—seeking compensation for a diminished quality of life brought about by use of their various products.

The ratio of caregivers-to-elders is projected to shrink substantially in the near future. Individuals, families, and businesses will all be affected somewhat negatively. The incidence of caregiver fraud and abuse, inflicted by children and friends, guardians, even institutional personnel, is already on the rise.

New concerns are surfacing about staffing policies and training procedures in nursing home and other congregate-care facilities. States will need to strengthen their inspections and prosecutions to protect America's most helpless seniors.

We can expect a rewriting of tax laws in the twenty-first century. Boomers will likely push hard for changes in the laws dealing with pensions, savings, capital gains, and estates. The changes will all be aimed at promoting, rather than deterring, personal savings and investments. Tomorrow's retirees will rely more on income from private savings, IRAs, and 401(k) or 403(b) plans, and less on Social Security. Any attempts to raise taxes on these private-sector-based revenues will face serious opposition from this "pig in the python" group.

Today's retirees are more likely to oppose new or higher state and local taxes than federal taxes. They benefit more directly from the huge entitlement programs funded by the federal government (Social Security, Medicare).

Changing demographics will force alterations in education policy. Seniors will continue to vote against many school tax and bond referenda if the current educational system doesn't improve. Exit polls show that seniors vote against these measures because they do not want to pump more money into a broken system.

The education community is in the midst of rethinking old policies about restricting citizens' after-hour use of school grounds and facilities. Upwards of two-thirds of all voters do not have children in school, nor have they been on any school grounds in years. Thus, administrators are rushing to establish programs that bring seniors back to K-12 settings (as volunteers, mentors, and tutors, for example). Projected teacher shortages are prompting states to reexamine teacher certification requirements, in anticipation of hiring retirees to teach in the classroom. Many colleges and universities are investigating the possibility of building retirement communities for their alumni. They envision the senior centers as living laboratories for their current students and benefactors for future generations.

What about moral and social issues? New forms of individual expression and lifestyles always seem to provoke intergenerational debates. By the close of the twentieth century, abortion, gay and lesbian rights, gun control, and unrestricted Internet "speech" sparked the greatest differences. But for the most part, the differences were in degree rather than direction. During the 1980s and 1990s, age-group differences on gender roles, racial equality, and environmental policy narrowed. The new moral battles of the twenty-first century will be about health and privacy issues—prioritization (rationing) of health care, disease research, organ donation recipients, along with euthanasia, nontraditional healing, and the privacy and security of one's medical records.

In foreign policy, national security is the top concern of today's retirees. Drug trafficking, international terrorism, and foreign dictators rank among the problems they feel need the most attention. The next generation of seniors (ages 50–64) has more interest in protecting America's place in the global economy. Younger citizens rank health, environmental, and human rights concerns ahead of security or economic concerns. All age groups agree that the national government should continue to play a major role in mounting a strong defense. Health care issues are destined to gain prominence as veterans age and more attention is focused on the impacts—physical and mental—of exposure to chemicals or biological germs early in their military careers.

Among domestic issues, transportation will create increasing concern. In the normal course of aging, an individual's vision, reflex time, physical strength, and memory may decline somewhat. Until recently, seniors have strongly resisted any state-level efforts to require more frequent driver's tests or shorter licensing periods for them. But safety concerns are starting to trump age-discrimination complaints, even among older drivers. The challenge will be to find accessible alternative forms of transportation for seniors as they give up their car keys. Paratransit may be more viable and cost-effective than traditional mass transit (buses, light rail, subways). The question of "who pays?" looms large in the early 2000s.

While older Americans are frustrated with government, politicians, the news media, political parties, and special interest groups, they are not ready to bow out of the political process. Older voters are the most likely to care who wins the presidency and to see differences between the two major political parties. They also want to know a lot about candidates from childhood to adulthood (issue stances, personal attributes, and character). But presidential candidates who want to win their votes have to start early because seniors make up their minds more quickly than other age groups.

# 7

+

# Targeting Seniors
# in the Twenty-First Century:

## *A Review of Some Basic Dos and Don'ts*

*Photo 7.1   Targeting senior voters in the twenty-first century will be challenging. Seniors will be more diverse—politically, economically, and health-wise.*

Science demonstrates that genes account for only about 50% of the aging
process. Change in lifestyle can tip the odds in favor of a longer, healthier,
more productive life. Just how long and healthy is still open for debate. How
soon will we be 90 and feel and look like we are 40? Is such a day really on
the horizon?

Andrew Olivastro, *IntellectualCapital.com*, Sept. 9, 1999

Targeting seniors will be a critical element of virtually every campaign's strategic plan in the twenty-first century. Candidates and political parties will continue to salivate over this fast-growing, high turnout group of voters.

Candidates committed to targeting senior voters must obtain a clear picture
of precisely who *are* these older constituents. This analysis needs to include the
following:

- The type of community in which most seniors live (age-segregated or age-integrated).
- Where seniors reside (mobile home parks, condominiums, townhomes, assisted-living facilities, nursing homes, apartments, single-family dwellings).
- Voter registration patterns (Democrat, Republican, third parties, independents).
- Age profile ("young-old" versus "old-old").
- Socioeconomic status (income; education; race/ethnicity; retirement status).
- Gender ratio (females-to-males).
- Health and disability status.
- TV and radio stations/programs with larger senior audiences.
- Professional organizations with large senior memberships and/or active local organizations (e.g., AARP, veterans' groups).

Aiming for twenty-first century seniors will be more challenging than in the
past. As a group, they will be less homogeneous, particularly as the baby boomers
reach retirement age. The boomer generation is considerably more diverse in its
demographic, socioeconomic, and political composition than today's senior population. In fact, the definition of "senior" will itself become mushier and likely
will vary issue by issue. An individual's health status will increasingly be a key
determinant of whether he or she is considered "old" or "elderly."

While the average senior can expect to live longer, the number who will
experience some type of chronic health problem (sight, hearing, mobility) will
increase. Political candidates who want to win must figure out better ways to
engage seniors with such disabilities. It is foolish to write off their votes at a
time when politics is becoming more partisan-competitive throughout the
United States.

# TIPS ON SURVEYING SENIOR VOTERS: LESSONS FOR PHONE INTERVIEWERS AND FOCUS GROUP MODERATORS

Listening to senior voices on everything from advertising formats to issues is a much more scientific endeavor than it used to be. Telephone surveys, focus groups, and in-person interviews are designed, conducted, and analyzed by professional market researchers and pollsters, more than by the candidates themselves or political parties.

Some firms are more attuned to the special needs of seniors than others and have been more successful at tapping into their opinions. Step one is to identify who is a "senior." The answer to this question is contextual—it varies from issue to issue, community to community, and across generations and databases.

Survey firms need to break down their data by a larger number of age categories. Typically, politically oriented polling firms have used four or five age breaks, while marketing firms have tended to use more. Narrower age categories, when analyzed over time, may help political firms to detect shifts in opinions driven by generational replacement a bit earlier.

## Telephone Interviews: Training of Interviewers Is Critical

Many survey firms need to strengthen their training of telephone interviewers who seek seniors' opinions. Firms that already do this advise interviewers to do the following:

Let the phone ring seven or more times; give seniors time to get there.
Speak more slowly and clearly; repeat the question and response options more often, but use slightly different words so as not to insult them.
Keep a low pitch to one's voice; don't shout.
Inform seniors it is *not* a solicitation call.
Use seniors to talk to seniors.
Be courteous and respectful; rudeness is particularly repulsive for seniors.
Be sensitive to the special concerns of older females (titles; suspicions and fears; gender bias).
Maintain control of the interview; stay on track.
Allow longer time for an interview.
Offer to call back if the respondent appears to be tiring.
Be prepared to offer a mail survey as an alternative for the hard-of-hearing or sight-impaired respondent.
Just hang up if the interview becomes problematic.

To date, less than one-third of the major survey firms acknowledge they do anything specific in surveying people with disabilities. Most acknowledge they simply end the interview (especially when they encounter hearing-impaired individuals) and drop these people out of the survey. But this is not a particularly wise strategy, especially as the number of persons with hearing problems increases.

### In-Person Interviews, Focus Groups

Politically oriented focus groups generally involve eight to twelve persons brought together to discuss a particular issue, candidate, or advertisement. They play a critical role in testing messages and devising campaign slogans, platforms, and advertisements. More attention must be paid to accessibility, facilities, time of day, food, and transportation when planning and conducting focus groups consisting of seniors.

Experienced firms suggest the following:

When first contacting a potential participant, use a trained interviewer to listen for coherency.

Choose accessible locations closer to where the participants live; wheelchair accessibility at the site is critical.

Select first-floor locations (or easy elevator access).

Choose facilities that are close to the parking lot and restrooms; make sure there is plenty of handicapped parking.

Provide transportation for those who need it; personal pick-ups or taxis are preferable to buses.

Hold sessions at convenient times; schedule mid-morning to early afternoon; avoid times of day when traffic is worst.

Be more sensitive to safety concerns of the participants.

Give clear, simple directions to the location.

Make reminder calls and send letters several times before the session.

Include instructions to bring eyeglasses or hearing aids.

Conduct shorter sessions.

Make print on handouts and charts big and bold.

Mix colors and shapes on charts; don't use highlighters.

Use fewer words in written materials.

Avoid high tech jargon.

Avoid using electronic or computer-based response mechanisms that intimidate many seniors. (This will be less of a problem in the future.)

Take frequent breaks.

Speak loudly and clearly; don't talk too fast.

Offer better food than you would to college students!

Use smaller groups than normal.

Select a moderator who has experience interacting with seniors.

Offer extra reassurance about how the results will be used; privacy is a key concern of seniors.

## TIPS FOR CAMPAIGN OUTREACH

Knowing where to find senior voters among one's constituents is a requisite to pitching a political message to them. Favorite spots identified by state and local candidates are civic clubs with older membership, senior citizen centers, and retirement communities. Nursing homes and assisted-living facilities are often bypassed by candidates. But this likely will change in the future as more seniors move into such facilities.

### Reaching Seniors in Nursing Homes, ALFs, and Other Closed Communities

Smart candidates know that not all residents of these facilities are frail and/or demented. Nor are they incapable of, or disinterested in, following politics. Attitudes of both candidates and nursing home/ALF administrators need to change. In the case of the latter, too many congregate-care facilities have policies that close the door to candidates running for office. Accustomed to protecting their residents from salespersons pushing products or services, administrators do not realize that they might be deterring democracy by treating candidates for office in the same way. These facilities, as well as other senior-oriented communities—mobile home parks, condominiums, and gated communities—need to rethink their policies if they want to make the most of their residents' political clout.

Some within the nursing home/ALF community *are* advocating more open-door policies. They would like to see campaigns brought to their facilities because most of their residents cannot go to campaign events—debates, candidate forums, and the like. Campaigns can be brought to these residents via the following:

Candidate visits.
Literature—large-print ads and brochures.
Candidate videos delivered to the facility.
Candidate forums or coffees held at the facility.
Candidate audio cassettes distributed to the visually impaired.
Video tapes of televised debates and candidate forums produced and delivered by TV stations (to show at a more convenient time than late night).
Candidate giveaways such as posters, bumper stickers, and buttons.

Shrewd candidates realize that an appearance at a nursing home or ALF has tremendous spillover effects. It signals a genuine concern about older voters to administrators, staff, family, friends, and advocates.

### Seniors, the Internet, and Multimedia Technology

Another strategy that will pay off for candidates and senior advocacy groups is to provide seniors with training on computers and the Internet. Just as seniors are more likely to follow politics via newspapers, magazines, television, and radio, they will likely do the same on the Internet.

Blind and visually impaired persons are the most in need but the least well-served by currently available multimedia technology. The ability of these individuals to follow politics via the electronic media is limited. TV and radio news programs typically pick just a few highly contested races to cover. Detailed coverage of ballot initiatives and down-ballot contests is seldom available.

Groups like the National Council on Disabilities are pushing hard for manufacturers to design multimedia machines that allow users to do the following:

Customize sizes and types of fonts.
Customize colors for fonts and backgrounds.
Customize interface timings.
Focus and enlarge parts of screens.
Have a keyboard alternative to a mouse.
Interface with speech programs.
Choose graphical images with video descriptions.
Have more accessible documentation.
Have aural and visual status messages.
Detect the presence and direction of hypertext links.
Have controls that can be operated without having to see them.

For the hearing-impaired, advocates are pressing for improvements to TTY phone systems, along with an expansion of closed captioning on television, especially on cable television.

## Campaign Literature: Direct Mail, Brochures, Door Hangers, Postcards

Campaign literature, usually arriving via the mailbox, is extremely important in educating seniors about lower- or down-ballot contests and ballot initiatives. In those contests, television ads are either too expensive or reach too broad an audience to be cost-effective.

But some seniors (approximately 15%) have trouble reading campaign literature. Word choice, message length, colors, individuals featured, layout, print font, paper texture and opaqueness, folding techniques, brochure size, and method of delivery make a difference.

Our research shows that candidates need to produce literature that is written simply, translated in different languages (when targeting senior immigrants), and printed in big, bold lettering.

Campaigns should avoid unusually folded brochures and stapled mail pieces because they are hard to open. Certain types of paper (mostly glossy paper and newsprint) are difficult for some seniors to handle. Several colors (blue, black, green, red) pose problems for a sizable portion of the senior audience.

Postcards and door hangers have limitations as well. The print on postcards is often too small to read. Door hangers anger some seniors who fear they attract burglars.

Candidates going door to door to deliver their literature often gain points with senior voters by simply offering to spend time reading the brochure or handout to them.

### Television Campaign Ads

Seniors pay close attention to anything political that appears on television—from regular news programs, to news magazine shows, to paid political advertisements. They often do not distinguish between paid and free air time, making it important for a candidate to appear in as many TV venues as possible.

When asked which features about television political ads they like best, many seniors say "positive" ones, with substance (platforms, promises, issue stances, candidate backgrounds, past voting records).

Ads that are highly repetitious are particularly annoying to seniors.

Short ads, especially 20-second spots, that have fast sound tracks and constantly repeat the same information are hard for some elderly to hear.

Candidates need to avoid running ads that are too loud, too fast, have lots of background music, or feature women's or children's voices (too high-pitched). Strong accents should be avoided in most cases.

Running ads exclusively around news programs on broadcast television stations is a myopic—and expensive—strategy. Successful candidates confess they have begun to run more political ads around popular non-news programs heavily watched by seniors (*Wheel of Fortune* and *Jeopardy*, for example). Cable television and radio, more easily targeted and cheaper, have become more attractive advertising venues as well.

### Campaigning among Disabled Senior Voters

Most candidates acknowledge that they encounter persons with disabilities in the course of their campaigns. Candidate forums, absentee voting assistance, and telephone surveys are, in their judgment, the best means to reach this audience. However, disabled seniors or those with disabled friends or relatives advocate other means—large-print ads and brochures, videos and audiotapes. In their judgment, health, mobility, and logistics make candidate forums a less pragmatic way to reach disabled seniors.

Candidates should seriously consider involving seniors in all phases of a campaign—from developing the messages to appearing in campaign literature, to selecting television programs around which political ads will be run. Seniors know best how they can be targeted!

## IMPROVING REGISTRATION AND VOTING PROCEDURES

America's senior citizens register and vote at considerably higher rates than other age groups. While most prefer to vote in person on election day, others cannot travel to the polling place to cast their ballots. Viable options to in-person voting include absentee balloting, early voting, mail-ballot elections, and, in the near future, the Internet. But whether registering or voting, a sizable number of seniors must rely on others to help them. Better safeguards need to be put in place.

### Improving the Registration Process

Most states have made registering to vote an easier task in recent years. Following passage of the National Voter Registration Act of 1993 (the "Motor Voter" Act), citizens may register at a wide variety of places or via postcard. For many seniors, however, certain aspects of the registration process need to be improved.

State legislators and local election officials should consider the following:

Adopting more proactive signature update programs (to prevent the voiding of an absentee ballot).

Increasing publicity about how to move one's registration in areas to which seniors move.

Re-examining automated answering systems; offer an option to "talk to a real person" at the *beginning* of the message, activated by voice.

Preparing and more widely distributing informational videos on how to register, change one's polling place, and otherwise participate in the political process.

Paying more attention to the accessibility of registration sites largely frequented by seniors (parking, paths of travel, signage, service animals, Braille availability, interpreters, listening devices, auxiliary aids and services).

Initiating more safeguards to lessen the likelihood of fraudulent registration information submitted by someone assisting the senior.

Placing registration materials in the offices of agencies that work with the disabled and making them more aware of their responsibility to offer voter registration to their clients under the National Voter Registration Act.

Dedicating toll-free TTY lines to registration-related activities; better publicizing their availability to citizens with hearing problems.

### Improving Get-Out-the-Vote Efforts

Almost everyone appreciates being reminded that an election is just around the corner. For some seniors, changing the way candidates and political parties present these reminders can make the difference in whether they vote and how they vote (in-person versus alternatives).

Historically, phone banks have been a critical GOTV effort. They have been proven more effective with older, rather than younger, voters. Typically, these GOTV phone bank efforts begin the Saturday before a Tuesday election. But this may be too late for some seniors, especially those who need to arrange for transportation or to receive an absentee ballot.

Postcard and door hanger reminders are also popular GOTV techniques. They can be particularly effective in informing a voter about a change in polling place location. But for some, the print on postcards is too small and cluttered. Door hangers have the same drawback, but also add stress to seniors who believe they invite burglary.

The mass media can help boost GOTV efforts in many areas. News stories and public service announcements are needed that call attention to registration book closings (cut-off dates), specific election dates, changes in precinct lines and voting locations, assistance available from the local election office, and contact numbers for advocacy groups interested in getting seniors to the polls. Seniors pay considerably more attention to political information presented in newspapers and on television than other age groups.

## Making Voting Easier and More Secure

Historically, voter turnout rates for seniors have far exceeded those of other age groups, although they start to decline somewhat among persons 75 and older. This tapering off of participation tracks closely with rising disability rates.

### Re-Examining Transportation Plans

Getting to the polls is a big obstacle for more seniors who no longer drive or are afraid to drive too far from home and in highly congested areas. Some popular transportation-related recommendations are the following:

Advocacy groups, with adequate liability insurance and accessible vehicles, should increase their efforts to provide transportation to the polls on election day.

More polling places should be located at facilities heavily frequented by, and familiar and accessible to, seniors—community senior centers, condo or townhome recreation centers, civic centers, libraries, and churches.

Create mobile polling place programs; use mobile vans staffed by election-office personnel to travel to nursing homes and ALFs to conduct voting at a specific time. Encourage civic groups, foundations, or private benefactors to donate mobile voting vans in the same way that they have donated mobile registration vans.

Expand and improve "curbside voting" programs that allow disabled persons to drive up to the polling place and have a ballot brought to them; develop better ways to secure ballot secrecy.

## Better Training for Election Officials, Poll Workers, Candidates, and Consultants

Poll workers need more and better training about how to deal with seniors with disabilities. Professional development organizations for election officials need to provide more workshops dealing with this issue. Advocacy group representatives should be invited to make presentations at such events.

New video materials need to be developed and made readily available to election offices, poll workers, candidates, and political consultants. These materials need to include discussions of the special problems encountered by persons with vision, hearing, mobility, communication, and/or dexterity limitations, as well as tips on how to effectively and courteously assist citizens experiencing such difficulties. (Review chapter 5.)

## Improving Balloting System Accessibility

Election officials should consider offering multiple types of ballot systems at the same polling location. (This may require legislative approval in some states.) Each of the five major systems (paper, mechanical lever machines, punch cards, Marksense [optical scan], and Direct Recording Electronic [DRE] systems) has limitations. For example, paper ballots may be printed in fonts that are too small or too light for elders to see. The height of mechanical lever machines, which cannot be adjusted, makes them difficult for those in wheelchairs. Punch cards create problems for seniors with dexterity and sight disabilities because font sizes on ballots are usually small, the stylus is difficult to grip, and aligning the ballot properly is a challenge. Optical scan systems cause a senior's vote to be voided if marks are too light or misplaced. DRE systems (touch screen) are intimidating to some seniors, although this problem is likely to diminish as this age group becomes more computer literate.

At a minimum, voting system manufacturers need to involve more seniors in their design and testing activities.

## Adopting Alternative Voting Arrangements

The three most common alternatives to in-person voting are absentee voting, mail-ballot elections, and early voting. (As previously noted, Internet voting is likely to become a fourth.)

Seniors have always taken greater advantage of absentee balloting than other age groups. Candidates know this and have made it a vital part of their campaign strategy to help seniors secure, complete, and mail absentee ballots. Sometimes this tactic can be perceived by seniors as overly aggressive and, thus, offensive. Candidates and political parties should be aware that when seniors request an absentee ballot from an election official, they do not appreciate being sent another one, along with partisan campaign literature, from a candidate or party.

Unfortunately, absentee balloting sometimes invites fraudulent activities by those who would steal or manipulate votes. To stem this growing problem, especially among nursing home residents, election officials need to develop better techniques for verifying witness signatures. Another safeguard is to give more responsibility to election officials—and less to individuals—in conducting absentee balloting.

Mail-ballot voting poses similar concerns about the potential for fraud. Specifically, someone may alter the senior's choices on the ballot before dropping it in the mail. One recommendation, although not cheap, is to enclose a pre-addressed, stamped return envelope with the ballot to reduce the senior's reliance upon a third party.

Another concern, based upon the tendency of seniors to cast their votes earlier than others, is that candidates will run two separate campaigns—an early one targeted to seniors, and a late one to others, possibly with counter promises. Such a scenario would put seniors at a disadvantage because they would not be able to "correct" their vote choice.

Early voting is highly appealing to seniors, the disabled, and election officials. It allows people to vote at a more convenient time, when the polling place is less congested and when election officials have more time to offer assistance. However, early voting poses the same drawback as mail balloting—namely, the possibility that candidates will run two different campaigns. At any rate, states considering the early voting option need to remember that when polling places are well-frequented, socially familiar locations, the number of citizens who choose to vote early increases.

Internet voting, a method rapidly gaining attention, must overcome one significant hurdle: citizen concerns about ballot tampering. Seniors are more skeptical of "virtual voting" than other age groups for two reasons—fear of fraud and a concern about the loss of community that one feels when voting in person. Candidates and parties who advocate Internet voting need to address these concerns. They also need to urge multimedia manufacturers to make computers that are more accessible and user friendly for sight- and hearing-impaired individuals.


## A PARTING LOOK AT AMERICANS' VIEWS OF THE FUTURE: THE NATION, GOVERNMENT, AND LONGER LIVES

Regardless of the political challenges confronting an aging nation, the vast majority of all age groups of Americans remain optimistic about the future of the United

States over the next fifty years. (See figure 7.1.) Most believe that government will be as or more important in the twenty-first century than in the twentieth. (See figure 7.2.)

For all their optimism about government, Americans look with skepticism at the prospect of ever-increasing life spans. Although medical and technological advances have prolonged life and softened the dreaded effects of aging, many Americans harbor real concerns about living "too long." When asked whether they would like to live another 100 years—to the twenty-second century—the majority of all age groups say "No." (See figure 7.3.)

Inherent in this concern is the uncertainty about what the years will do to the body and the mind—the failing eyesight, the stiffening bones, the slowing of mental functioning. Most Americans anticipate that at some point in their lives they will need assistance in getting around and carrying out the basic activities of living. Those needing assistance will multiply as the baby boomers enter their twilight years. In anticipation of that time, we need to forge ahead in our efforts to keep democracy accessible to them and future generations.

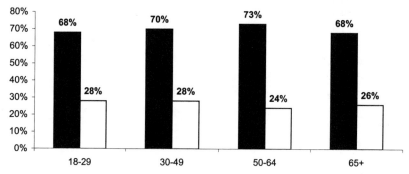

*Figure 7.1*   *Percentage of People by Age Group Who Are Optimistic and Pessimistic about the U.S. in the Next 50 Years*
*Source: The Pew Research Center for the People & the Press. Telephone survey of a random sample of 1,546 adults, 18 years of age or older, conducted April 6–May 6, 1999. The margin sampling error is +/- 3 percent.*

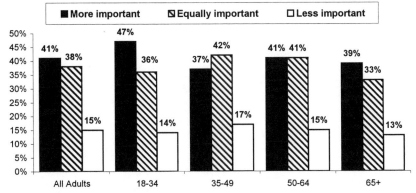

Figure 7.2   *Importance of Government in the Twenty-First Century*
Source: *The Council for Excellence in Government, 1999 poll of 1,214 adults, conducted May 21–June 1 by the firms of Peter Hart and Robert Teeter, margin of error +/– 3.2 percent. Used with permission.*

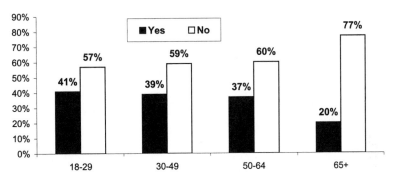

Figure 7.3   *Would You Like to Live Another 100 Years?*
Note: *Respondents were asked: "If it were possible, would you like to live to the twenty-second century—that is another 100 years—or do you think you would prefer not to?"*
Source: *The Pew Research Center for the People & the Press. Telephone survey of a random sample of 1,546 adults, 18 years of age or older, conducted April 6–May 6, 1999. The margin sampling error is +/- 3 percent.*

# Appendix A

# Relevant Federal Laws and Applicable Guidelines/Standards

Five federal statutes pertain to the accessibility of the election process to persons with disabilities. These laws work together to ensure that all persons with disabilities, young and old, can enter a facility, cast their vote, and exit the polling place along with their fellow citizens. The following federal laws apply to all State and local jurisdictions:

## THE VOTING RIGHTS ACT OF 1965 (42 U.S.C. 1973aa-6)

The Voting Rights Act of 1965 was originally designed to protect and facilitate the voting rights of racial minority groups. Subsequent amendments have, however, expanded it to include other minority groups as well as more general matters regarding voting qualifications and procedures. Section 208 of that Act applies to all elections in all jurisdictions and reads in its entirety:

"Any voter who requires assistance to vote by reason of blindness, disability, or inability to read or write may be given assistance by a person of the voter's choice, other than the voter's employer or agent of that employer or agent of the voter's union."

This provision supersedes any incompatible State law that may restrict the number of voters a person may assist or that may place restrictions, such as on children, on who may enter a polling booth with a voter requiring assistance. It does not, however, preclude obtaining a signed and sworn affidavit from any person providing voter assistance.

## THE REHABILITATION ACT OF 1973 (29 U.S.C. 791 et seq)

Section 504 of the Rehabilitation Act of 1973 requires recipients of federal funds to make their programs and activities accessible to persons with disabilities. Included are both private and public entities. State and local governments that receive some type of federal funding, such as Community Development Block Grants, are considered to be covered by Section 504.

The accepted standards for newly constructed or altered facilities under Section 504 are the Uniform Federal Accessibility Standards (UFAS) issued jointly by the General Services Administration, Department of Housing and Urban Development, Department of Defense, and the U.S. Postal Service.

## THE VOTING ACCESSIBILITY FOR THE ELDERLY AND HANDICAPPED ACT OF 1984 (42 U.S.C.1973ee THROUGH 1973ee-6)

The Voting Accessibility for the Elderly and Handicapped Act (VAA) of 1984 contains provisions expressly intended to "promote the fundamental right to vote by improving access for handicapped and elderly individuals to registration facilities and polling places for Federal elections." Key provisions require:

- that each political subdivision responsible for conducting elections within each State assure that all polling places for federal elections are accessible to elderly and handicapped voters *except* in the case of an emergency as determined by the State's chief election officer or *unless* the State's chief election officer
  - determines, by surveying all potential polling places, that no such place in the area is accessible nor can be made temporarily accessible, *and*
  - assures that any handicapped voter assigned to an inaccessible polling place will, upon advanced request under established State procedures, either be assigned to an accessible polling place or be provided an alternative means of casting a ballot on election day.
- that each State or political subdivision responsible for voter registration for federal elections provide a reasonable number of accessible permanent registration facilities *unless* the State has in effect a system which provides potential voters an opportunity to register by mail or at their residence.
- that each State make available to handicapped and elderly individuals registration and voting aids for federal elections *including* large-type instructions conspicuously displayed in every permanent registration facility and polling place *and* information by telecommunication devices for the deaf (TDD's).
- the elimination of any notarization or medical certification requirement for handicapped voters to obtain (or apply for) an absentee ballot *except* for medical certifications required to establish eligibility, under State law, for

automatically receiving such an application or ballot on a continuing basis *or* for applying for an absentee ballot after the deadline has passed.

- that each State's chief election officer provide public notice, calculated to reach elderly and handicapped voters, of the availability
  - of the registration and voting aids required above
  - of the voter assistance provisions under Section 208 of the Voting Rights Act of 1965, *and*
  - of the procedures for voting by absentee ballot not later than general public notice of registration and voting is provided.

Although it was not the intent of this Act to impose any national standard of accessibility, the chairman of the House Subcommittee on Elections (in Hearings conducted in 1987) asked the Federal Election Commission to explore ways of achieving a greater commonality of approach in the various States. Accordingly, the FEC's National Clearinghouse on Election Administration joined with the National Association of Secretaries of State and the Coalition for Voter Accessibility in an effort to devise a polling place evaluation and reporting form which might be adopted voluntarily by the States. This form was designed to be comprehensive, flexible enough to accommodate variations in individual States specifications, yet fairly easy to complete.

## THE AMERICANS WITH DISABILITIES ACT OF 1990 (42 U.S.C.)

Title II of the Americans with Disabilities Act (ADA) prohibits discrimination by State or local entities in any of its services, programs, or activities—including the election process. State and local election entities are thereby obliged to ensure the accessibility of the election process by qualified persons with disabilities.

The applicable standards for assessing public facilities under this Act are either the Uniform Federal Accessibility Standards (UFAS) or the Americans with Disability Accessibility Guidelines/ADA Standards for Accessible Design (ADAAG).

## A NOTE ON THE RELATIONSHIP OF THE VOTING ACCESSIBILITY FOR THE ELDERLY AND HANDICAPPED ACT TO THE AMERICANS WITH DISABILITIES ACT

A number of State and local election officials were concerned in 1993 about the impact of the Americans with Disabilities Act on their efforts to comply with the Voting Accessibility for the Elderly and Handicapped Act of 1984. For although there are no direct statutory linkages between the Acts, they both address the same subject.

Indeed, the House Subcommittee on Elections, in their 1991 Hearings on the VAA requested the Federal Election Commission's understanding of the relationship between the two Acts.

## THE NATIONAL VOTER REGISTRATION
## ACT OF 1993 (42 U.S.C. 1973gg)

This Act applies to all federal elections in all States except Idaho, Minnesota, New Hampshire, North Dakota, Wisconsin, and Wyoming which are exempted by 42 U.S.C. 1973gg-2 as amended. In all other States, this Act, among many other things:

- requires that individuals be given an opportunity to register by mail using either a State mail voter registration form or the national mail voter registration form
- requires that individuals be given an opportunity to register to vote (or to update their voter registration data) when applying for or renewing a driver's license or other personal indentification document issued by a State  motor vehicle authority
- requires that individuals be given the opportunity to register to vote (or to change their voter registration address) when applying for services or assistance
    - at any office in the State that provides public assistance including, but not limited to, the Food Stamp program; the Medicaid program; the Special Supplemental Food Program for Women, Infants, and Children (WIC) program; and the Aid to Families with Dependent Children (AFDC) program;
    - at other offices designated by the State;
    - at Armed Forces recruitment offices;
    and most important for the purposes of this volume
    - at or through any office in the State that provides State funded programs primarily engaged in providing services to persons with disabilities.

Local election officials should consult their chief State election official to learn which agencies within their State have been designated as voter registration facilities.

*Source:* Federal Election Commission, "Ensuring the Accessibility of the Election Process: Innovations in Election Administration," vol. 15, Washington, D.C.: Office of Election Administration, Federal Election Commission, August 1996.

# Appendix B

# Florida Statute: Absentee Balloting in Nursing Homes and ALFs

## 101.655 SUPERVISED VOTING BY ABSENT ELECTORS IN CERTAIN FACILITIES

(1) The supervisor of elections of a county shall provide supervised voting for absent electors residing in any assisted living facility, as defined in s. 400.402, or nursing home facility, as defined in s. 400.021, within that county at the request of any administrator of such a facility. Such request for supervised voting in the facility shall be made by submitting a written request to the supervisor of elections no later than 21 days prior to the election for which that request is submitted. The request shall specify the name and address of the facility and the name of the electors who wish to vote absentee in that election. If the request contains the names of fewer than five voters, the supervisor of elections is not required to provide supervised voting.

(2) The supervisor of elections may, in the absence of a request from the administrator of a facility, provide for supervised voting in the facility for those persons who have requested absentee ballots. The supervisor of elections shall notify the administrator of the facility that supervised voting will occur.

(3) The supervisor of elections shall, in cooperation with the administrator of the facility, select a date and time when the supervised voting will occur.

(4) The supervisor of elections shall designate supervised voting teams to provide the services prescribed by this section. Each supervised voting team shall include at least two persons. Each supervised voting team must include representatives of more than one political party; however, in any

primary election to nominate party nominees in which only one party has candidates appearing on the ballot, all supervised voting team members may be of that party. No candidate may provide supervised voting services.

(5) The supervised voting team shall deliver the ballots to the respective absent electors, and each member of the team shall jointly supervise the voting of the ballots. If any elector requests assistance in voting, the oath prescribed in s. 101.051 shall be completed and the elector may receive the assistance of two members of the supervised voting team or some other person of the elector's choice to assist the elector in casting the elector's ballot.

(6) Before providing assistance, the supervised voting team shall disclose to the elector that the ballot may be retained to vote at a later time and that the elector has the right to seek assistance in voting from some other person of the elector's choice without the presence of the supervised voting team.

(7) If any elector declines to vote a ballot or is unable to vote a ballot, the supervised voting team shall mark the ballot "refused to vote" or "unable to vote."

(8) After the ballots have been voted or marked in accordance with the provisions of this section, the supervised voting team shall deliver the ballots to the supervisor of elections, who shall retain them pursuant to s. 101.67.

# Notes

## CHAPTER 1

1. Ken Dychtwald, *Age Power: How the 21st Century Will Be Ruled by the New Old* (New York: Jeremy P. Tarcher/Putnam, 1999), 208.

2. Peter G. Peterson, *Gray Dawn* (New York: Times Books, Random House, 1999): 208.

3. The Council on Excellence in Government, *America Unplugged: Citizens and Their Government*: 3. Nationwide survey of 1,124 adults conducted between May 21 and June 1, 1999 by Peter D. Hart and Robert Teeter for the Council.

4. Quoted in Robin Toner, "Parties Watch Older Voters Shift to Right," *New York Times*, reprinted in *Ledger*, June 1, 1999.

5. Voter News Service, used with permission.

6. Some define the "near elderly" as 55 to 64.

7. "Old-old" is often defined as 85 and older, although in the future, some demographers are projecting it will be defined as 90 and older. Still others refer to centenarians, those 100 and older, as the "old-old."

## CHAPTER 2

1. U.S. Bureau of the Census, *Sixty-Five Plus in the United States: A Statistical Brief*, May 1995.

2. Alliance for Aging Research, "Independence for Older Americans: An Investment for Our Nation's Future," 1999, <http://www.agingresearch.org/Resources/brochures/indep.htm>.

3. U.S. Census Bureau, "New Census Report Shows Exponential Growth in Number of Centenarians," June 16, 1999.

4. Peter G. Peterson, "The Graying of the Developed Economies," *IntellectualCapital.com*. 4 (September 9–16, 1999).

5. Ken Dychtwald, *Age Power: How the 21st Century Will Be Ruled by the New Old* (New York: Jeremy P. Tarcher/Putnam, 1999): 1.

6. Frank B. Hobbs, *65+ in the United States*. Washington, D.C.: U.S. Department of Commerce, Bureau of the Census and U.S. Department of Health and Human Services, National Institute on Aging: 3–1.

7. Andrew Olivastro, "Issue of the Week: The New Elderly," *IntellectualCapital.com* 4 no. 36 (September 9–16, 1999).

8. U.S. Bureau of the Census, *Statistical Abstract of the United States 1997*: 9.

9. Bureau of the Census, *Statistical Brief: Sixty-Five Plus in the United States,* May 1995.

10. Bureau of the Census, *Statistical Brief*.

11. Hispanic origin may be of any race. Bureau of the Census, *Statistical Brief,* 2:14–15.

12. However, the life expectancies of any Asian women living in Hawaii and Puerto Rican women (living in Puerto Rico) exceed that of white women. Hispanic women have a longer life expectancy (more than 77 years) than either black American or American Indian/Alaska Native women (both more than 74 years). From the National Women's Health Information Center *Women of Color Health Data Book*, <http://www.4woman.org/owh/pub/woc/figure1.htm>.

13. Susan A. MacManus, "Retiree Recruitment: How Florida's Burgeoning Senior Population Is Transforming State and Local Politics," *Responses to an Aging Florida,* Fall 1998.

14. Voter News Service. Used with permission.

15. Susan A. MacManus, "The Widening Gap between Florida's Schools and Their Communities: Taxes and a Changing Age Profile." Tallahassee, Fla.: *The James Madison Institute Backgrounder,* February 1996.

16. Typical illnesses striking older age groups are arthritis, diabetes, osteoporosis, and senile dementia. Bureau of the Census, *Statistical Brief: Sixty-Five Plus in the United States,* May 1995.

17. Alliance for Aging Research, "Independence for Older Americans."

18. National Institute on Aging, "Age Page: Hearing and Older People," <http://www.nih.gov/nia/health/pubpub/hearing.htm>.

19. National Center for Health Statistics, Centers for Disease Control, *Disability Among Older People: United States and Canada,* March 1995: 11.

## CHAPTER 3

1. Mail survey of candidates for state legislative seats and cabinet posts conducted by the author in December 1998; funded by the University of South Florida Institute on Aging.

2. A national telephone survey of 103 political pollsters and market research firms listed on the Web site of *Campaigns & Elections* magazine. It was conducted by the author in September–October 1999.

3. See, for example, Mohamed Abdel-Ghany and Deanna L. Sharpe, "Consumption Patterns among the Young-Old and Old-Old," *Journal of Consumer Affairs* 31 (Summer 1997): 90–112.

4. See Celinda Lake, "Contours of the Senior Electorate," *The Polling Report* 15 (September 20, 1999): 1, 7.

5. For an example of the changing profile of older Americans, see Sharon Yntema, ed., *Americans 55 & Older: A Changing Market* (Ithaca, N.Y.: New Strategist Publications, 1997).

6. For an example of research focusing on the role of senior discounts in advertising, see Ellen Day and Marla Royne Stafford, "Age-Related Cues in Retail Services Advertising: Their Effects on Younger Consumers," *Journal of Retailing* 73, no. 2 (1997): 211–233.

7. Frank Conaway, "Segmenting Will Unleash Mature Market Potential," *Public Relations Journal* 47, no. 5 (May 1991): 18–20.

8. George P. Moschis, "Life Stages of the Mature Market," *American Demographics* 18, no. 9 (September 1996): 44–45.

9. Cheryl Russell, "Baby Boom Turns 50," *American Demographics* 17 (December 1997): 22–33. Quote is from a review of this article from the AARP Research Center's Web site AgeLine <http://research.aarp.org>, "Marketing to Adults 50 and Over, A Bibliography with Abstracts."

10. John Rowe and Robert L. Kahn, *Successful Aging* (New York: Pantheon Books, 1998).

11. Carter, Henderson, "Today's Affluent Oldsters: Marketers See Gold in Gray," *The Futurist* 32, no. 8 (November 1998): 19–24.

12. Quoted in Monika, Guttman, "Facing the Facts of Life: Marketers Find New Ways of Appealing to Gradually Graying Baby Boomers," *U.S. News & World Report* 120, no. 16 (April 22, 1996): 57–59.

13. Nursing study reported in "Older Adults as Customers," *Caring for an Aging Population* (Larchmont, N.Y.: Vericom, Inc., 1999), 21–22.

14. Sandra Timmermann, director of MetLife Mature Market Institute, as quoted in "Older Adults as Customers," *Caring for an Aging Population*.

15. Marilyn Moats Kennedy, founder of Career Strategies consulting firm, as quoted in "Older Adults as Customers," *Caring for an Aging Population*.

16. Scott Walker, "How to Conduct a $10,000 Focus Group for Less Than a Grand," in *The Road to Victory 2000: The Complete Guide to Winning Political Campaigns—Local, State and Federal*, 2nd ed., ed. Ron Faucheux (Dubuque, Iowa: Kendall/Hunt Publishing Co., 1998), 120–124.

17. Louis M. Rea and Richard A. Parker, *Designing and Conducting Survey Research: A Comprehensive Guide*, 2nd ed. (San Francisco, Calif.: Jossey-Bass Publishers, 1997), Chapter 5.

18. For good discussions of focus groups, see David W. Stewart and Prem N. Shamdasani, *Focus Groups: Theory and Practice*, Applied Social Research Methods Series, 20 (Newbury Park, Calif.: SAGE Publications, 1990); Richard A. Krueger, *Focus Groups: A Practical Guide for Applied Research*, 2nd ed. (Thousand Oaks, Calif.: SAGE Publications, 1994).

19. For excellent discussions of the mechanics of targeting, see Murray Fishel, "Electoral Targeting, Part I, Do-it-Yourself" and "Electoral Targeting, Part II, Analyzing the Data"; Wayne C. Johnson, "Targeting Voters Without Boosting Your Negatives"; Mark Gersh, "The Key to Effective Targeting"; Robert Blaemire, "Targeting Your Message" in *The Road to Victory 2000*, Chapter 4.

## CHAPTER 4

1. Ron Faucheux, "Hitting the Bull's Eye," *Campaigns & Elections* (July 1999): 20.

2. Center for Congressional and Presidential Studies, "Are Political Consultants Hurting or Helping Democracy? Who They Are, How They Evaluate the Process of Electing Candidates and What They Reveal about Their Ethical Practices" (Washington, D.C.: American University, June 1999).

3. Mail survey of nursing home and assisted-living facilities activity directors in three Florida counties: Hillsborough (13% 65+ population), Pasco (32.3%), and Pinellas (24.9%). Lists of facilities obtained from county supervisors of elections. Survey conducted by the author, December 1998; response rate 36% (76 of 210).

4. Mail survey by the author of Florida supervisors of elections, conducted September 1999. Response rate 90% (60 out of 67).

5. See Gary W. Selnow, *Electronic Whistle-Stops: The Impact of the Internet on American Politics* (Westport, Conn.: Praeger, 1998); Shannon E. Martin and Kathleen A. Hansen, *Newspapers of Record in a Digital Age: From Hot Type to Hot Link* (Westport, Conn.: Praeger, 1998).

6. National Council on Disability, *Access to Multimedia Technology by People with Sensory Disabilities* (Washington, D.C.: March 13, 1998).

7. National Council on Disability, *Access to Multimedia Technology*: 26–27.

8. National Council on Disability, *Access to Multimedia Technology*: 21.

9. National Council on Disability, *Access to Multimedia Technology*: 22.

10. Telephone interviews conducted under the direction of Princeton Survey Research Associates for the Pew Research Center for the People & the Press, Nov. 6–10, 1998. It is based on a nationwide sample of 1,005 adults, 18 years of age or older. The sampling error (at the 95% confidence level) is plus or minus 4.5 percentage points.

11. The breakdowns by age group of those who said they did not learn enough from the campaign were 18 to 29, 50%; 30 to 49, 38%; 50 to 64, 31%.

12. Telephone survey conducted by Princeton Survey Research Associates for the Pew Research Center for the People & the Press, Feb. 18–21, 1999. The sampling error for the 1,293 adults is plus or minus 3 percentage points (95% confidence level).

13. Telephone survey conducted by Princeton Survey Research Associates for The Pew Research Center, Feb. 18–21, 1999.

14. Mary Anne Moffitt, *Campaign Strategies and Message Design: A Practitioner's Guide from Start to Finish* (Westport, Conn.: Praeger, 1999): 140.

15. Dave Gold and Tony Marsh, "How to Move Votes Through the Mail," in *The Road to Victory 2000: The Complete Guide to Winning Political Campaigns—Local, State and Federal*, 2nd ed., Ron Faucheux (Dubuque, Iowa: Kendall/Hunt Publishing Co., 1998), 305.

16. Gold and March, "How to Move Votes," 308.

17. Richard Schlackman and Michael Hoffman, "Targeted Direct Mail," in *The Road to Victory 2000*: 312.

18. Robert E. Denton, Jr. and Gary C. Woodward, *Political Communication in America*, 3rd ed. (Westport, Conn.: Praeger, 1998).

19. Ross Bates, "Blending Media with Mail," in *The Road to Victory 2000*: 315.

20. Wayne C. Johnson, "How to Personalize Direct Mail," in *The Road to Victory 2000*: 17.

21. Richard Schlackman and Jamie "Buster" Douglas, "Attack Mail: The Silent Killer," in *The Road to Victory 2000*: 350.

22. "Older Adults as Customers," *Caring for an Aging Population* (Larchmont, N.Y.: Vericom, Inc., 1999), 21–22.

23. Ann Beaudry and Bob Schaeffer, *Winning Local and State Elections: The Guide to Organizing Your Campaign* (New York: The Free Press, 1986), 136.

24. Darrell M. West, *Air Wars: Television Advertising in Election Campaigns 1952–1996*, 2nd ed. (Washington, D.C.: Congressional Quarterly, 1997), 1.

25. See Dean Rindy, "Focusing Your TV Commercials," in *The Road to Victory 2000*: 391.

26. See, for example, Doug Bailey, "Effective Use of TV," in *The Road to Victory 2000*: 383–387.

27. Rindy, "Focusing Your TV Commercials," 392.

28. Karen S. Johnson-Cartee and Gary A. Copeland, *Manipulation of the American Voter: Political Campaign Commercials* (Westport, Conn.: Praeger, 1997), xxi.

29. Among the respondents, 43% won their races and 57% lost. As for the size of the senior constituency, 22% of the candidates had less than 25% seniors; 37% had 25–49%; 25% had 50–74%. Some 44% were incumbents.

30. Susan A. MacManus, *Young v. Old: Generational Combat in the 21st Century.* (Boulder, Colo.: Westview Press, 1996).

## CHAPTER 5

1. "102-year-old voter: 'It's quite a privilege,'" <http://jacksonville.com/tu-online/stories/100298/>.

2. See Larry Sabato and Glenn R. Simpson, "Vote Fraud!" *Campaigns & Elections* (June 1996); Isabelle de Pommereau, "Miami's Ballot Fraud Trial May Affect How America Can Vote," *The Christian Science Monitor* (March 4, 1998); Jorge Fitz-Gibbon, "2 Fined For School Vote Fraud," *New York Daily News*, Jan. 19, 1999; Bruce C. Smith, "Voter Fraud Probe Remains an Option," *The Indianapolis Star*, Aug. 7, 1999; Grace Schneider, "Ex-Sheriff Pleads Guilty in Vote-Fraud Case," *The Courier-Journal*, Oct. 5, 1999.

3. See Susan A. MacManus, *Young v. Old: Generational Combat in the 21st Century* (Boulder, Colo.: Westview Press, 1996), 39.

4. For an overview of voter registration laws and procedures, see MacManus, *Young v. Old*, Chapter 2.

5. See Robert S. Montjoy, *Mail Voter Registration Programs*. Washington, D.C.: (National Clearinghouse on Election Administration, Federal Election Commission, April 1994).

6. Federal Election Commission figures for 1995–96 show that 33% of Americans registered at motor vehicle offices, 29.7% by mail, 6% at public assistance offices, 0.4% at disability services agencies, 0.2% at Armed Forces offices, 4% at state designated sites, and 26% at all other sources. See <www.fec.gov/votregis/nvra2.htm>.

7. See "Voting Early and Often," *Wall Street Journal*, Nov. 6, 1999.

8. For a state-by-state list of voter registration requirements, see the Federal Election Commission Web site: <www.fec.gov/pages/Voteinst.htm>.

9. A Florida legislative committee in March 1999 approved a proposed bill requiring elections supervisors to mail signature-update cards to voters 65 and older every four years. The bill, H 919, was initiated by State Rep. Manny Prieguez of Miami. "Absentee ballots: Elderly voters could update signatures," <http://www.hearld.com/florida/digdocs/>.

10. Mail survey of Florida Supervisors of Elections, conducted July–September, 1999 by the author, funded by the University of South Florida Institute on Aging. Responses were received from 60 of the 67 supervisors.

11. Telephone survey of a random sample of 600 Floridians age 60 or older, conducted in December 1998, by Independent Market Research, Inc. for the author. The USF Institute on Aging funded the research.

12. "Voting Access for All," distributed at the 1997 IACREDOT (International Association of Clerks, Recorders, Election Officials, and Treasurers) annual conference, May 28, 1997.

13. AARP/VOTE, <http://www.arp.org/aarpvote>.

14. For an overview of the nature of state statutes in the early 1980s, see Rita Ann Reimer and M. Ann Wolfe and Carolyn Fletcher, "Survey of State Statutes Affecting Voting by the Physically Handicapped." Washington, D.C.: Congressional Research Service, May 30, 1983, updated July 8, 1983.

15. William C. Kimberling, ed. *Ensuring the Accessibility of the Election Process.* (Washington, D.C.: Office of Election Administration, Federal Election Commission, August 1996).

16. Kimberling, ed. *Ensuring the Accessibility of the Election Process:* 3.

17. See, for example, National Council on Disability, *Disabled Citizens at the Polls: A Guide for Election Officials* (Washington, D.C.: National Council, 1988).

18. Todd Shields, Kay F. Schriner, and Ken Schriner, "The Disability Voice in American Politics: Political Participation of People with Disabilities in the 1994 Election," *Journal of Disability Policy Studies,* 9 (2): 33-52; Douglas L. Kruse, Kay Schriner, Lisa Schur, and Todd Shields, "Empowerment Through Civic Participation: A Study of the Political Behavior of People with Disabilities." Final Report to the Disability Research Consortium, Bureau of Economic Research, Rutgers University and the New Jersey Developmental Disabilities Council, March 1999.

19. Kay Fletcher Schriner, Todd G. Shields, and Ken Schriner, "The Effect of Gender and Race on the Political Participation of People with Disabilities in the 1994 Mid-Term Election," *Journal of Disability Policy Studies* 9, no. 2 (1998): 72.

20. Editorial, "A Smart Way to Help Disabled Voters," *The Tampa Tribune,* May 16, 1996.

21. National Organization on Disability, "National Organization on Disability Launches Campaign for Disability Vote in the Year 2000," press release, Oct. 6, 1999.

22. National Organization on Disability, "Voter Implementation Guide for Nonprofits: NOD VOTE!2000 Campaign," no date.

23. Kay Schriner and Todd G. Shields, "Empowerment of the Political Kind: The Role of Disability Service Organizations in Encouraging People with Disabilities to Vote." *Journal of Rehabilitation* (April/May/June 1998): 34–35.

24. National Organization on Disability, *Disabled Citizens at the Polls: A Guide for Election Officials.* (Washington, D.C.: National Organization, January 1988).

25. Supervisor responses did not vary by either the size of the senior population or the number of nursing homes and ALFs in the county.

26. Cathy Allen, "Grassroots GOTV," in *The Road to Victory 2000,* 2nd ed., edited by Ron Faucheux (Dubuque, Iowa: Kendall/Hunt Publishing Co., 1998), 620.

27. MacManus, *Young v. Old.*

28. Kruse, Schriner, Schur, and Shields, "Empowerment Through Civic Participation: A Study of the Political Behavior of People With Disabilities," iv.

29. Kruse, Schriner, Schur, and Shields, "Empowerment Through Civic Participation."

30. The 1998 survey used disability questions to be used in the 2000 Census, but supplemented them with additional questions about the nature, severity, and duration of the disability. See Kruse, Schriner, Schur, and Shields, "Empowerment Through Civic Participation": Table 2.

31. Lisa Schur, Todd Shields, Douglas Kruse, and Kay Schriner, "Enabling Democracy: Disability and Voter Turnout in the 1998 Elections," paper presented at the American Political Science Association annual meeting, Atlanta, September 1999.

32. Kay Schriner and Todd G. Shields, "Empowerment of the Political Kind: The Role of Disability Service Organizations in Encouraging People with Disabilities to Vote." *Journal of Rehabilitation* (April/May/June 1998): 34–35.

33. Kimberling, ed. *Ensuring the Accessibility of the Election Process*: 9.

34. Schriner, Batavia, and Shields, "The Americans with Disabilities Act."

35. Government of the District of Columbia Board of Elections and Ethics, "Voting Access Services for the Elderly and Handicapped Community." Washington, D.C.: D.C. Board of Elections, Bulletin no. 3, Aug. 7, 1986.

36. Schriner, Batavia, and Shields, "The Americans with Disabilities Act."

37. Federal Election Commission, *Polling Place Accessibility in the 1992 General Election* (Washington, D.C.: Federal Election Commission, 1992), 5.

38. National Organization on Disability, "N.O.D. VOTE! 2000 Campaign: Disabled Citizens at the Polls," no date.

39. See Kay Schriner, Andrew I. Batavia, and Todd G. Shields, "The Americans with Disabilities Act: Does It Secure the Fundamental Right to Vote?" *Policy Studies Journal* (forthcoming 2000).

40. Bev Graham, "Accessibility Task Force Begins Work," *The Oklahoma Ballot Box* 16, no. 12 (November 1989).

41. Federal Election Commission, *Polling Place Accessibility*: Appendix B.

42. Schriner, Batavia, and Shields, "The Americans with Disabilities Act."

43. For a detailed look at these restrictions, see Alexander J. Bott, *Handbook of United States Election Laws and Practices: Political Rights*. (Westport, Conn.: Greenwood Press, 1990); for an argument in favor of extending voting rights to these individuals, see Kay Schriner, Lisa A. Ochs, and Todd G. Shields, "The Last Suffrage Movement: Voting Rights for Persons with Cognitive and Emotional Disabilities," *Publius* 27 (Summer 1997): 75–96. States with NO constitutional restrictions on voting by mentally impaired people are Colorado, Indiana, Kansas, Michigan, New Hampshire, North Carolina, Pennsylvania, and Tennessee. See Martha T. Moore, "The Vote to All Mentally Ill," *USA Today*, Oct. 30, 1997.

44. Section 208 of the Voting Rights Act (42 U.S.C. 1973aa-6) states: "Any voter who requires assistance to vote by reason of blindness, disability, or inability to read or write may be given assistance by a person of the voter's choice, other than the voter's employer or agent of that employer or officer or agent of the voter's union."

45. "Disabled Citizens at the Polls," information card distributed by the National Easter Seal Society and the National Organization on Disability, no date.

46. Royal National Institute for the Blind, "Access to Elections: The Problems Faced by Blind and Partially Sighted People." (*See It Right,* no date.)

47. Federal Election Commission, *Polling Place Accessibility:* 51.

48. Letter to Interested Parties from Al Davidson, Marion County Clerk, and Sharon Ricks, Elections Supervisor, July 1998. A tactile mask covers the ballot with raised markings to guide a voter to the appropriate locations on the ballot and openings to allow the voter to insert a marking instrument to mark the ballot.

49. Local governments would be required to provide privacy for blind and disabled voters under a bill introduced in the U.S. Senate in March 1999 by Senator John McCain of Arizona. The bill, an amendment to the Voting Accessibility for the Elderly and Handicapped Act, would expand the role of federal and state authorities in ensuring compliance, rather than leaving decisions to local governments. The bill would apply to all elections conducted by the states. "McCain Bill Would Mandate States to Provide Blind Voters with Way to Vote in Private at All Polls," *Election Administration Reports* 29, no. 6 (March 15, 1999): 1–3.

50. Rhode Island Governor's Commission on Disabilities, "Rhode Island's 39 Cities and Towns Voting Accessibility Project: May 1997–November 1998" (Providence, R.I.: Author, no date).

51. Schriner, Batavia, and Shields, "The Americans with Disabilities Act." The system is detailed in a memo from Bernard LaFleur, president of Quad Media, "Election Systems and Software, Inc. to Exclusively Distribute Quad Media's Accessibility Products to the Voting/Election Industry." Draft memo dated Aug. 11, 1998. "Through the use of an armored telephone handset or stereo headphone jack, users who are blind or sight impaired, are given a verbal description of options available within the program. Users who are deaf are able to use a close captioning system similar to that available on most modern television sets. The users are then able to select a desired choice by pushing an easily locatable green diamond button labeled with the official International Standards Organization "HP" logo. An integrated bi-directional infrared communications port allows users who may be deaf, blind, or severely motor restricted, to communicate with Quad Media's PiK (Portable Interactive Kiosk) voting terminal using a Braille Lite or wheelchair based interpreting device.

52. Richard G. Smolka, "Must Blind Be Offered Unassisted Secret Voting Method?" *IIMC News Digest* (February 1997): 14.

53. Letter from Stewart B. Oneglia, Chief, Coordination and Review Section, Civil Rights Section, U.S. Department of Justice, to Dorothy Walker Ruggles, Supervisor of Elections, Pinellas County, Florida, Aug. 26, 1993.

54. City of Chicago, Mayor's Office for People with Disabilities, MOPD Services and Programs, Jan. 13, 1995.

55. Schriner, Batavia, and Shields, "The Americans with Disabilities Act."

56. For a more detailed discussion of this type of voting machine, see <www.fec.gov/pages/lever.htm>.

57. For a more detailed description of punch cards, see <www.fec.gov/pages/punchrd.htm>.

58. See <www.fec.gov/pages/marksnse.htm>.

59. See <www.fec.gov/pages/dre.htm>.

60. See Benjamin Highton, "Easy Registration and Voter Turnout," *Journal of Politics,* 59 (May 1997): 565–575; J. Eric Oliver, "Who Votes at Home? The Influence of State

Law and Party Activity on Absentee Voting and Overall Turnout," *American Journal of Political Science* 40 (May 1996): 498–513; Samuel C. Patterson and Gregory Caldeira, "Mailing in the Vote: Correlates and Consequences of Absentee Voting," *American Journal of Political Science* 29 (1985): 766–788.

61. Lois Romano, "Growing Use of Mail Voting Puts Its Stamp on Campaigns," *Washington Post*, Nov. 29, 1998.

62. Norman Ornstein, "Vote No on Mail Ballots," *USA Today*, Oct. 15, 1995; also see Ornstein, "Vote-by-Mail: Is It Good for Democracy? An 'Anti' Perspective," *Campaigns & Elections* 17 (May 1996): 47–49.

63. Robert M. Stein, "Early Voting," *Public Opinion Quarterly* 62 (Spring 1998): 57–70.

64. Craig Varoga, "Absentee and Early Voting: Watching Recounts," *Campaigns & Elections* 16 (December 1995): 76.

65. Andrew E. Busch, "Early Voting: Convenient, But . . .?" *State Legislatures* 22 (September 1996): 24–28.

66. For the pros and cons of unrestricted absentee voting, see Busch, "Early Voting."

67. Richard Smolka, ed., *Election Administration Reports* (March 1998).

68. Sabato and Simpson, "Vote Fraud!"

69. Sabato and Simpson, "Vote Fraud!"

70. Sabato and Simpson, "Vote Fraud!"

71. This is probably a conservative number. It was generated by identifying precincts with nursing homes and/or ALFs, determining the number of voters in those precincts who returned absentee ballots, and calculating the number of voters living at nursing home/ALF addresses who returned an absentee ballot. Data were collected for the first primary, the runoff primary, and the general election in 1998.

72. For an excellent account of this "first," see David Beiler, "It's in the Mail: How Liberal Ron Wyden Won a U.S. Senate Seat in Oregon's Revolutionary Special Election," *Campaigns & Elections* 17 (April 1996): 34–40.

73. Steve Welchert and John Britz, "Mail Balloting: Do Early Voting Laws Impact Election Results?" *Campaigns & Elections* (August 1997): 35–36, 50.

74. Overview presented in *Election Administration Reports* (Sept. 22, 1997): 5.

75. For example, see Kieran Nicholson, "Jeffco Mail-In Ballots Slowed Tally Process; Last-Day Voters Created Bottleneck, Late Final Returns," *Denver Post*, Nov. 4, 1999.

76. Robert Sullivan, "Mail Order," *The New Republic* 214 (Feb. 26, 1996): 14–16.

77. Deborah Phillips, "Voting by Mail Hurts Electoral Process," op-ed in *Detroit News*, July 2, 1999.

78. Welchert and Britz, "Mail Balloting": 35.

79. Welchert and Britz, "Mail Balloting": 36.

80. Sullivan, "Mail Order."

81. Stein, "Early Voting."

82. Margaret Rosenfield, "Early Voting," *Innovations in Election Administration*, (Washington, D.C.: Federal Election Commission, April 1994): 9.

83. Busch, "Early Voting"; Romano, "Growing Use of Mail Voting."

84. Welchert and Britz, "Mail Balloting": 50.

85. See Robert M. Stein and Patricia A. Garcia-Monet, "Voting Early But Not Often," *Social Science Quarterly* 78 (September 1997): 657–671.

86. Welchert and Britz, "Mail Balloting": 50.

87. Robert M. Stein, "Early Voting," *Public Opinion Quarterly* 62 (Spring 1998): 57–70.

88. In 1997, the Texas Legislature passed a law to allow a person on a space flight to vote; the law instructed the Secretary of State's Office to set out the procedures. (This legislation no doubt was stimulated by an astronaut who had asked to vote in the 1996 presidential election from the Mir Space Station but was turned down because there was no law allowing this sort of voting.) Subsequently, in the November 1997 City of Houston and constitutional amendment elections, an astronaut voted from space using a carefully orchestrated system. The Secretary of State's Office worked with NASA and authorized an e-mail system in which an electronic ballot image was made with an embedded password. The ballot was e-mailed from the Houston County Clerk's Office to the Johnson Space Center and e-mailed to Russia, which then uplinked the ballot to the Mir Space Station. The crew member on Mir opened it with his password, voted, downlinked it to Russia, which e-mailed it to the Johnson Space Center, which e-mailed it to the Harris County Clerk's Office, which opened it with the password. Since the bill passed, this astronaut has been the only one to date to use this voting method. As the elections supervisor noted, "I don't think this will be one of our larger sources of voter turnout!"

89. "Arizona Democrats Plan an Online Vote," *New York Times*, Dec. 5, 1999: 22.

90. "Iowa Counties Experiment with Voting on the Internet," *Election Administration Reports* 29, no. 23 (Nov. 22, 1999): 4.

91. James Evans, "Cybervoting for the People," *Government Technology* (February 1998): 22.

92. Evans, "Cybervoting."

93. Gary Langer, "Virtual Voting: Poll Finds Most Oppose Online Ballots," <www.abcnews.go.com/sections/political/DailyNews/poll990721.html>.

94. See Gary W. Selnow, *Electronic Whistle-Stops: The Impact of the Internet on American Politics* (Westport, Conn.: Praeger, 1998).

95. "Congressional Bill Calls for Study of Internet Voting," *Election Administration Reports* 29, no. 23 (Nov. 22, 1999): 1–2.

96. See Sabato and Simpson, "Vote Fraud!"

97. Ronnie Green and Tyler Bridges, "Reforms in Absentee Voting to be Postponed," *Miami Herald*, Aug. 18, 1998.

## CHAPTER 6

1. Richard Morin, "Fix Social Security Now, They Say," *Washington Post National Weekly Edition* (May 31, 1999): 34.

2. *Wall Street Journal*, "'Gen Xers' Bypass Social Security," *St. Petersburg Times*, March 13, 1999: 4A.

3. Robert J. Samuelson, "Financing America's Elderly," *St. Petersburg Times*, July 10, 1999: 15A.

4. Peter G. Peterson, *Gray Dawn* (New York: Times Books, 1999); Peter G. Peterson, *Will America Grow Up Before It Grows Old?* (New York: Random House, 1996).

5. See, for example, Sam Beard, *Restoring Hope in America: The Social Security Solution* (New Castle, Del.: Economic Security, 2000).

6. The law raises earning limits until 2003 when it will be indexed to growth in average wages: 2000—$17,000; 2001—$26,000; 2002—$30,000. *Toledo Blade*, "Rising Earnings Limit Lifts Retirees," *St. Petersburg Times*, May 5. 1996: 5H.

7. Miles Benson, Newhouse News Service, "Trend Reversed," *Tampa Tribune*: 1; Commentary, *Los Angeles Times*; "Report Upbeat About Boomers' Aging," *St. Petersburg Times*, Jan. 13, 1999. The report, titled "Demography Is Not Destiny" was written by the National Academy on an Aging Society.

8. "Opinion Pulse: Social Security and the Alternatives," *The American Enterprise*, 10 (March/April 1999): 92–93.

9. The eligibility age will rise to 66 in 2009 and to 67 in 2027. Robert J. Samuelson, "Getting Serious," *Newsweek* (Sept. 18, 1995): 41.

10. Elizabeth Crowley, "Social Security Reform: The Great Divide," *Wall Street Journal*, American Opinion, March 11, 1999: 14A.

11. Albert R. Hunt, "Senior Vote Could Decide 2000 Election, But the Bloc Can Be Fickle," *Wall Street Journal*, March 11, 1999: 9A.

12. See, for example, William Sterling, *Boomernomics* (New York: Library of Contemporary Thought, 1998).

13. Albert R. Hunt, "Fundamental Shift in What It Means to Be a Senior," *Wall Street Journal*, American Opinion, March 11, 1999: 9A.

14. The Henry J. Kaiser Family Foundation, "Medicare: The Basics," 1998:10.

15. National Bipartisan Commission on the Future of Medicare, "Talking Points: Breaux-Thomas Proposal." <http://rs9.loc.gov/medicare/talking.htm>.

16. Howard Fineman, "MediScare," *Newsweek* (Sept. 18, 1995): 38.

17. For a complete description of the Medicare program, see <www.medicare.gov/whatis.html>.

18. Health Care Financing Administration, "Medicare & You," pamphlet, no date.

19. The Commission's Final Report, *Building a Better Medicare for Today and Tomorrow*, can be found at <http://rs9.loc.gov/medicare/bbmtt31599.html>.

20. League of Women Voters Education Fund, *How Americans Talk About Medicare Reform: The Public Voice* (Washington, D.C.: League of Women Voters, 1999), 5.

21. Michelle Kitchman, "The Role of Medicare." The author is a senior policy analyst for the Henry J. Kaiser Family Foundation, March 4, 1999.

22. Peterson, *Gray Dawn*, 201.

23. Peterson, *Gray Dawn*, 201.

24. League of Women Voters, *How Americans Talk About Medicare*: 26.

25. League of Women Voters, *How Americans Talk About Medicare*: 31.

26. The other half is paid out-of-pocket by beneficiaries, supplemental private insurance, Medicaid, and other public payers. Martha P. King and Stephen M. Christian, *Medicaid Survival Kit* (Denver, Colo.: National Conference of State Legislatures, November 1996): 4-3.

27. Henry J. Kaiser Family Foundation, "Medicare: The Basics," 1998.

28. National Medical Expenditure Survey, 1996, reported in "Social Security Braces for Boomers," *Tampa Tribune*, Feb. 16, 1998: 7 (Nation/World).

29. Lucette Lagnado, "The Uncovered: Drug Costs Can Leave Elderly a Grim Choice: Pills or Other Needs," *Wall Street Journal*, Nov. 17, 1998: 1A.

30. People who qualify for both Medicare and Medicaid do so based on income, resources, and need. In general, Medicaid covers elderly individuals who qualify for Sup-

plemental Security Income (SSI) or similar cash assistance programs or others who become eligible after spending down their assets on long-term care services. King and Christian, *Medicaid Survival Kit*: 4-3.

31. "State Medicaid programs must cover nursing facility services and home health care for people eligible for nursing facility services. Among the services covered at each state's option that especially benefit elderly recipients are prescription drugs, eyeglasses, private duty nursing, personal care services, hospice services, physical therapy, services for dentures and nursing facility services for the aged in an institution for mental diseases." King and Christian, *Medicaid Survival Kit*: 4-6.

32. American Seniors Housing Association, "Seniors Housing: Solving America's Long-Term Care Crisis" (pamphlet), 1999: 5.

33. National Institute on Aging, "Age Page: Planning for Long-Term Care." See <www.nih.gov/nia/health/pubpub/longterm.htm> (Nov. 14, 1999).

34. King and Christian, *Medicaid Survival Kit*: 4-2. According to one estimate, nursing homes providing basic care can easily cost $40,000 a year. Sara Rimer, "Families Hit with Costs of Elder Care," *Tampa Tribune*, June 8, 1998: 1 (Nation/World).

35. National Bipartisan Commission on the Future of Medicare, "Building a Better Medicare for Today and Tomorrow," March 16, 1999. See < http://rs9.loc.gov/medicare/bbmtt31599.html>.

36. King and Christian, *Medicaid Survival Kit*: 4-10–4-11.

37. The telephone survey of 1,105 noninstitutionalized adults age 50 and older, was conducted Sept. 1–18, 1995. The margin of error was plus or minus 3%. American Seniors Housing Association, "Seniors Housing: Solving America's Long-Term Care Crisis," 1999: 6.

38. Laurie McGinley, "Assisted-Living Centers Criticized in Study," *Wall Street Journal*, April 26, 1999: 20A.

39. Rimer, "Families Hit with Costs of Elder Care."

40. Genevieve W. Strahan, "An Overview of Nursing Homes and Their Current Residents: Data from the 1995 National Nursing Home Survey," *Advance Data*, no. 280 (Jan. 23, 1997).

41. Strahan, "An Overview of Nursing Homes."

42. Achintya N. Dey, "Characteristics of Elderly Nursing Home Residents: Data from the 1995 National Nursing Home Survey," *Advance Data*, no. 289 (July 2, 1997): 2.

43. Bruce Vladeck, "The Future of Home- and Community-Based Long Term Care," *Aging Research & Policy Report*, no. 8 (October 1998): 30.

44. *CQ Weekly* (Jan. 16, 1999): 131.

45. Pollster Frank I. Luntz, in Craig Crawford, "Hotline Extra," *National Journal* (May 30, 1998): 1256.

46. Albert R. Hunt, "Public Is Split on How to Pay for Access," *Wall Street Journal*, American Opinion, June 25, 1998: 10A.

47. Pollster Peter Hart and Robert Teeter quoted in Albert R. Hunt, "Politicians Risk Voter Backlash This Autumn If They Ignore Call for Action," *Wall Street Journal*, June 25, 1998.

48. See Judith Kline Leavitt, "Does Our Nation Have the Will to Provide Care for Elders and Children? The Bases of Cross-Generational Advocacy," *The Public Policy and Aging Report* (Winter 1997): 7–9.

49. Douglas Belkin, "Abuse of Seniors Sometimes Hard to Detect," *Palm Beach Post*, April 11, 1999.

50. Belkin, "Abuse of Seniors."

51. Lindsey Peterson, "Elder Abuse Has Another Likely Cause," *Tampa Tribune*, July 20 1999: 3 (Baylife).

52. Rimer, "Families Hit with Costs of Elder Care."

53. Associated Press, "Survey Finds Elder Care Cuts into Job Time." *St. Petersburg Times,* June 19, 1997: 1E.

54. Maturity News Service, "Long-Distance Caregiving Becoming a Growing Concern," *St. Petersburg Times*, April 29, 1997, 15G.

55. Belkin, "Abuse of Seniors."

56. "Money or Mercy?" A Special Report by *Tampa Tribune*, Nov. 15, 1998.

57. Michael Moss, "Fighting a Nursing Home's Closing," *Wall Street Journal*, Jan. 4, 1999: 13A.

58. Moss, "Fighting a Nursing Home's Closing," 13-14A.

59. Associated Press, "In Radio Address, President Details Plans to Protect Older Americans," *Miami Herald*, April 17, 1999.

60. Associated Press, "In Radio Address, President Details Plans."

61. Belkin, "Abuse of Seniors."

62. Peter Weaver, "Guardians Drawing Increased Scrutiny," *AARP Bulletin*, May 1999.

63. Horace B. Deets, "Age Discrimination Still on the Rise," *Modern Maturity* (May-June 1999): 80.

64. The U.S. Equal Employment Opportunity Commission, "Federal Laws Prohibiting Job Discrimination: Questions and Answers,"< www.eeoc.gov/facts/qanda.html>.

65. "Courts Make Age-Discrimination Cases Harder to Win, Plaintiffs Lawyers Say," *Wall Street Journal*, May 18, 1999: 1A.

66. Deets, "Age Discrimination Still on the Rise."

67. Sara E. Dix, "Frequently Asked Questions: What DO People Want to Know about Older Workers and an Aging Labor Force?" *The Public Policy and Aging Report* 7 (Fall 1996): 10–11.

68. Dix, "Frequently Asked Questions," 11.

69. Ellen E. Schultz, "Older Workers Fight 'Cash Balance' Plans," *Wall Street Journal*, Feb.11, 1999, 1C.

70. Albert R. Crenshaw, "Finding a Haven from Taxes," *Washington Post National Weekly Edition* (May 7, 1999).

71. Elizabeth Crowley, "Social Security Reform: The Great Divide," *Wall Street Journal*, March 11, 1999, American Opinion, 14A.

72. Kevin Sack, "Faith Shifts over Secure Retirement Funds," *New York Times* (July 7, 1999): 12; Ann Kates Smith, "Roads to Riches," *U.S. News & World Report* (June 28, 1999): 66–73.

73. Ron Faucheux, "Politics of the New Stockholder Majority," *Campaigns & Elections* (July 1999): 7.

74. Lawrence Kudlow, quoted in Faucheux, "Politics of the New Stockholder."

75. Norman Ornstein, "Boomers Beware: Estate Tax Now Not Just for the Rich," *USA Today*, April 23, 1997: 15A.

76. Susan A. MacManus, *Young v. Old* (Boulder, Colo.: Westview Press, 1996), Chapter 5.

77. Telephone survey of a random sample of 1,200 adults, 18 years of age or older, conducted July 13–18, 1999. The sampling error for the split sample is plus or minus 4.5 percentage points.

78. Susan A. MacManus, "Selling School Taxes and Bond Issues to a Generationally Diverse Electorate: Lessons from Florida Referenda," *Government Finance Review* 13 (April 1997): 17–22.

79. Cindy Loose, "Going Back for Post-Postgraduate Studies," *Washington Post National Weekly Edition* (Nov. 16, 1998).

80. Loose, "Going Back For Post-Postgraduate Studies."

81. Christopher T. Cross, "Lure Retirees Back to Class to Solve Social Problems," *Tampa Tribune-Times*, Jan. 10 1999: 6 (Commentary).

82. The Pew Research Center for the People & the Press. Telephone survey of a random sample of 1,200 adults, 18 years of age or older, conducted July 13–18, 1999. The margin of error for the split sample is plus or minus 4.5 percentage points.

83. MacManus, *Young v. Old.*

84. 71% of persons 65+ (but 65% of persons 18-29) favor requiring that women younger than 18 years of age get the consent of at least one parent before they are allowed to have an abortion. The Pew Research Center for the People & the Press, survey conducted Sept. 1–12, 1999, margin of error plus or minus 3 percentage points.

85. The vast majority of each age group thinks controlling gun ownership is more important than protecting the right of Americans to own guns. However, 40% of the 50-to-64-year-olds believe protecting the right to own guns is more important, compared to just 23% of the 18-to-29-year-olds. The Pew Research Center for the People & the Press, survey conducted June 9-13, 1999, margin of error plus or minus 3.5 percentage points.

86. Among 18-to-29-year-olds, 49% favor allowing gays and lesbians to adopt children; only 21% of those 65 and older agree. The Pew Research Center for the People & the Press, survey conducted Sept. 1–12, 1999, margin of error plus or minus 3 percentage points.

87. Roger W. Cobb, Joseph F. Coughlin, and Richard Marottoli, "Older Adults and Transportation: Technology's Promise to Reinvent Paratransit," *The Public Policy and Aging Report* 10 (Spring 1999): 10.

88. Diane C. Lade, "Accident Analysis: A Breakdown by Age Groups," (Ft. Lauderdale) *Sun-Sentinel*, Nov. 15, 1998.

89. Diane C. Lade, "Testing Based on Age Gaining Support of Older Voters," (Ft. Lauderdale) *Sun-Sentinel*, Nov. 15, 1998.

90. Telephone survey of a random sample of 600 Floridians age 60 or older, conducted December 1998.

91. Diane C. Lade, "Test of Time: A Look at South Florida's Elderly Drivers," series published in the (Ft. Lauderdale) *Sun-Sentinel*, Nov. 15–16, 1998.

92. Lade, "Testing Based on Age."

93. Diane C. Lade, "Some Seniors Go Back to Driver's Ed," (Ft. Lauderdale) *Sun-Sentinel*, Nov. 16, 1998.

94. Cobb, Coughlin, and Marottoli, "Older Adults and Transportation," 11.

95. Susan A. MacManus, *Public Transportation in Florida: A Survey of Resident Use Patterns, Assessments, and Preferences* (Tallahassee, Fla.: Florida Department of Transportation, Office of Public Transportation, July 1997).

96. Cobb, Coughlin, and Marottoli, "Older Adults and Transportation," 12.

97. See Curtis B. Gans, "The Internet as Political Villain," *IntellectualCapital.com* (May 20, 1999); see <www.intellectualcapital.com/issues/Issue233/item4522.asp>; Marc Strassman, "Internet Voting Circa 2002," *IntellectualCapital.com* (May 6, 1999), <www.intellectualcapital.com/issues/Issue228/item4339.asp>; Marc Strassman, "Could the Internet Change Everything?" *IntellectualCapital.com* (June 17, 1999), <www.intellectualcapital.com/issues/Issue249/item5418.asp>.

# Index

AARP, 23, 32, 141, 176; advocacy by, 6, 138, 142; on age discrimination/action, 142; driving issue and, 157, 159; on older worker stereotypes, 143; prescription drug coverage and, 130; registration/voting and, 80, 115; senior definition of, 9

AARP/VOTE, 6, 80

ABC News: on Internet voting, 113; on voting fraud, 113

abortion issue, 151, 152, 172, 208n84

absentee balloting, 8, 84, 91, 92, 116, 182, 193–94; disabled voters and, 181; fraud problems with, 93, 107–8, 110, 185; help with, 62, 67, 106 (fig.), 108 (fig.); mailing, 185; no-fault, 105; patterns with, 110; procedures for, 109 (table); registration and, 114; requesting, 106; using, 72, 105–8, 110, 184

abuse: elder, 138–41; nursing home, 140; physical/mental, 138

accessibility, 115; attentiveness to, 63 (photo); balloting system, 184; facility, 78–79; issues about, 94–95, 189; parking, 91, 92 (photo), 99; polling place, 93, 100, 183; registration site, 78–79, 182; voting booth, 91, 99; wheelchair, 98, 178

*Access to Multimedia Technology by People with Sensory Disabilities* (National Council on Disabilities), 43

accident rates, 155–57; reducing, 159

Activities of Daily Living (ADLs), 131, 135; help with, 130; percentage needing assistance with, 131 (fig.)

activities, percentage of requiring assistance (by age group), 19 (fig.)

activity directors, consulting with, 36–40

ADA. *See* Americans with Disabilities Act

ADAAG. *See* Americans with Disability Accessibility

211

# About the Author

Susan A. MacManus is the Distinguished University Professor of Public Administration and Political Science and past chair of the department of government and international affairs at the University of South Florida, Tampa. She is also a member of the teaching faculty of the Ph.D. in Aging Studies Program at USF. Her book *Young v. Old: Generational Combat in the 21st Century* (1996) was designated an Outstanding Academic Book. MacManus chairs the Florida Elections Commission and routinely serves as a political analyst for national, state, and local news media. She has served as president of the Urban Politics Section of the American Political Science Association, the Southern Political Science Association, and the Florida Political Science Association.